Fighting Fans

Fighting Fans

Football Hooliganism as a World Phenomenon

edited by

Eric Dunning Patrick Murphy
Ivan Waddington Antonios E. Astrinakis

University College Dublin Press
Preas Choláiste Ollscoile
Bhaile Átha Cliath

First published 2002
by University College Dublin Press
Newman House
86 St Stephen's Green
Dublin 2
Ireland

www.ucdpress.ie

ISBN 1 900621 73 8 (hardcover)
1 900621 74 6 (paperback)

Cataloguing in Publication data available from the British Library

Typeset in Ireland in Adobe Garamond and Trade Gothic
by Elaine Shiels, Bantry, Co. Cork
Text design by Lyn Davies
Printed on acid-free paper in Ireland by Betaprint

Contents

Preface

In deciding whom to ask to contribute to *Fighting Fans*, we sought to achieve a reasonably balanced geographical coverage of an issue that became in the course of the twentieth century quite literally a worldwide problem. Football hooliganism, and its equivalents in countries where soccer is not played, came to be seen by many people as one of the negative accompaniments of the compelling processes of globalisation in which humankind are currently enmeshed.

It has not been possible to cover fighting fans in every country and doubtless there will be those who disagree with our selections. Given that the 2002 World Cup Finals, the first in Asia, are being co-hosted by Japan and Korea, we wanted a chapter on spectator behaviour in at least one of these countries. Even though it does not deal with soccer, we also wanted a chapter on sports spectator violence in the United States and Canada. That is because they are often wrongly held up as countries in which there is little or no sports spectator violence. In addition, we thought it would be a good idea if some of our authors on this quintessentially male subject were females. And finally, we tried to strike a reasonable balance between new authors and more established ones.

We do not seek to deny that a prime motive for compiling this book was to use the occasion of the first World Cup Finals in Asia to draw attention to the fact that fighting and disorder connected with football are worldwide problems, as well as demonstrating that disinterested academic research is a *sine qua non* for understanding and effectively tackling them.

We should like to thank the contributors for the speed and courtesy with which they responded to our requests. Thanks are also due to Sue Smith for typing the initial proposal, and to Lisa Heggs and Mary Needham for the onerous task of word-processing the final manuscript. Last but not least, we offer our thanks to Barbara Mennell of UCD Press and to Professor Stephen Mennell for all their help and advice. It has been a pleasure to work with them.

ERIC DUNNING
PATRICK MURPHY
IVAN WADDINGTON
ANTONIOS E. ASTRINAKIS
Leicester, January 2002

Contributors to this volume

Pablo Alabarces is Professor in Popular Culture at the University of Buenos Aires. He is a researcher for the National Council for Scientific Research in Argentina and the Coordinator of the Working Group 'Sport and Society' of the Latin American Council for Social Sciences (CLACSO). A specialist in cultural analysis and popular cultures, his research has focused especially on rock 'n roll, youth and football cultures. His major publications include *Cuestión de pelotas. Fútbol, deporte, sociedad, cultura* (1996), *Deporte y sociedad* (1998, editor) and *Peligro de gol. Estudios sobre deporte y sociedad en América Latina* (2000, editor).

Antonios E. Astrinakis is Assistant Professor in Sociology in the Department of Philosophy and Social Studies, University of Crete. He holds degrees from Budapest, Paris and the Panteion University, Athens, where he completed his PhD in 1990. He was a Research Fellow in the Centre for Research into Sport and Society, University of Leicester in 1997. His main publications include *Youth Subcultures: The British Subcultural Theorization and the Greek Research Experience* (Athens, 1991) and *Heavy Metal, Rockabilly and Hardcore Fans. Youth Cultures and Subcultures in West Attica* (co-edited with L. Stylianoudis, Athens, 1996). His current research interests focus on the sociology of culture and deviance and the social construction of emotions.

Alan Bairner is Professor in Sports Studies at the University of Ulster at Jordanstown. He is the author of *Sport, Nationalism and Globalization: European and North American Perspectives* (2001), the co-author of *Sport, Sectarianism and Society in a Divided Ireland* (1993) and joint editor of *Sport in Divided Societies* (1999). He has written extensively on sport and identity in Ireland, Scotland and Sweden and was a member of the ministerial advisory panel on the future of soccer in Northern Ireland. He is currently preparing a monograph on sport and politics for Pluto Press.

Carlo Balestri lives and works in Bologna. He has long worked on the subcultures linked to football fans, publishing a number of papers on the subject. Since 1996 he has been in charge of Progetto Ultrà, promoted by UISP Emilia-Romagna, which has the goals of restricting violent behaviour through social work with the fans' groups, of evaluating the popular culture of fans, and organising Mondiali Antirazzisti, an annual tournament of fan groups and migrants' communities.

CORA BURNETT is a professor in the Department of Sport and Movement Studies at the Rand Afrikaans University in Johannesburg, South Africa. She lectures in sport sociology and research methodology. In 1984 she completed a PhD at the University of Stellenbosch on ethnic dance and in 1996 she obtained another doctorate in social anthropology investigating violence within the context of poverty in South Africa. She has published and delivered papers at international conferences in the areas of sport and gender, violence, sport development (impact assessment) and dance ethnology. She also co-ordinates a national research project relating to indigenous knowledge and games.

VIC DUKE is Senior Research Fellow in the Football Industry Group at the University of Liverpool. He is the author of *Football, Nationality and the State* (1996), *A Measure of Thatcherism* (1991), as well as numerous articles on political and sociological aspects of football. He has recently written on football spectator behaviour in the Czech Republic, the politics of football in Argentina and the growing number of mergers among Belgian football clubs. In addition he is researching aspects of semi-professional football in England.

ERIC DUNNING is Emeritus Professor at the University of Leicester and Visiting Professor at University College Dublin and the University of Ulster at Jordanstown. He studied sociology under Norbert Elias at both the undergraduate and postgraduate levels, later coming to write *Quest for Excitement* (Blackwell, 1986) and several articles with Elias. Dunning's main research interest is in sport and violence, and his latest books are *Sport Matters: Sociological Studies of Sport, Violence and Civilization* (Routledge, 1999) and *Handbook of Sport Studies* (Sage, 2000) co-edited with Jay Coakley. He is also co-author of *Barbarians, Gentlemen and Players* (Martin Robertson, 1979), *The Roots of Football Hooliganism* (Routledge, 1988), *Football on Trial* (Routledge, 1990) and *Sport and Leisure in the Civilizing Process* (Macmillan, 1992).

HUBERT DWERTMANN studied physical education and German language and literature at the Universities of Berlin and Hanover, Germany. He completed his dissertation and Habilitation in the sociology of sport at the University of Hanover and researches into historical and sociological problems of the development of sport. His publications and contributions in social and cultural history and sociology of sport include *Sportalltag und Dorfkultur. Eine Studie über den Konstitutionsprozess des Sports in einem ländlichen Verein* (1991), *Zwischen deutscher Kulturtradition und zivilgesellschäftlichem Aufbruch. Eine entwicklungssoziologische Studie zur Arbeiter-Turn- und Sportbewegung in Hannover* (1997).

JOHN HUGHSON is Principal Research Fellow in Cultural Studies at the University of Wolverhampton, UK. He is Reviews Editor for the journal *Ethnography* and co-author of the forthcoming book *Confronting Culture: Sociological Vistas* (Polity). He is also co-writing a book on sport and cultural studies, *The Uses of Sport: A Critical Study*, for Routledge. He has published a number of papers on football supporter subcultures, an area of interest that stems from his doctoral research which presented an ethnographic study of youth, ethnicity and soccer support in western Sydney, Australia.

SALOMÉ MARIVOET has lectured in the sociology of sport in the Faculdade de Motricidade Humana of the Universidade Técnicas de Lisboa since 1992. Between 1986 and 1991 she was a researcher in the Direcção Geral dos Desporto of the Ministério da Educaçã. She has carried out research into violence in sport and the sporting habits of the Portuguese and had technical responsibility for the campaign '1991 Ano da Ética Desportiva'. Among other publications she is author of the books *Aspectos Sociológicos do Desporto* and *Hábitos Desportivos da População Portuguesa.*

PATRICK MIGNON is head of the sociology of sport research centre in INSEP (Institut National des Sports et de l'Education Physique) in Paris. His fields of research are the evolution of sport and physical activities in France, the transformation of high-level sport and the relations between sport and ethics. He has been working on different aspects of popular culture, including drug use, popular music and sport, and is the author of *Le rock, de l'histoire au mythe*, Anthropos, 1991 (with A. Hennion) and *Drogues, politiques et sociétés*, Le Monde Editions, 1992 (with A. Ehrenberg). For ten years, he has researched football supporterism and doping in sport and published *La passion du football,* 1998, and produced a report, *Les clubs de football professionel et le supportérisme: quelle politique?* in the account of the Commission nationale mixte de sécurité, Ligue National de Football-Ministère de la Jeunesse et des Sports, 1999.

PATRICK MURPHY is Co-Director of the Centre for Research into Sport and Society at the University of Leicester. He is co-author of *The Roots of Football Hooliganism, Football on Trial* and *Hooligans Abroad.* He is also the editor of the *Singer and Friedlander Seasonal Review.* He was one of the founders of the Sir Norman Chester Centre for Football Research and co-founder of the Centre for Research into Sport and Society. The latter centre has pioneered the global development of distance learning Masters programmes in sports management and the sociology of sport and has more post-graduate students of sport than any other European university centre.

ALDO PANFICHI is a sociologist who directs the Masters programme in Sociology at the Catholic University of Peru. He earned his BA and MA in Sociology from the Catholic University of Peru and his PhD from the New School for Social Research in New York. His main areas of interest are civil society and democracy, urban poverty, youth, ethnicity and politics. He is also a member of the board of directors of Alianza Lima, a major professional football club in Peru.

ORSOLYA PINTÉR is a PhD student of the Semmelweis University, Faculty of Physical Education and Sport Sciences, Budapest. Her main interests are in the fields of sport for people with disabilities and football hooliganism. She is currently enrolled in a European Masters degree programme in Adapted Physical Activity at the Katholieke Universiteit Leuven, Belgium.

BERO RIGAUER studied sociology at the Institute for Social Research of the University of Frankfurt/Main, and physical education at the same university. He is a Professor (emeritus) in the Institute of Sport Science at the University of Oldenburg, Germany, where he still teaches the sociology of sport and the methodology of sciences, and researches into the social and group dynamics of sport games. His publications include *Sport and Work* (translated 1981), other sociological books and contributions, and most recently, *Soziodynamische Prozesse in Sportspielen. Eine feld- und figurationssoziologische Untersuchung* (2001).

ANTONIO ROVERSI is Professor of Sociology and Communication at the Faculty of Education, University of Bologna, Italy. His main research interests are in the area of sport and violence and, more recently, in the field of Internet studies. He is the author of several books on football hooliganism in Europe and Italy. In 2001 he published a book in Italian with the title *Chat Lines: Places and Experiences of the Life Online*. He is a member of the Scientific Board of the Italian Encyclopaedia of Sport.

PAVEL SLEPIČKA is currently Professor of Sport Psychology in the Faculty of Physical Education and Sport at Charles University in Prague. He is a member of the Czech Olympic Academy, Vice-President of the Czech Association of Sports Psychologists and a representative of the Czech Republic in the European Federation of Sports Psychologists. His many books include *Social Interaction and Sport, Psychology of Sport, Sport Spectators* and *Problems of Doping and the Possibility of Doping Prevention*. He is currently researching aspects of sports spectatorship and problems of aggression and violence in sport.

YOSHIO TAKAHASHI is Assistant Professor in the Research Centre for Health, Physical Fitness and Sports at Nagoya University, Japan. He is a member of the World Cup Japan 2002 Bidding Committee Secretariat and of the Japan Organising Committee for the 2002 World Cup Korea–Japan staff. He has also worked with a variety of other sport-related organisations. His major interests are in sport sociology and sport management, social change, modernisation, globalisation and the acculturation of sport in Japan.

JORGE THIEROLDT is a sociologist from the Catholic University of Peru. His main areas of interest include the sociology of youth, urban violence, and popular culture.

JAN VAN GESTEL completed his undergraduate studies at University College Chester (University of Liverpool) and his Master's degree in the sociology of sport at the University of Leicester. He is currently a scientific associate at the Research Unit in Socio-cultural Kinesiology of the Katholieke Universiteit Leuven, Belgium. He is also the editor of *Body Talk*, a sport-scientific magazine available in Dutch and French. His interests include social theory, globalisation and health issues.

IVAN WADDINGTON is a Director of the Centre for Research into Sport and Society at the University of Leicester and Visiting Professor in the Sociology of Sport, University College Chester. He has published extensively in the sociology of health and the sociology of sport and much of his work has focused on the interface between health and sport. He has written about several aspects of football and is the senior author of a major study of club doctors and physiotherapists in English professional football clubs. He is also a specialist in the study of doping in sport. He is the author of *Sport, Health and Drugs* (Spon, London, 2000) and a co-author of *Drugs in Sport: The Pressure to Perform* (British Medical Journal Books, 2002), which is the official policy statement of the British Medical Association on doping in sport. He has also provided expert advice on doping to the European Commission.

KEVIN YOUNG is Senior Research Fellow in the Department of Physical Education, Sports Science and Recreation Management at Loughborough University. He has published on a variety of sports-related topics such as violence and subcultural identity, and is the co-editor of *Sport and Gender in Canada* (Oxford University Press, 1999) and *Theory, Sport and Society* (Elsevier Science Press, forthcoming). He has served on the editorial boards of *Sociology of Sport Journal, Avante,* and *Soccer and Society,* and on the executive board of the North American Society for the Sociology of Sport. He is currently Vice-President of the International Sociology of Sport Association.

Chapter 1

Towards a sociological understanding of football hooliganism as a world phenomenon

Eric Dunning
Patrick Murphy
Ivan Waddington

Writing in 1966, the only year in which the English inventors of the game staged and won the Finals of the football World Cup, the journalist Lawrence Kitchin (1966) pithily described the soccer form of football[1] as 'the only global idiom apart from science'. Since neither soccer nor science has spread throughout the entire world, and since the degree of their diffusion was even less at the time when he was writing, it would, of course, have been better had Kitchin referred to them as 'emergent' global idioms rather than as idioms which are global *tout court*. Moreover, although it was not so well known or well publicised at that time, Kitchin might have added that forms of 'hooliganism'[2] – meaning crowd and fan[3] disorderliness – have historically been a near-universal addendum to this emergent 'global idiom'. Indeed, at particular times and places, such as England in the 1980s, they have constituted a threat to the popularity of the game and perhaps even to its continuing viability as a top-level spectator sport.[4] In this chapter, we shall endeavour to construct a sociological diagnosis of football hooliganism as a world pheno-menon, exploring how far it can be understood using data and theories – popular as well as academic – that were first generated using the case of England.

Our first task must be to attend to the question of definition. Probably the most important thing to stress is that the label 'football hooliganism' is not so much a scientific sociological or social psychological concept as a construct of politicians and the media. As such, it lacks precision and is used to cover a variety of forms of behaviour which take place in contexts that are related to football to a greater or lesser degree. These forms of behaviour also vary in the kinds and levels of violence that they tend to involve. More particularly, the politicians and media personnel who employ the term are liable to use 'football hooliganism' in a 'cover-all' sense which includes *inter alia*: forms of verbal as well as physical violence; the throwing of missiles at players, match officials, club officials and other fans; the vandalising of club and private property; fist fights; fights involving kicking; and fights involving weapons such as knives and even guns. It is also important to realise that such behaviour does not only take place at or in the vicinity of football grounds but also in locations – pubs, clubs, railway and bus stations; such encounters are often pre-arranged – that are sometimes far removed from stadia. Nor does it take place only on match days. The main common feature is fights between groups of males (these groups occasionally include females), who share a common allegiance to opposing football clubs. Intra-fan group fights have also been known to occur and the label 'football hooliganism' is also sometimes loosely used to cover politically orientated behaviour, such as that of groups on the political right. Then again, it is used in relation to protests against the owners and managers of clubs; to racist behaviour in football-related contexts and protests against such behaviour; and to fighting which is related in differing degrees to football matches *per se*. 'Football hooliganism' is therefore a complex and many-sided phenomenon. Let us examine some data, generated through an analysis of English newspaper coverage, which shed light on football hooliganism as a world phenomenon.

In the early stages of the research into football hooliganism that we started at the University of Leicester in the late 1970s,[5] we examined (as a sideline to the main study which was systematically historical as well as contemporary in its focus) a range of English newspapers and we recorded references to football-related violence involving fans rather than players reported as having occurred outside Great Britain. We looked at newspapers from 1890 onwards, ceased recording at the end of 1983 and did not use newspapers as a data source again until 1996. This means that, whilst our figures cover most of the twentieth century, they do not cover the years between 1983 and 1996. In that sense, they are incomplete. Nevertheless, until more systematic and intensive research along similar lines has been carried out, they can usefully serve as a rough indication of the worldwide incidence of football hooliganism in the twentieth century. In the course of this part of our research we came across reports of 101 incidents of football-related violence involving spectators or fans, which were reported as having occurred in 37 countries between 1908 and 1983. The countries and the number of incidents are given in table 1.

As can be seen, 16 of the reported countries – 17 if the former USSR is included – were European. This was, not surprisingly given their proximity to England, the highest geographical concentration of reported incidents. Central and South America, with hooliganism reported as having occurred in

Table 1 **Worldwide incidence of football-related violence as reported in English newspapers, 1908–83**

Argentina	c. 1936, 1965, 1968	Italy	1920, 1955, 1959,
Australia	1981		1963 (2 incidents),
Austria	c. 1965		1965 (2 incidents),
Belgium	1974, 1981		1973, 1975, 1979,
Bermuda	1980		1980, 1981, 1982
Brazil	1982	Jamaica	1965
Canada	1927	Lebanon	1964
China	1979, 1981, 1983	Malta	1975, 1980
Colombia	1982	Mexico	1983
Egypt	1966	New Zealand	1981
France	1960, 1975,	Nigeria	1983
	1977 (2 incidents), 1980	Norway	1981
Gabon	1981	Peru	1964
Germany[1]	1931, 1965 (2 incidents),	Portugal	1970
	1971, 1978, 1979 (2 incidents),	Rumania	1979
	1980, 1981 (3 incidents),	Spain	1950, 1980 (2 incidents),
	1982 (6 incidents)		1981, 1982
Greece	1980 (2 incidents), 1982, 1983	Sweden	1946
Guatemala	1980	Switzerland	1981
Holland	1974, 1982	Turkey	1964, 1967
Hungary	1908	USSR	1960, 1982
India	1931, 1982	USA	1980
Ireland[2]	1913, 1919, 1920 (3 incidents),	Yugoslavia	1955 (2 incidents)
	1930, 1955, 1970,		1982 (2 incidents)
	1979 (3 incidents), 1981		

1　Apart from the reported incident in 1931, these incidents were reported as having taken place in the former Federal Republic (West Germany).
2　Includes incidents reported as having taken place in both the Republic and Northern Ireland as well as incidents reported before the partition.

Source: Williams, J. et al. (1984/1989)

five countries, came second. 'Topping the poll' among the European countries were Germany, with 17 incidents reported between 1931 and 1982, Italy with 13 incidents between 1920 and 1982, and Ireland with 12 incidents between 1913 and 1982. Interestingly, if the data reported in a 20-page dossier published by the Council of the European Union in 1999 are adequate as a measure of the nation-by-nation incidence of football hooliganism – and the behaviour of a group of German hooligans in Lens (France) in 1998 at the World Cup Finals suggests that they may be – Germany continues by some way to lead what the authors of the dossier call 'the division of dishonour'.[6] This

...e fact contrasts markedly with the dominant stereotype which ...nues to mark out football hooliganism as a mainly 'English disease'.

The overwhelming majority of the incidents referred to in table 1 were reported in the 1960s, 1970s and 1980s. More particularly, 17 were reported in the 1960s, 20 in the 1970s, and no fewer than 40 in the first three years of the 1980s. This pattern arguably reflects both a factual increase in the incidence of football hooliganism during that 30-year period and a correlative increase of media interest in football hooliganism as a 'newsworthy' subject. The rise in media interest also occurred correlatively with growing popular and political interest in football hooliganism as a social problem, and with what one might jargonistically call the 'tabloidisation' of the popular press. Largely as a result of intensifying competition with television news, popular newspapers in the sensationalising tabloid form have risen to prominence, and one of the repercussions of this process has been a parallel, though lesser, trend towards the sensationalising of reporting in the more 'serious' or 'broadsheet' press.

Probably more than any other single incident, it was the Heysel tragedy, which took place in Brussels at the 1985 European Cup Final between Liverpool and Juventus, that fixed the idea of football hooliganism as an 'English disease' firmly in the minds of people around the world. What happened was that a charge of Liverpool hooligans across an inadequately segregated and under-policed terrace led to the flight of the targeted Italian fans (who were not 'ultras', the Italian equivalents of English football hooligans, although 'ultras' were there in force in other parts of the ground),[7] the build-up of pressure leading a defective wall to collapse and 39 Italians to lose their lives. Probably a majority of people, perhaps especially in Western countries, would, if asked, identify Heysel as the worst directly hooligan-related football tragedy to have occurred in modern times. The data in table 2, however, suggest that it was not the worst, and that football and football hooliganism outside Europe have involved a greater number of fatalities and perhaps also a greater incidence of murderous violence than have their counterparts in Europe – the continent where people consider themselves to stand at the apex of 'civilisation' and where, if Norbert Elias ([1939] 2000) is right, a 'civilising process' can be demonstrated factually to have occurred since the Middle Ages.

Sketchy though they are, the figures on football-related murders in table 3 point in the same direction. Italy, the European country with the highest incidence of football-related murders reported in the years 1996–99, had five, whereas Argentina, largely as a result of the activities of the notorious *barras bravas*, had a reported 39 murders, almost eight times as many.

The Heysel tragedy occurred at or near the crest of a rising wave of English-inspired hooligan incidents in continental countries, the first of which occurred in the late 1960s and early 1970s (Williams et al., 1984/1989). Associated with this wave was the adoption and adaptation of English hooligan styles by

Table 2 **Selected incidents at which serious crowd violence was reported**

Country	Year	Match	Number of deaths	Number of injuries
Argentina	1968	River Plate v Boca Juniors	74	150
Brazil	1982	San Luis v Fortaleza	3	25
Colombia	1982	Deportivo Cali v Club Argentina	22	200
Peru	1964	Peru v Argentina	287–328	5000
Turkey	1964	Kayseri v Sivas	44	600
USSR	1982	Moscow Sparta v Haarlem	69	100

Source: Williams et al., 1984/1989.

Table 3 **Number of football-related murders reported in selected English newspapers, June 1996–October 1999**

Country	Number
Argentina	39
England	3
Italy	5
Netherlands	1
Total	48

Sources: The Times; The Leicester Mercury; The Guardian; The Observer; The Sunday Times.

continental fans, although this is not something that we propose to discuss further.[8] More to the point for present purposes is that Heysel and the overall reaction to it also represented a peak in the politicisation of the English hooligan problem. It did so in the sense of leading for the first time to direct Prime Ministerial involvement in the problem and contributing to the introduction in Parliament of the Football Spectators Bill, Part I of which demanded computerised entry to matches. It also led the Union Européenne de Football Associations (UEFA) to ban English clubs – though not the national side – from European competition *sine die* and to an annual attempt by the English Football Association (FA) to secure their readmission. Between them, the passage of the Football Spectators Bill through Parliament and the annual attempt of the FA to secure the readmission of the English clubs helped to sustain media and popular interest in the hooligan problem. In its turn, the intense media searchlight led to large numbers of incidents being regularly observed and reported, amplifying the problem in two senses: first perceptually, by making it appear that more (and more serious) incidents were occurring than was objectively the case; and secondly by providing the oxygen of anonymous publicity which so many hooligans crave, in that way helping to sustain and even to increase the frequency of their hooligan involvements.

The Hillsborough tragedy of 1989, in which 96 people lost their lives at an (abandoned) FA Cup Semi-Final match between Liverpool and Nottingham Forest, constituted another watershed. The tragedy was indirectly related to hooliganism in three ways. First, as part of the official attempt to contain and control the hooligan threat, terrace fans in England – those who used to stand rather than sit to watch matches[9] – were forced to watch from inside what were, in effect, wire cages. Secondly, the hooligan-related alcohol ban led many supporters to linger on in pubs until the last moment, thus contributing to a panic to gain entry to the ground and a panic response by the police. Thirdly, the police interpreted as a hooligan pitch invasion what was in fact an attempt by Liverpool fans to escape from the terrace at the Leppings Lane end of Sheffield Wednesday's Hillsborough Stadium, which had become lethally overcrowded. Overcrowding had resulted from fans being forced into a space from which there was no escape, and 96 of them were crushed to death. The central relevance of Hillsborough for present purposes, however, lies in the fact that, in his official enquiry into the tragedy, Lord Justice Taylor concluded that computerised entry was more likely to increase than decrease the incidence of crowd fatalities. As a result, the Government was forced to climb down and, in 1990, Part 1 of the Football Spectators Bill was withdrawn. This contributed in its turn to consequences such as: (i) the relative and gradual depoliticisation of the English hooligan problem; (ii) the correlative withdrawal by UEFA of its ban on English clubs; (iii) a decline in the perceived newsworthiness of the hooligan problem; (iv) a decrease in the frequency with which it was reported; and (v) a growing impression that, in England, football hooliganism was becoming 'unfashionable', a 'thing of the past'. This impression was given graphic expression by the late Ian Taylor when he wrote in the *Independent on Sunday* (21 April 1991) that: 'An astonishing sea-change is taking place in the culture of some of (England's) football terraces.' He attributed this supposed process to a conjuncture of what he called 'the BBC's packaging' of 'Italia 90' with the removal of perimeter fences from grounds in response to the report of Lord Justice Taylor. According to Ian Taylor, the dynamics of this process worked according to something like the following pattern: the removal of 'cages' reduced the frequency of 'animal-like' behaviour among the fans, and this interacted with the TV packaging of the 1990 World Cup Finals in which, as he put it, 'the opera of Pavarotti would meld ethereally into a poetic display of European football', producing a re-emphasis on 'style'. As a result, Ian Taylor argued, 'hooliganism [became] suddenly decidedly unfashionable, passé, irrelevant'.

Despite the elegance of Ian Taylor's language, the problem with this kind of impressionistic, non-research-based analysis is that it involves a gross oversimplification of the hooligan problem and is in many respects simply empirically false. What happened in England during the 1990s was not so much that football hooliganism itself declined, as that, in conjunction largely with the relative depoliticisation of the problem, the reporting of football hooliganism became less fashionable. This was especially true of the reporting practices of the national media and in relation to 'bread and butter' domestic matches. It was less true of international matches, because of – among other things – their higher profile and the fact that the international media were there. For example, the 1990 World Cup Finals were accompanied in England by a hitherto virtually unprecedented form of hooliganism, namely outbreaks around the country of rioting, fighting and attacks on foreigners and foreign cars by fans who had been watching England's Italia 90 matches on TV. Similar outbreaks occurred during Euro 96 and the 1998 World Cup Finals. Events during Euro 96 are particularly instructive.

It is widely believed in England that Euro 96 passed off without the occurrence of hooliganism on any substantial scale. For example, discussing the hopes of the English FA that FIFA might allow England to host the 2006 World Cup, the journalist Martin Thorpe wrote of Euro 96 that: 'UEFA's ability to turn a handsome profit on a tournament in which England matched the best teams on the field and avoided trouble off it will go down well with FIFA when it chooses a venue for the second World Cup of the new century' (*The Guardian*, 12 October 1996). In his personal message, which fronted England's ultimately unsuccessful bid to host the 2006 World Cup Finals, the Prime Minister, Tony Blair, wrote of his belief that: 'the carnival atmosphere of Euro 96, I feel sure, has amply demonstrated our passion for football and our capacity for friendship and organisation. Our commitment to sport is unrivalled' (Football Association, n.d.). Later on in the same publication, Euro 96 was given the following fulsome praise:

> Ask anyone who was there. Euro 96 was one of the finest celebrations of international football ever staged. It was fun and friendly, yet superbly run in a safe and secure environment. No crowd problems marred the event, despite the complete absence of any perimeter fences. Almost 1.3 million spectators attended – an average of 41,270 per game – yielding profits of nearly £70 million. Euro 96 proved that England has put behind it the problems of the 1980s and is back to its best on the international stage (Football Association, London, n.d.).

There is no doubt that Euro 96 was in many respects a great success. The England team's standard of play (they reached the semi-finals only to be beaten by Germany in a penalty shoot-out), and the standard of football produced in the tournament overall exceeded many people's expectations. The Prime Minister, Tony Blair, following authors such as Richard Giulianotti, was led rightly to describe 'the carnival atmosphere' generated by the majority of people in the crowds. There was also a relative absence of serious disorders

inside and in the immediate vicinity of stadia. What is problematic is the
extent to which trouble was avoided in the broader context of match days.
There is ample evidence that it was widespread. For example, crowds gathered
in London's Trafalgar Square following England's game against Spain on 22
June and had to be dispersed by riot police. Disturbances were also reported
in Hull, and fights between Englishmen and Spaniards were reported as
having broken out in Fuengirola and Torremolinos on Spain's Costa del Sol
(*The Independent*, 24 June 1996). By far the most serious rioting, however,
occurred following England's defeat by West Germany in the semi-finals
when trouble was reported, not only in London, but in Basingstoke, Bedford,
Birmingham, Bournemouth, Bradford, Brighton (where a Russian teenager
was mistaken for a German, stabbed in the neck and almost killed),
Dunstable, Exeter, Haywards Heath, Mansfield, Norwich, Nottingham,
Portsmouth, Shropshire and Swindon (*Daily Mail*, 28 June 1996). The events
in London's Trafalgar Square were reported in the *Daily Mail* as follows:

> The agonising moment when Gareth Southgate's penalty was saved . . . was the
> trigger for a night of sustained hooliganism. Draped in flags and brandishing
> bottles, thousands spilled out of the pubs and bars . . . within moments of
> Germany's victory . . . The worst flashpoint came in Trafalgar Square . . . [I]t was
> the centre of . . . orchestrated rampage . . . Up to 2,000 people poured into the
> square shortly after 10.06 pm . . . [T]he situation rapidly deteriorated . . . Cars and
> motorists . . . found themselves engulfed in the rapidly-escalating violence with
> German Volkswagens and Mercedes singled out. A hard core of 400 hooligans . . .
> burst out of the square and attacked a police patrol car. The two officers inside
> had to flee for their lives as in less than a minute the car was smashed to pieces.
> The hooligans surged towards the Thames, shattering windscreens, turning one
> vehicle over and setting fire to a Japanese sports car . . . Between 10.10 p.m. and
> midnight, police received over 2,500 calls requesting urgent help. Of these 730
> were related to violent disturbances . . . The final toll around Trafalgar Square was
> 40 vehicles damaged, six overturned and two set alight. Seven buildings were
> damaged with 25 police officers and 23 members of the public injured across
> London, as well as a further 18 casualties, both police and civilians, in Trafalgar
> Square itself . . . Nearly 200 people were arrested across London with 40 held
> during ugly scenes in Trafalgar Square (*Daily Mail*, 28 June 1996)

These events were the most violent among a series, varying in violence and
scale, which took place across England during Euro 96. They took place
despite a co-ordinated police effort which had been planned for some three
years, cost an estimated £20 million (BBC1, 10 July 1996), and involved the
well publicised arrest of 'known hooligans' up and down the country before
the tournament. John Goodbody, the sports correspondent of *The Times*,

concluded not unrealistically that: 'What Wednesday night emphasised is that whenever the English supporters are taking part in an international tournament, it is inevitable that there will be trouble. However careful the preparations, troublemakers will ensure that there will be confrontations' (*The Times*, 28 June 1996).

Events in France in July 1998, especially in Marseilles, offered support for John Goodbody's view. Earlier, England fans had rioted in Sweden in 1992, in Amsterdam and Rotterdam in 1993, and in Dublin in 1995. In Dublin, they forced the abandonment of an Ireland–England match. Proponents of the 'hooliganism is a thing of the past' thesis, such as Helgadottir (1993) and I. Taylor (*Independent on Sunday*, 21 April 1991), can only account for such incidents by claiming with tortuous logic that the English hooligans have become peaceful at home and engage only in violence abroad. Alternatively, they suggest that the fans of Premiership teams have become peaceable as a result of an interaction between more effective police and club controls, and fashion changes among fans in the direction of both more carnival-like and consumer-orientated behaviour (Giulianotti, 1999). Hooliganism, they suggest, remains more stubbornly entrenched at the lower levels of the game. Yet the evidence is against them. Hooliganism continues to occur at all levels of the English game, suggesting the use of a kind of Ptolemaic logic on their part.[10] Take the figures in tables 4, 5 and 6. Table 4 offers a selection of incidents known to the police which took place at or in conjunction with Premiership, Football League and other top-level (e.g. pre-season 'friendly') matches in England and Wales during 1992–93.

Table 5 summarises data furnished by the British Transport Police (BTP) for the period 21 August 1990 to 22 December 1993, a period during which they recorded 655 incidents of varying levels of seriousness which had taken place at or in the vicinity of railway stations or on trains.

Table 6 is based on 69 reports of football hooliganism that appeared in 13 English newspapers between June 1996 and October 1999. A total of 110 incidents were referred to and/or described in these reports. Sixty-nine of them were reported as having occurred in England or Wales, and a further 20 as having involved English fans abroad. In 12 of the latter cases, the English fans were reported as aggressors and in the remaining eight as victims. Of the 21 incidents that remain, five were reported as involving Dutch fans, four Argentinian fans, four Italian fans, two German fans, two Russian fans, one an Iranian fan and the final one a Scottish fan. Twenty-four of the incidents were reported in 1996, 19 in 1997, 59 in 1998 and eight in the months January to October 1999. The larger numbers reported in 1996 and 1998, the years of Euro 96 and the last World Cup Finals respectively, are clearly in part a reflection of the heightened media interest in hooliganism that is generated in conjunction with major tournaments. Furthermore, independently of the

Table 4 **Selected hooligan incidents at or in conjunction with Premiership, Football League, international, pre-season friendly and other matches in England and Wales**

Date	Match/fans involved	Type of incident
7.10.92	Notts. Forest *v* Stockport	CS gas used, 8 policemen hurt
18.10.92	Sunderland *v* Newcastle	30 arrests, 200 ejected
31.10.92	Leyton Orient *v* Swansea	Fights in London (Marble Arch)
31.10.92	Grimsby *v* Portsmouth	Missiles thrown at players
14.11.92	Darlington *v* Hull	Pub fights in city centre and station
16.11.92 and 24.11.92	Stoke *v* Port Vale	Fights inside/ outside ground/ town centre
19.12.92	Chelsea *v* Manchester Utd	CS gas thrown in Covent Garden pub
12.1.93	Southend *v* Millwall	Pitch invasion, pub fights
16.1.93	Tranmere	Fan beaten to death (racial more than football-related)
19.1.93	Cardiff *v* Swansea	Pitch invasion, pub fights*
30.1.93	Leicester *v* West Ham	Fights outside ground, CS gas thrown in pub
20.2.93	Tottenham *v* Leeds	300 in fight, CS gas thrown in pub*
5.3.93	Tottenham and Blackpool	Fans fighting in Blackpool prior to Spurs/Man. City match
7.3.93	Man. City *v* Tottenham	Pitch invasion, fighting outside ground*
17.3.93	England U18 *v* Ghana	Attack on police
17.3.93	Sheffield Wed. *v* Sheffield Utd	Fighting, murder*
24.3.93	Peterborough *v* Leicester	Pitch invasion, arson
3.4.93	Millwall *v* Portsmouth	Pub fights, missiles thrown*
28.4.93	England *v* Holland	Pub fights, police attached
1.5.93	Reading *v* Swansea	Fighting inside/outside ground, pitch invasion*
2.5.93	Aston Villa *v* Oldham	Disturbances in Oldham; riot police used
4.5.93	Exeter *v* Port Vale	Attack by fans on referee
8.5.93	Millwall *v* Bristol Rovers	Pitch invasion, missiles thrown*
8.5.93	Halifax *v* Hereford	Mounted police used. Fighting inside ground
Div 1 Play-off Semi-Final	Portsmouth *v* Leicester (at Nottingham's City ground)	Fights outside the ground
Div 1 Play-off Final	Swindon *v* Leicester City (at Wembley)	Leicester fans ransacked Wembley pub. Disturbances in Swindon

* Denotes police judgement of disturbances sufficiently serious to 'stretch' available police resources.

Source: These data were provided by Ian Stanier, a Leicester postgraduate student.

Table 5 **Football-related incidents known to the British Transport Police, 1990–93**

Season		No. of incidents
1990–91	(21.8.90–5.6.91. Includes end-of-season play-offs)	204
1991–92	(17.8.91–3.6.92. Includes end-of-season play-offs and one international)	260
1992–93	(8.8.92–31.5.93)	127
1993–94	(24.7.93–22.12.93. First half season only)	64
Total		655

The remaining 12 incidents known to the BTP took place in conjunction with pre-season matches.

Table 6 **Number of hooligan incidents reported in selected English newspapers, June 1996–October 1999**[1]

Incidents reported as occurring in England and Wales	69
Incidents reported as involving English fans abroad as:	
(a) attackers	12
(b) attacked	8
Incidents reported as involving fans from Argentina (4); France (2); Germany (2); Iran (1); Italy (4); Netherlands (5); Russia (2); Scotland (1)	21
Total	110

1   23 of these reports appeared in *The Guardian*, 18 in the *Leicester Mercury* and 15 in *The Observer*.

effects produced by media reporting, it can be unequivocally stated that these data indicate unambiguously that football hooliganism is alive and kicking.

Who are the football hooligans and why do they behave as they do? An examination of some popular and academic explanations of the phenomenon of football hooliganism in Britain will start to shed light on these issues.

In Britain, five main popular explanations of football hooliganism have been proposed, each of them espoused by the media, politicians and members of the general public. These explanations – some of them at least partly contradicting the others – are that football hooliganism is 'caused' by: excessive alcohol consumption; violent incidents on the field of play or biased and incompetent refereeing; unemployment; affluence; and 'permissiveness'. Available evidence does not show that any of these factors plays any deeper, more enduring part in generating football hooliganism. This does not mean, of course, that they cannot be an element in a more complex explanation. Alcohol consumption cannot be said to be a 'cause' of football hooliganism, because not every fan who drinks in a football context fights, not even those who drink heavily. The converse is also true, that is not all hooligans drink before fighting because they need a clear head in order (*a*) to avoid being caught unawares by rivals or the police and (*b*) to play a part in determining strategy (Dunning et al., 1988). Some, of course, drink or take other drugs for 'Dutch courage'. There is an *indirect* connection between soccer hooliganism and alcohol consumption, however, in that the masculinity norms of the groups involved tend to stress ability to fight, 'hardness' and ability to 'hold one's ale' as marks of being a 'man', and tests of masculinity are one of the things that football hooliganism is all about.

Violence on the field of play and refereeing that is, or is perceived to be, biased can similarly be dismissed as lying at the roots of football hooliganism. That is because incidents take place before and after as well as during matches, often at considerable distances from grounds. Nor can unemployment – a favoured 'cause' of the political left – be said in some simple sense to produce football hooliganism. For example, during the 1930s when unemployment in England was high, the incidence of reported match-related violence was at an all-time low. Similarly, when English football hooliganism began to enter its current phase in the 1960s, the national rate of unemployment was at its lowest ever recorded level. And today, the rate of participation in football hooliganism by the unemployed varies regionally, being higher in areas such as the North of England where unemployment is high and lower in usually low unemployment areas such as London and the South-East. In fact, almost every major English club has its soccer hooligans, in part independently of the local rate of unemployment, and fans from more affluent areas in the 1980s regularly used to taunt their less fortunate rivals by waving bundles of £5 or £10 notes at them en masse, singing (to the tune of 'You'll never walk alone') 'You'll never work again'. However, unemployment can be said to be an indirect 'cause' of soccer hooliganism in the sense of being one among a complex of processes which help to perpetuate the norms of aggressive masculinity which appear to be centrally involved.

The fourth popular explanation of soccer hooliganism, namely that 'affluence' rather than unemployment is the principal 'cause', tends to be favoured by the political right. This is in direct contradiction of the explanation by reference to unemployment. It is also sometimes associated with the explanation in terms of 'permissiveness', for example when it is suggested that football hooliganism is an attribute of the 'too much, too soon' generation. Whatever form it takes, however, the explanation by reference to 'affluence' is contradicted by the available evidence; it seems largely to result from an ideologically driven misreading of the fashion-switch on the part of young British football fans during the 1980s from the 'skinhead' to the 'casual' style. The skinhead style was, of course, openly working class; the casual style, by contrast, is apparently 'classless'. The clothes worn by devotees of the casual style may be, but are not necessarily, expensive. Sometimes they are stolen and sometimes only appear expensive as when 'designer labels' are sewn onto cheap, sometimes stolen, sweaters or when they are 'seconds'. Of course, some soccer hooligans are at least temporarily affluent, either because they have well-paid jobs or prosperous parents, or because they make money through black market activities or involvement in crime. But the bulk of the available evidence runs counter to the 'affluence thesis'. Data on the social origins of football hooligans first began to become available in the 1960s and they have been, on the whole, remarkably consistent since that time: while hooligans come from all levels in the class hierarchy, the majority come from the ranks of the working class and have low levels of formal education (Dunning et al., 1988). We shall return to this issue later.

The popular explanation by reference to 'permissiveness' appears to be similarly deficient. It is superficially plausible in that the advent of the so-called 'permissive society' in Britain in the 1960s coincided with the authorities and the media coming increasingly to perceive the behaviour of football fans as problematic. Yet football hooliganism in Britain as a fact if not by name can be traced back to the 1870s and 1880s (Dunning et al., 1988), and the *coup de grâce* is given to the 'permissive society' argument by the fact that, since football hooliganism began to be recognised in Britain as a social problem in the 1960s, soccer matches have become more heavily policed and subject to tighter controls. Watching British football has thus become anything but 'permissive'. Moreover, during the 1980s, members of the Thatcher government sought explicitly, by means of 'authoritarian', 'law and order' policies, to reverse what they saw as the generally deleterious 'permissiveness' of the 1960s and 1970s. Nevertheless, football hooliganism, along with crime in general, continued to grow for some time.

Let us turn now from the *popular* explanations of football hooliganism to the principal explanations of football hooliganism that have so far been proposed by British *academics* and which deal mainly with the English problem.

Besides the 'figurational' or 'process-sociological' approach on which this chapter is based,[11] six main academic approaches to the study of football hooliganism can be distinguished: the 'anthropological' approach of Armstrong and Harris (1991) and Armstrong (1998); what is perhaps best called the 'postmodernist' approach of Giulianotti (1999); the Marxist approaches of Ian Taylor (1971a; 1971b; 1982b), Clarke (1978) and Hargreaves (1986); the 'ethogenic' approach of Marsh et al. (1978) and Marsh (1978); the 'psychological reversal theory' approach advocated by Kerr (1994); and the historically sensitive/historical approaches of King (1997a; 1997b) and Robson (2000), which variously apply aspects of the theories of Durkheim, Weber, Goffman, Bernstein and Bourdieu to the problem. Each of these approaches to explanation has its particular strengths. But each has its particular weaknesses too. Since the approaches of King and Robson are broadly consistent with that of the 'figurationalists', in the discussion that follows we shall focus on the approaches of Armstrong and Harris, Giulianotti, Taylor, Clarke, Hargreaves and Kerr.

The anthropological work on football hooliganism by Armstrong and Harris is based on rich, in-depth description of the behaviour of hooligan fans from Sheffield, a two-club city. It is theoretically eclectic, present-centred and, as is often the case with ethnographic or participant observation research, its principal author (Armstrong) seems insufficiently aware of the limitations which derive from reliance on the unsupported testimony of an individual. This is true of the work of Giulianotti, too. Armstrong also pays insufficient attention to the ways in which the dynamics of fan behaviour and relationships may have been affected by the fact that Sheffield is a two-club city; and the need for comparative observation of one-club cities such as Leicester and other two-club cities such as Liverpool and Nottingham was apparently not recognised. Nor, and this again holds good for the work of Giulianotti, is sufficient attention paid to change over time. These limitations are compounded by the authors' peremptory dismissal of virtually all research in the field other than their own, a stance which is not conducive to open dialogue and hence to the possibility of publicly establishing the degree to which the – in many ways – rich, deep and dense Sheffield findings and the rather more abstract Aberdeen findings confirm or refute the findings of others.

The work of Taylor, Clarke and Hargreaves is insightful in showing how developments in English football have been bound up with the capitalist character of the economy (see also King, 1998). None of these authors has carried out systematic in-depth research into soccer hooliganism, however, and they all neglect the significance of the fact that the phenomenon principally involves conflict *between* working-class groups – groups that only become involved in regular conflict with the football authorities and the police, and less directly with other representatives of the state – as part of an attempt to fight *among themselves.* In his early work, Taylor even romantically described football hooliganism as a 'working class resistance movement' (Taylor, 1971b). Marsh et al. do not make such mistakes. Nevertheless, their work lacks an historical dimension, with the consequence that they tend to see hooligan fighting – or what they call 'aggro' – as an unchanging historical constant. Moreover, in their stress on 'aggro' as 'ritual violence' (that is, violence which is mainly symbolic or metonymic in the sense of involving aggressive posturing but not the completion or 'consummation' of aggressive acts), they neglect the fact that ritualised aggression can be seriously violent.

Finally, through his use of 'reversal' theory, Kerr seems to do little more than dress up in complex psychological jargon some relatively simple sociological ideas. For example, he writes:

The metamotivational state combination operative during most types of soccer hooliganism activity is paratelic-negativistic-autic-mastery. The paratelic-negativism element within this combination (with accompanying high levels of felt arousal and felt negativism) gives rise to the type of provocative, playful paratelic aggression that characterizes so many examples of soccer hooligan activity. Hooligan behaviour in these circumstances is not necessarily malicious, but is engaged in with the major purpose of generating excitement and the pleasures of release from rules (Kerr, 1994: 109).

Kerr seems to think that the football hooligans' quest for excitement through violent, deviant and delinquent acts in soccer-related contexts can be explained as a simple 'reversal' from one 'metamotivational state', 'boredom' (Kerr, 1994: 33ff), to another, 'excitement'. It is difficult to see how what he writes does more than dress up in psychological jargon what Elias and Dunning (1986) had written more than twenty years before (although we wrote about routinisation in this connection and not simple boredom), at the same time reducing a complex and graduated socio-behavioural reality to a simple dichotomy. Above all, there is no reference in what Kerr writes to what is also arguably at stake in football hooligan fighting, namely norms of masculinity. These figure centrally in the figurational/process sociological explanation (see also King, 1997a; 1997b; and Robson, 2000).

The figurational approach to football hooliganism does not constitute some kind of 'super theory' which purportedly explains everything. It is offered rather as a beginning on which to build. Its distinctive features include the fact that it is based on a synthesis of psychology, sociology and history. It also involves (i) an exploration of the meanings of hooligan behaviour via an analysis of verbatim statements by the hooligans themselves; (ii) the location of football hooligans in the overall social structure, especially the class system; and (iii) an examination of the dynamics of the relationships between them and groups in the wider society. Shortage of space means that here we can only briefly examine some of our data on the meanings and social locations of English football hooligans. Let us simply give some verbatim quotations that shed light on English football hooligans' characteristic values and motives, which have remained relatively stable over time.

Reminiscing about the emotions he experienced during his days of active hooligan involvement in the 1960s, E. Taylor wrote in *The Guardian* in 1984 of:

The excitement of battle, the danger, the heightened activity of body and mind as the adrenaline raced, the fear and the triumph of overcoming it. To this day, when trouble starts at a game I come alive and close to getting involved. I may not forget the dangers of physical injury and criminal proceedings but I do ignore them (*The Guardian*, 28 March 1984).

Similar sentiments were expressed by a 26-year-old lorry driver interviewed in conjunction with the 1974 Cardiff City *v* Manchester United game, a match in which serious trouble had rightly been anticipated by the authorities and the media. He said:

> I go to a match for one reason only: the aggro. It's an obsession. I get so much pleasure when I'm having aggro that I nearly wet my pants . . . I go all over the country looking for it. . . . [E]very night during the week we go round looking respectable . . . [T]hen if we see someone who looks like the enemy, we ask him the time; if he answers in a foreign accent, we do him over, and if he's . . . got any money on him, we'll roll him as well (Harrison, 1974: 602–4).

Here is how one of our Leicester informants put it in 1981. His words illustrate the sort of rationality which tends to be involved:

> If you can baffle the coppers, you'll win. You've just gotta think how they're gonna think. And you know, half the time you know what they're gonna do 'cos they're gonna take the same route every week, week in, week out. If you can figure out a way to beat 'em, you're fuckin' laughin': you'll have a good fuckin' raut ['Raut' is Leicester slang for a fight].

Finally, when interviewed in 1984–85 for the Thames TV documentary, *Hooligan*, which was centred on the Leicester research, a member of West Ham United's 'Inter City Firm' (ICF), England's most notorious football hooligan gang at the time, said:

> We don't – we don't well, we *do* go with the intention of fighting, you know what I mean . . . We look forward to it . . . It's great. You know, if you've got, say, 500 kids coming for you, like, and you know they're going to be waiting for you, it's – it's good to know, like. Like being a tennis player, you know. You get all geed up to play, like. We get geed up to fight . . . I think I fight, like, so I can make a name for meself and that, you know. Hope people, like, respect me for what I did like.

Despite the fact that they cover a period of more than 20 years, these statements are broadly consistent. What they reveal is that, for the (mainly) young men involved, football hooligan fighting is basically about masculinity, struggle to control territory, and excitement. For them, fighting is a central source of meaning, status or 'reputation', and pleasurable emotional arousal. Thus, Taylor spoke of 'battle excitement' and 'the adrenaline racing'; the ICF member referred not only to the excitement generated in fighting but also to the respect among his peers that he hoped his involvement would bring; and the lorry driver spoke of 'aggro' as a pleasurable, almost erotically arousing obsession. This latter point received substantiation when Jay Allan, a leading member of 'the Aberdeen Casuals', a Scottish football hooligan 'firm', wrote of fighting at football as being even more pleasurable than sex (Allan, 1989). Another non-English expression of this kind of sentiment was provided in 1994 by a 17-year-old Brazilian *torcida* who told a reporter for the Rio paper, *Journal do Brasil*: 'For me fighting is fun. I feel a great emotion when the other guy screams in pain. I don't care about how other people feel as long as I'm happy' (reported in *The Australian*, 15 December 1994). This resembles the delight taken in injuring and inflicting pain on others reported of some leading members of the Chelsea 'Headhunters', a neo-Nazi hooligan crew exposed by Donal Macintyre in a television documentary on BBC2 on 10 November 1999. American author Bill Buford, who spent around a year following a group of hooligans, expressed the same basic idea in more literary terms when he wrote in 1991 that:

> [The hooligans] talk about the crack, the buzz and the fix. They talk about having to have it, of being unable to forget it when they do, of not wanting to forget it – ever . . . They talk about it with the pride of the privileged . . . They talk about it in the way that another generation talked about drugs and drink. One lad, a publican, talks about it as though it were a chemical thing . . . once it's in the air, once an act of violence has been committed, other acts will follow inevitably – necessarily . . . Violence is one of the most intensely lived experiences and, for those capable of giving themselves over to it, one of the most intense pleasures . . . crowd violence was their drug (Buford, 1991: 206–7).

What about the social class antecedents and locations of the football hooligans? Social class raises complex and contentious sociological issues of definition and measurement. The available data on the social origins and current stratificational rankings of English football hooligans remain relatively scanty and cannot be described as definitive or 'hard'. What they suggest, however, is that while football hooligans come from most levels of the class hierarchy, the majority, some 70–80 per cent, are working class in their social origins and most usually in terms of their present stratificational standings as well. That is, the majority of their parents had low levels of formal education and worked or work in manual occupations, whilst the majority of the hooligans themselves have failed to rise above their parents' social level. The data also suggest, with one main possible exception, that this sort of distribution has remained relatively stable since the 1960s when English football hooliganism first began to attract public concern. More particularly, the data of Harrington (1968) on the 1960s, of Trivizas (1980) on the 1970s, of Stuttard (1985), Armstrong (1999), and the Leicester group (Stuttard, 1985; Dunning et al., 1988) on the 1980s, and of the Leicester group again on the

1990s, all suggest that the majority of English football hooligans come from the lower reaches of the social scale. A small proportion, however, is recruited from around the middle, and an even smaller one is from at or near the top. Let us explore this pattern and the data which support it in greater detail.

Harrington's 1968 analysis of the occupations of 497 convicted soccer hooligans showed a preponderance of labourers and unskilled workers (see table 7). Over a decade later, Trivizas (1980) reached a similar conclusion. More particularly, on the basis of data about 520 offences committed at 'football crowd events' in London's Metropolitan Police Area during the years 1974–76, he found that:

> More than two-thirds (68.1%) of those charged with football-related offences were manual workers . . . Only 8 football-related offences were committed by people in 'intermediate' occupations. 6 were committed by students, 3 by individuals in professional occupations, and 3 by members of the armed forces (Trivizas, 1980: 281–3).

Harrison's impressionistic account of Cardiff City's 'committed rowdies' in 1974 paints a similar picture. He depicted them as coming from 'Canton and Grangetown, rows of terraced houses with few open spaces, and from Llanrumney, a massive council estate with an appalling record of vandalism' (Harrison, 1974: 602). Although Marsh et al. did not directly address the issue of social class in their 1978 study of Oxford United fans, some of their informants provided relevant comments. For example, one of them said: 'If you live up on the Leys (an Oxford council estate) then you have to fight or else people piss you about and think you're a bit soft or something' (Marsh et al., 1978: 69). In fact, over half of the large contingent of Oxford fans arrested during serious disturbances at the Coventry City–Oxford United FA Cup match in January 1981 came from the estate in question (*Oxford Mail*, 9 January 1981). Evidence from Leicester supports this general picture. One council estate alone contributed 87, or 20.32 per cent, of the 428 local persons arrested in a football context in the years 1976–80. In 1981 and 1982, the years in which the participant observation part of the Leicester research was carried out on this estate, the occupations of 23 active football hooligans from the estate were as follows: two drivers, one barman, one slaughterhouse man, three bouncers, one bookmaker's assistant, three factory workers (two in the hosiery trade and one in boots and shoes), one milkman, one apprentice printer, one apprentice electrician, one builder's labourer, and eight unemployed. The data in table 7 suggest a possible change in this overall pattern: Harrington's 1968 data indicate that 12.9 per cent of his arrested football hooligans were skilled workers, compared with 24.1 per cent in the Stuttard and Dunning et al. figures for West Ham United's 'Inter City Firm' (ICF) in

1985, and 46.8 per cent in Armstrong's 1987 data on Sheffield United's 'Blades' (published in Armstrong, 1998). In short, these data suggest that an increase in the participation in football hooliganism of skilled relative to unskilled and semi-skilled males may have occurred in the 1980s as compared with the 1960s and 1970s.

Table 7 **Trends in the occupational class of employed English football hooligans, 1968–87**[1]

Occupational class	Harrington, 1968		Stuttard/Dunning et al., 1985		Armstrong, 1987[2]	
	No	%	No	%	No	%
Professional	2	0.5[3]			3	2.1
Intermediate			8	5.7	7	4.9
Skilled non-manual	19	4.9	2	1.42	24	16.8
Skilled manual	50	12.9[4]	34	24.1	67	46.8
Semi-skilled	112	28.8	10	7.0	14	9.8
Unskilled	206	52.9	25	17.7[5]	28	19.6

1   Figures exclude those for schoolboys, apprentices, the unemployed and those with occupations unclassifiable in terms of the Registrar General's scheme.
2   Armstrong's 1987 data published in Armstrong (1998).
3   Professional and intermediate classified together.
4   Harrington uses different categories.
5   32 (22.7 per cent) of our ICF sample were unemployed at the time and 30 (21.2 per cent) were unclassifiable using the Registrar General's categories. Twelve of the latter earned a living as ticket touts and eight were members of the armed forces.

Assuming that this putative increase in the participation of young skilled workers in football hooliganism did in fact occur, it seems to have corresponded with the abandonment by football hooligans and by young fans in general of the avowedly working-class 'skinhead' style, and their adoption of the apparently middle-class or classless style of the so-called football 'casuals'. Although the figures it contains are very scanty and perhaps more than usually unreliable, the data culled from English newspapers and reported in table 8 appear to confirm the continuation of this pattern into the late 1990s. The description of himself as a 'property tycoon' by one English hooligan was, however, probably a 'wind-up'.

Research on the social class of football hooligans in Scotland, Belgium, The Netherlands and Italy suggests that hooligans in other countries tend to come from social backgrounds similar to those of their English counterparts. A study of Scottish 'football casuals', for example, found that:

All the evidence points to the fact that 'football casuals' come predominantly from the lower levels of the social scale and are basically working class youths. (In the Edinburgh survey, 75% of the 'casuals' arrested fell into the 'unskilled manual' or 'unemployed' category. None came within the 'managerial-professional' category) (Harper, 1989: 90).

Table 8 **Occupational data from selected British newspapers on arrested English hooligans, 1997–98**[12]

Upper and middle class	
Property tycoon	1
Intermediate and indeterminate	
IT worker (City of London); clerical worker; engineer; bank worker; self-employed glazier.	5
Working class	
Hospital worker; factory worker; parcelforce worker; post-office worker; postman; railway workers (2); floor layer; roofer; RAF fireman; tiler; soldier; mould operator; builder.	14
Total	**20**

Sources: The Times; The Leicester Mercury; The Guardian; The Observer; The Sunday Times.

Similarly, a study of soccer hooliganism in Belgium concluded that 'most of [Belgium's] "hard core" football hooligans . . . had a short and frustrating school career. Most . . . come from unstable working class families. Almost none . . . have a regular job . . . Their material situation is poor, the casuals get their expensive clothes by theft' (Van Limbergen et al., 1987: 8). According to the research of Van der Brug in Holland, typical Dutch hooligans: tend to resent and resist formal education; are more likely than non-hooligans to be unemployed; have parents who display a relatively tolerant attitude towards the use of violence and aggression; and gain prestige and status from fighting and generally displaying macho characteristics (Van der Brug, 1986). Finally, on the basis of a survey of Bologna 'ultras', Roversi concluded that:

> The majority of young '*ultras*' are from the working class. The group in employment contains 169 males and 46 females. In this group the skilled and unskilled blue-collar workers visibly predominate, both compared to workers of other kinds and within the sample as a whole; they represent 80.3% and 51.9% respectively. They are warehousemen, porters, shop-assistants, bricklayers, carpenters but above all shop-floor workers . . . It must be emphasised that only 3.9% of the entire sample admitted to being unemployed (Roversi, 1994: 359–81).

Despite differences of theoretical, conceptual and methodological orientation, there is substantial consistency between these Scottish, Belgian, Dutch and Italian findings, those of Harrington, Armstrong and Trivizas and those of the Leicester research. Soccer is the world's most popular team sport; worldwide, a majority of its spectators tend to be male and, despite inter-societal variations in the stratificational location of the game, they tend to come from the lower reaches of the social scale. That is, they tend to come from social backgrounds where shared norms legitimate a more ready resort to overt violence and aggressiveness in everyday social relations than is usually sanctioned among the middle and upper classes. Members of these higher groups are more liable to conform in public (though not necessarily in private) with official standards.[13] To express the same point differently, lower-class males are more likely to develop an overtly violent and aggressive habitus and mode of presenting themselves to the world than tends to be the case with the male members of higher social strata. The lower-class male habitus tends to involve a complex of learned traits which seem to derive principally from: (i) a pattern of early socialisation characterised by ready resort to violence by parents, older relatives, siblings, neighbours and other children; and (ii) adolescent socialisation on the streets in the company mainly of age peers, in adolescent 'gangs' (Dunning et al., 1988).[14] In these gangs, ability and willingness to use violence and to fight tend to become criteria for member-ship of and prestige within the group – for the status of these males in their own and each others' eyes as 'men'. As a result, they learn to associate adrenaline arousal in fights and physical confrontations with warm, rewarding and thus pleasurable feelings, rather than with the anxiety and guilt that tend to accompany the performance and witnessing of 'real' (as opposed to 'mimetic' [Elias and Dunning, 1986]) violence in the broader context of societies in which a majority of people consider themselves to be 'civilised'.[15]

The violent and aggressive habitus of these males will tend to be reinforced when they live and work in circumstances characterised by high levels of gender and age-group segregation. That is, this habitus will tend to be rein-forced to the extent that 'softening' pressure from females and older males is lacking.[16] In most societies, furthermore, the members of groups lower down the social scale are likely, by reason for example of the relative homogeneity of their work experiences, to be less highly individualised and more likely readily to form intense 'we-group' bonds and identifications (Elias, 1978: 134–48) which involve an equally intense hostility towards 'outsiders' (Elias [1939] 2000) than is the case among the more powerful, more self-steering and usually more inhibited groups who stand above them. At a soccer match, of course, the outsiders are the opposing team and its supporters, as well as, in some cases, the match officials. These groups tend to choose soccer as a context in which to fight because it, too, is about masculinity, territory and excitement. Given a widespread pattern of travel to away matches, the game also regularly provides a set of ready-made opponents with whom to fight.

Large crowds form a milieu, furthermore, where it is possible to behave violently and in other deviant ways with a relatively good chance of escaping detection and arrest.

The above argument is not meant to imply that soccer hooliganism is always and everywhere a consequence solely or mainly of social class. As a basis for further research, it is reasonable to hypothesise that the problem will be contoured and fuelled, *ceteris paribus*, by what one might call the major 'fault-lines' of particular countries. In England, now and in the recent past, that means by class and regional differences and inequalities; in Scotland (at least in Glasgow) and Northern Ireland, by religious sectarianism; in Spain, by the partly language-based subnationalisms of the Catalans, Castilians and Basques; in Italy, by city-based particularism and perhaps the division between North and South as expressed in the formation of the 'Northern League'; and in Germany, by relations between the generations (Heitmeyer and Peter, 1992; Elias, 1996) and between East and West.[16] Religious, subnational, city-based, regional and generation-based fault-lines may draw into football hooliganism more people from higher up the social scale than has tended to be the case in England up to now. Indeed, it is possible that future social changes may produce the same effect in England, too. Arguably, however, a shared characteristic of all these fault-lines – and, of course, each can overlap and interact with others in a variety of complex ways – is that they are social formations which involve intense 'we-group' bonds ('us') and correspondingly intense antagonisms towards 'outsiders' or 'they-groups' ('them'). The relative violence and persistence of such 'we-group'/'they-group' figurations is likely to be a consequence, *ceteris paribus*, of the degree to which they involve an overlap between class, sectarian and perhaps other inequalities and rivalries.

By way of conclusion, let us make ourselves perfectly clear. We do not consider this argument about 'fault-lines' as having the status of anything more than a working hypothesis. It needs to be subjected to public discussion and tested by means of systematic, theory-guided, cross-national empirical research. Doubtless in that context, it will need to be revised, expanded, modified and perhaps even rejected altogether. It is our hope, though, that this Introduction and the chapters in this book which follow will serve as a basis from which a programme of cross-national research on football hooliganism can be constructed, leading to an expanded understanding of the phenomenon and forming the basis for more effective policies for tackling the problem at the world, European and national levels. Such policies are urgently needed if the great social invention of soccer is to be protected from the serious threat currently posed by a combination of hooligan fans, complacent politicians, and money-driven owners, managers and players.

Chapter 2

'Aguante' and repression: football, politics and violence in Argentina

Pablo Alabarces

Introduction: the 'last' conflict

After 68 years of professional football, during which 137 people had been killed and more than 20,000 wounded in football-related violence,[1] the intervention of a judge, Victor Perrotta, led to the first ever suspension of the Argentine football championships as a result of violence. In an order of Wednesday 13 May 1998, the judge decided provisionally to suspend all matches in the premier division organised by the Argentine Football Association (AFA). The AFA, for its part, decided to extend the measure to include the suspension of matches in the Regional, Women's and Youth Leagues. The suspension was extended for a further two weeks in the period immediately preceding the 1998 World Cup Finals in France in which the Argentine team was due to participate.

Judge Perrotta's action was initially supported as a necessary means of trying to bring an end to the violence associated with football. However, it increasingly came under attack, particularly by those who had economic interests in television and journalism. More generally, the judge's action came to be seen as an excessive measure which disorganised the football calendar both for football clubs and the media and which did not in itself produce any solution to the problem of violence. Finally, the judge authorised the restarting of football competitions but demanded the adoption of a series of essentially repressive measures. The judge understood that those responsible for the violence were relatively small numbers of people who were members of the so-called 'barras bravas' and he ordered that those who were known to have been involved in violence should not be admitted to the stadia. In this

This chapter was written in collaboration with Ramiro Coelho, Mariana Conde, Christian Dodaro, José Garriga, Betina Guindi, Andrea Lobos, María Verónica Moreira, María Graciela Rodríguez, Juan Sanguinetti and Angel Srabszteni.
This research has been financed by the University of Buenos Aires and CONICET, Argentina.

connection, he demanded that the clubs and the police should provide lists of participants who had been involved in violence and, after some initial resistance, both the police and the clubs provided such lists, thus demonstrating that club administrators and police chiefs knew the names of the members of the 'barras' and of other violent fans. These people were denied admittance to the stadia. The judge also banned the use of fireworks (their use was already prohibited under other legislation) and the use of flags greater than two metres long, alleging that weapons and fireworks were hidden in the giant flags used by some supporters. Judge Perrotta also demanded the installation in all the stadia of audiovisual systems of control, similar to the system of closed circuit television (CCTV) used in English football grounds; this proposal was unanimously rejected by the clubs who were to be required to bear the costs of installing and running these devices.

The restarting of football led to a great deal of discussion, argument and controversy. Clubs were required to bear increasing costs for additional police protection and, in some cases, these costs were higher than the income from admission charges; some of those who were barred from entering the stadia went to the ground accompanied by lawyers who claimed that their exclusion from the ground was illegal and unconstitutional; fans protested vehemently against the ban on the carrying of large flags, claiming they were a fundamental component of the football fiesta. The major beneficiaries were the police forces who received extra income because of the larger numbers of police who were mobilised at football matches.[2]

None of these measures had a major effect in terms of controlling violence. Violence returned almost immediately in August 1998 when football matches resumed and, after several violent incidents, some of them very serious, the judge again suspended football matches in December 1998. But this suspension, imposed after judicial arguments in a higher court, resulted in an even greater crisis in football. In the light of the problems confronting their colleagues in the poorest teams, the Premier League players called for a strike of solidarity in February, thus delaying the start of the 1999 season. This led to feverish negotiations between clubs, judges, political authorities (who were worried about the possible social consequences of a country without football) and television managers. After a delay of three weeks, football resumed in March 1999. On the day the judicial suspension of football was removed, the 'hinchadas' (groups of supporters) of Boca and Chacarita fought violently after a training match, with several people being wounded and arrested.

Approaches to the problem of football-related violence

The introduction outlined the current situation in relation to violence in football in Argentina. The phenomenon of football-related violence has been the subject of relatively little systematic, specialised, scientific study in Argentina, though it has been extensively discussed in journalistic and political circles. But, with the exceptions that I shall analyse later, academics in Argentina have rarely studied the topic.

The approach of most journalists to the problem of football-related violence is characterised by what Ford and Longo (1991) call the 'logic of cases'; the 'trouble' appears on the front pages every time there is a new 'case' of violence. But this focus on football-related violence lasts only a few days, until the next 'case' occurs, and the papers offer little more than the dominant or 'common-sense' view of the violence; 'investigation' is understood as the production of some statistical or other data with a comment from a so-called 'specialist' who is likely to be any well-known intellectual, even if his speciality is not in this field. There will also normally be newspaper editorials warning people of the dangers of violence and putting forward their own preferred policy. However, such discussions are largely closed discussions which reflect the preferred approach of journalists and do not draw upon the wider context of argument and explanation; such discussions privilege a narrative approach, but usually suspend the critical.

In their examination of media coverage of violence, Coelho et al. (1998)[3] noted that, despite strong formal and ideological differences between the different newspapers which were examined, there were common patterns in the treatment of news relating to violence. In all the papers, those responsible for the violence were placed outside a social normality that is presupposed rather than made explicit; in this general frame, *we* (the good) are implicitly contrasted with *they* (the evil and violent). This contrast can also be seen in the last anti-violence campaign run by the AFA and the monopoly owner of TV transmissions, TyC.[4] Moreover, those involved in violence are often described in terms of biological metaphors: they are aliens who should be extracted from the social body. This use of biological metaphors suggests, as De Ipola (1985) has argued, that journalism draws on discourses characteristic of right-wing thought.[5] Those who engage in violence may also be 'animalised' and described as beasts or wild animals; a similar reading can be seen in the work of Young (1986). This process of stigmatisation results in a paradox, however, because those involved in violent actions are defined as criminal and are also the object of warlike metaphors. The paradox resides in the fact that animalisation and biologisation define this behaviour as being outside the field of the rational, while its description as criminal conduct and its organisation in terms of warlike attitudes supposes a strong rationality: as some researchers have noted, the behaviour of supporters in episodes of violence often points to strong organisation and planning, except in those incidents which could be described as spontaneous, where rationality can be restored in the analysis of the behaviour, but not in the moment of the action itself.[6]

This use of narrative and stereotyping leads to the conclusion that it is not in journalism that we shall find a proper understanding of the phenomenon of football-related violence. On the other hand, however, there have been almost no academic studies in this area. Problems related to violence in sport are defined as belonging to the greater classificatory system of 'sport', an area which has been largely ignored by sociologists and anthropologists in Argentina. There has, of course, been some important work on other areas of violence: on political violence, an area of concern in Argentinian society between the 1950s and the 1980s; on urban violence, which is related to the insecurity associated with the new conditions of life in the big metropolises and the growing impoverishment of large groups of the population in neo-conservative regimes; and also on police violence. Some of these areas provide potential bridges with the study of sports-related violence, though the link has not been made by researchers.

The only important work on the topic has been undertaken by the anthropologist Edward Archetti (who now works at the University of Oslo) and the journalist Amílcar Romero. Archetti is the founder of anthropological studies of Argentine football and, in one of his first works on the topic, he analysed the repertoires of masculinity among Argentine fans, with the symbolic violence that these codes imply being seen as fundamentally bound to a discursively aggressive sexuality (Archetti, 1985). In a later article, Archetti (1992) uses the anthropological category of ritual in order to examine the phenomenon of violence. In an historical journey, he describes Argentine football ritual as a mixture of tragic and comic elements, an oscillation between the violent and the carnivalesque which suggests that a classification of football simply as carnivalesque in a Bakhtinian sense (Bakhtin, 1987) is inadequate. Archetti's description also has a diachronic element: his hypothesis is that the comic elements would formerly have prevailed in the classical time of Argentine football, but that they have been progressively displaced by the tragic elements in the last three decades. He suggests that 'this creates a context in which the practice of violence becomes more and more legitimate' (Archetti, 1992: 242). As we shall see, that legitimacy does not have its roots only in football culture. If, on the one hand, the prevalence of tragic elements creates an immediate context for the production of acts of violence which are understood as legitimate – that is to say, it provides a frame of discursive reflexivity – on the other hand, the broader political context in Argentina creates a macro-frame of reference which has a similar effect.

Archetti and Romero (1994) described the phenomenon of football-related violence within a broader context that helped in the interpretation and understanding of the phenomenon. After outlining the English research on the topic, and pointing out some of the complexities and the richness of that research, they point to some particularly significant aspects of the history of football-related violence in Argentina. These include the fact that there have been as many deaths at the hands of police as have resulted from confrontations between supporters, and also that these events have to be understood in the context of political developments in Argentina since the 1970s. Archetti and Romero, far from proposing a simple solution or a simple interpretation, insist on the necessity of linking football-related violence with broader social and political contexts for, if this is not done, any analysis of the phenomenon cannot but be reductionist. They write:

> a change of scope in the study of hooliganism, should make it possible to conceive the moral issues and cultural dilemmas of death and violence in football as general sociological problems. How English society copes with death and violence seems to us a more relevant subject of study than to continue in the type of research which aims at a better understanding of the logic of a fan's behaviour. A better contextualisation of English hooliganism and different outcomes of acts of violence should enable a comparative analysis of the way English society conceives and tolerates death in football. This change in focus implies a movement from the analysis of the culture of football fans to the general field of cultural analysis. Football is then transformed into an arena in which social actors symbolize, reproduce or contest by means of their social practices the social values dominant in a given period. Consequently football, and sport in general, become a central dimension in the analysis of social and cultural processes (Archetti and Romero, 1994: 69–70).

I propose to follow the path recommended by Archetti and Romero. This does not involve understanding football as a 'reflex of society' – an old metaphor which, besides being theoretically erroneous, has no explanatory value. Instead, I propose to understand the game as a symbolically privileged arena from which general characteristics of Argentine society can be read. This involves prioritising, not the analysis of a football culture but the cultural analysis of Argentinian society as a whole. In that sense, our work in the University of Buenos Aires has defined violence in football as a particular segment (but not for that reason less privileged) of a general inquiry into the universe of Argentine sport.[7] Our research, developed in the context of a Department of Social Communication and strongly imbued with the influence of the cultural studies approach, avoids adopting the paradigm of a single discipline; we have used materials coming from sociology, anthropology, history and media analysis. Consequently, the methodologies we have used are also diverse: these include depth interviews with qualified informants;[8] analysis of media products using the techniques of semiotic and discourse analysis; and also analysis of statistical data from journalistic sources and from Romero's compilations (1987; 1994).

The crisis of football identities

The construction of identities through football is, we suggest, central to an understanding of violence in football and is a central axis of our research. Violent acts may be centrally bound up with the construction of identities and with imaginary (and sometimes) symbolic territories. As Eric Dunning (1999: 155) has noted:

> The probability of spectator violence in football contexts is also likely to be exacerbated by the degree to which spectators identify with the contending teams and the strength of their emotional investment in and commitment to the victory of the teams they support. . . . In turn, the strength of spectators' emotional investment in the victory of their sides is liable to be a function of the centrality and significance of football in their lives; that is, of whether it is one among a number of sources of meaning and satisfaction for them or just the only one.

In this context, it may be argued that, in Argentina in the 1990s, traditional forms of collective representation were becoming unclear at the same time as their centrality for many people was increasing. Particularly important in this regard are collective representations relating to class: Argentine football is not, neither is it perceived to be, the 'people's game'. Rather it appeals, statistically and symbolically, across all classes, although there is a slight prevalence of interest amongst the middle and lower-middle sectors.

Changes in the class structure in Argentina reveal many characteristics also found in Western societies, including the progressive disappearance of the industrial working class and a rapid increase in unemployment. These changes have meant that it has become increasingly difficult to designate a working class *stricto sensu*, while on the other hand, these changes have also been associated with the growth of those groups referred to by the category 'popular sectors'. However, this category is not clearly defined and does not provide those who are held to be members of this group with a clear collective identity.

In much the same way, the growth of what has been called a mediatic culture from the 1970s has had the effect of displacing class-based cultural classifications. The rapid development of communication technologies in the last few decades has weakened national-popular cultures, which have traditionally been important in Latin American societies, whilst strengthening international-popular cultures (Ortiz 1991, 1996). In these processes, football, a fundamental commodity of the culture industry, has also tended to extend its limits of representation in an increasing 'poly-classism'.

But at the same time as these limits were being expanded, mechanisms of exclusion were also being developed. The neo-conservative regimes, while weakening the traditional bases of class, have also generated processes of social exclusion, classical symptoms of which are the expulsion of large numbers of people from the labour market and the impoverishment of the middle class. Football has also been involved in this process of economic expulsion: in a Social Darwinist process which would have been unbelievable a few years ago, the costs of access to the stadia and to the services of cable television have tended to exclude the 'traditional' football public.

In Argentina, these mechanisms of exclusion have also impacted on those who play, or who would like to play, football at both the professional and amateur levels. In the case of professional football, the conditions of access to high performance sport require a threshold of nutrition in childhood that the lower classes cannot provide and this has been associated with a change in the origin of elite players, who today mostly come from the middle classes. In relation to recreational or amateur football, the progressive disappearance of public spaces and the absence of free time amongst workers – a product of the labour conditions of twenty-first century capitalism – have made it increasingly difficult to take part in recreational football which is increasingly restricted to those who enjoy greater resources of finance and time.

To this crisis (by exclusion) of social representation is added the expansion, in the form of a symbolic and cultural imperialism, of Argentine football culture. This imperialism is symbolised in the growth of football discourse, in the construction of a 'footballised' country without limits.[9] Football is an economic phenomenon in the growth of its turnover, direct or indirect, whether through the mass media or by merchandising, and in the increasing amount of capital involved, from the purchase of players to advertising and television investments.

In addition to the above processes is the constant movement of players, from small teams to 'big' teams, and from these towards European football or the 'new markets', especially Mexico and Japan. The traditional continuity of a player in one team for an extended period of time has disappeared: after a short while at one club, he is sold to a larger club, thus benefiting all those involved in football – except the fans. At an earlier period in the development of Argentine football, the strong axes of team identity were the spaces (the stadia), team colours and players who had symbolic significance for the club; today, with the constant changes in sponsorship of team shirts, the continuous changes in shirt designs, and the incessant flows of player sales, the establishment of a firm identity based on these axes is greatly weakened.[10]

Supporters have thus come to perceive themselves as the only custodians of team identity, as the only actors who *may* not produce economic surplus value, but who *do* produce symbolic surplus value. Confronted with the maximisation of economic profit in football, supporters seek to defend the production of their own 'surplus value', namely that involved in the production of pure symbolic excess. The continuity of the repertoires which guarantee the identity of a team thus appears to be deposited with the fans; they are the only ones who are faithful 'to the colours', and they demonstrate their continuing faith in front of 'traitors': the ever-mobile players, the managers guided by personal economic interest, the television managers busied in maximising profits, and the corrupt journalists involved in the transfer business. Supporters develop, in consequence, a self-perception based on militant commitment to carrying out the obligations involved in supporting their team: attending matches at the stadium is not only the execution of a weekly rite, but a double play, both pragmatic and symbolic. On the one hand, because of the persistence of the mythical mandate, supporting their team at the stadium implies a magical participation which makes it possible for fans to influence the outcome of the game. On the other hand, the continuity of their identity as fans depends on regular visits to the 'temple' where that identity is renewed and reinforced.

Tribal football

These processes have not, however, resulted in a simple restatement of traditional football identities; on the contrary, there has been a postmodern fragmentation of identities. This can be seen in a process of tribalisation (Maffesoli, 1990), which is revealed in two ways: firstly in the development of a radically negativised other; secondly, in the fragmentation within the group of supporters associated with a particular club.

With regard to the former, oppositions and confrontations – for example, between classical rivals such as Buenos Aires and the provinces, or between rival neighbourhoods within the same city – radicalise and configure primary and almost essentialised identities. The processes of antagonisation – the ways in which the several rivalries are structured – are very varied. Romero (1994) points out that globally, leaving aside confrontations between national sides, there are four ways of articulation of these rivalries:

i) Regional: between teams of different cities, regions or communities within a nation-state. Examples include relations between Madrid and the Basques or Catalans in Spain, or the opposition between Buenos Aires and the provinces in Argentina.

ii) Intra-city: between teams within a city with a history of dichotomic representation –usually, rich versus poor. Examples here include Nacional and Peñarol in Montevideo, Uruguay, or Rosario Central and Newell's Old Boys in Rosario, Argentina.

iii) Inter-neighbourhood: in this case the rivalry is once again between teams within a single city but, instead of representing a dichotomic symbolic reference, they are associated with the ownership of a defined territory as a neighbourhood. This is typically the case in Buenos Aires where there is a large number of teams within the city, each of which is associated with a local neighbourhood in opposition to other local neighbourhoods. The representation of the larger community – the city – disappears in this focus on micro-community, the neighbourhood. But in recent years, the category 'neighbourhood' has recovered its strong capacity to produce cultural subjects.

iv) Lastly, there are absolutely exceptional cases involving intra-neighbourhood antagonism. Romero sees this exemplified in the relationship between River and Boca, both of which are based in the same neighbourhood on the banks of the River Plate. However, the representation of both teams exceeds that purely local reference, for they are both 'national' teams in the sense that they command the loyalty of other regional communities outside Buenos Aires. We would suggest that the opposition between Independiente and Racing Club, in Avellaneda (near Buenos Aires), is a better example.

Although I am critical of Romero's use of the River–Boca example, the idea that Argentine football is characterised by a progressive and microscopic fragmentation of the represented spaces is absolutely valid. However, I differ from Romero in his suggestion that, insofar as the space of representation is reduced, it loses its power as a representation. On the contrary, I would suggest that the more segmented and atomised the territory becomes, so it becomes warmer and acquires an increased capacity for constituting its subjects. At the same time, however, the possibilities of transcending that local space and moving to a higher level – for example, to the national – are reduced.[11]

As we noted earlier, the development of tribal football has also been associated with a process of fragmentation within the group of supporters associated with a particular club. That is to say, at the level of the 'hinchada' it has produced a phenomenon of novel segmentation, involving the construction of particular identified groups with their own names and organisation. This fragmentation of groups may involve the allocation of functions, each group with its own flags and often identified with particular spaces within the ground, although in other cases differentiation between groups may be based on more contingent factors.[12] This hyper-segmentation may fracture the forms of support for a broader identity, sometimes scattering it in irreconcilable fragments. This phenomenon is similar to that of rock culture where this process has been going on for rather longer. Moreover, this could be taken as support for the hypothesis that there has taken place a transfer of practices from rock culture to football culture, a process which derives from the strong relationships between both cultural universes and the superimposition of their subjects (Alabarces and Rodriguez, 1996).

A ritual of violence

Like all ritual, football involves a suspension of the normal rules of social order. Yet, though the normal restraints on behaviour are lessened, it does not mean that there are no limits placed on what is regarded as permissible behaviour. This loosening of the normal restraints on behaviour opens up different possibilities of behaviour in a situation in which standards governing behaviour may be ambiguous or even contradictory. One such possibility involves the use of violence, which may be seen as a ritual of resistance and as a means of appropriating a territory and an identity.

Alessandro Portelli suggests that violence in football allows us to see the continuities between the stigmatised construction of the popular classes in the last century – the so-called 'dangerous classes' of the industrial revolution – and their reappearance in a similarly stigmatised manner in the period of the information revolution (Portelli, 1993: 78).[13] From this perspective, the revolt in the stadium has been associated with the development of a loose but stigmatised definition of those who take part in this violence. The use of violence is seen as threatening the private property of commodities and the body. It is also seen as threatening because it operates outside the monopoly of the state and, yet worse, it reproduces state mechanisms of outrage and racism and, in reproducing them, it leads them to be deployed and exposed.

Violence can also be seen, as Mignon (1992) has suggested, as a form of action which increases the visibility of those groups which use it. Several social crises – of participation and legitimisation in neo-conservative societies; of the status of the middle classes; of social exclusion affecting the popular sectors – have all led to a search, on the part of these different groups, for mechanisms of visibility. This search has, as Mignon has pointed out in relation to France, led to the use of violence in several forms: violent behaviours against oneself (through the consumption of drugs), against others (for example, vandalism) and through participation in the extreme right of politics. In that same sense, the social space of the stadium allows fans to assert a sense of ownership in relation to a community from which they feel excluded. The stadium is, however, also a stage where the mass media amplify the performance for millions of readers, listeners and viewers.

The dominant or hegemonic interpretations of football-related violence in Argentina, as previously indicated, involve stigmatisation: in this 'common-sense' view, these 'violent people' are seen as ill-adjusted young people operating under the influence of drugs and alcohol, and their actions are reduced to the unpredictable behaviour of people who should be excluded both from the stadium and the wider society. The stigmatisation deeply permeates, in turn, the discourse of militant fans, who interpret acts of violence as the acts of people from a different class and culture. They are, in reality, fellow countrymen who support the same team in the same stadium and they are all victims of police repression but they also stigmatise their fellow fans who are involved in violence. In this regard, the perception by the militant fans reveals an interesting contradiction. On the one hand, they do not see themselves as violent people; when they experience violence, they are placed in a passive position, like victims of a game that they cannot dominate and that they do not want to play. Also, they see institutional actors (police, the management of clubs etc.) as being directly responsible for violence; they understand repressive measures as part of a plot designed to remove the passion from football and to turn it into a commodity for the show-business industry. In that sense, hinchas understand themselves as sharing with those that they define as 'violent' (the 'barras' or action groups) the common defence of a space (the terraces), an identity (the team) and a practice (the football hinchada). On the other hand, however, imbued with the journalistic discourse of stigma, they do not hesitate to point to 'the violent' fans who may be defined as an outsider group 'they', perhaps with racial overtones ('the Negroes that are crazy'). In the poly-classism of football one sees the reappearance of class ethnocentrism and racism.[14]

Possibilities of interpretation

Violence in Argentine football raises a number of important questions in relation to how we understand football-related violence. The phrase 'violence in football' is too broad to be meaningful. In a similar way, the reduction of the problem simply to the actions of hooligans leaves aside deep differences between actors, practices and societies.

In Argentina, violence crosses daily life. This is the case not only in football but also in politics and the economy. The policies of recent governments have been more complex, with less obviously recognisable forms of repression than in the period of the last military dictatorship (1976–83). Nevertheless, recent policies have involved the persistence and worsening of social violence:

in forms of social exclusion; in the expulsion of groups from the labour market and from consumption; and in the deprivation of health and education. But they have also involved the continuity of state violence. The monopoly of legitimate violence has become the illegitimate exercise of that monopoly, directed in a systematic way against the popular classes.[15] When Archetti (1992) reviewed the different causes which have been suggested for violence in football, he did not consider the allegedly violent nature of the Argentine popular classes (or of all popular classes) as a plausible explanation; the history of our country, as Archetti points out, indicates that the dominant classes have systematically demonstrated a higher level of using violence than the popular classes.[16]

The observation of the phenomenon of contemporary violence, and the study of its historical antecedents, allow us to develop a classification that distinguishes different types of practices and which allows us to begin to understand the causes and meanings of violence. Basically, football-related violence in Argentina can be classified under the following headings:

(a) Actions organised and carried out by 'barras bravas'

Although Argentine 'barras bravas' are the groups with most similarity to the so-called hooligans, there are also important differences that prevent comparison. The major difference is that the origin of the 'barras bravas' is linked historically to the emergence of political violence in the mid-1960s. Not surprisingly, the first appearance of the 'barras bravas' led to their comparison, in the press, with the urban guerrillas and to demands for secret action to eliminate them (Coelho et al., 1998). Simultaneously, the development of the so-called 'Souto case' (1967)[17] pointed to the deep complicity of political leaders in sport. The explosive reappearance of the barras took place towards the end of the military dictatorship in 1983, with the case of 'Negro' Thompson, the leader of the barra of Quilmes who, following a murder, was protected by the club, the communal authorities and the Province of Buenos Aires Police. Thus, independently of any imitation of British hooligans, the barras preferred a native model. Configured like paramilitary task groups, they are able to carry out illegitimate tasks by means of violence and compulsion, and are used by sporting and political leaders for that purpose. As Peter Hudson (1999: 13) has noted:

> The reluctance to act comes partly from fear. But it is also because the barras bravas can be very useful. Within the clubs, directors have enlisted them to impose order, giving a hard time to players who are refusing to sign a new contract, for instance. In addition, many of the lower division clubs are the fiefdoms of political leaders who use the barras for packing rallies and settling scores with their opponents. 'Some clubs only have football as an excuse for their other activities', says Ezequiel Fernandez Moores, a local sports writer.

Football violence, in this perspective, cannot be seen simply as a 'reflection' of society. Drawing upon the work of Foucault, Tomás Abraham (1999: 16) says 'violence in football doesn't reflect anything, but rather . . . it is part of a wider device of power'. That mechanism of power, at the same time secret and public, can be observed in the dramatic arena of football.

(b) **Actions produced by, or as a response to, police violence, or to violence by private security organisations which have been established as part of the privatisation of the legitimate monopoly of violence**

The prominent role of the security forces in Argentine violence (not just in football but in other contexts) has not been sufficiently analysed. Romero (1994: 78) has noted:

> In Argentina the police have been responsible for 68% of the deaths at football grounds, a figure that includes the Door 12, where the Federal Police were unwilling to accept any responsibility, even indirect, and where no member of that force was interrogated or charged.[18]

To those killed and wounded directly by police bullets (with the 'Scaserra case' as the prototype[19]), one needs to add the systematically violent conduct of police in relation to match security. The whole treatment of fans by the police involves aggression: restrictions on travelling, the frisking of fans and bizarre prohibitions (for example, of newspapers and cigarette lighters). In all these situations, reproduced in their daily conduct, police abuse reflects an image of citizens as enemies; this is increased by the systematic persecution of the youth of the popular classes, who are judged guilty of incidents even before they have taken place. To this picture it is necessary to add that the processes of neo-conservative privatisation have resulted in the multiplication of private security forces which are allowed the unregulated use of weapons. These private security forces have become the refuge of former police members including, in some cases, those who have been expelled from the police force for their repressive excesses; in their new posts within private security forces, they are able to continue with their habitual, repressive practices.

(c) **Confrontations between rivals as part of a dispute for symbolic supremacy, or as a reaction to a sporting 'injustice' that supposes the imaginary reinstatement of a state of ideal justice**

In most of these cases, the actions of the 'barras' are supported by large numbers of fans. Violence against a radicalised other, as we indicated previously, is the logical result of the process of tribalisation. The defence of the territory, of a symbolic supremacy, involves violent action in a context where the discursive condemnation of violence hides its systematic practice. Also, it points to the desperation of young people among the popular classes who find in violence the only expression that confers visibility on them. Forgotten by the state, with all avenues, present and future, closed, they understand that the only way of being recognised is by gaining media coverage in the press and TV. The importance of football within the mass media guarantees them some recognition which confirms their existence; their appearance in the mass media is, however, contradictory, for at the same time that they obtain recognition, the behaviour which gained them that recognition also results in a new condemnation.

But the use of violence also facilitates the construction of a collectivity which is affirmed through physical conflict and the shared experience of the confrontation and which is founded in the rhetoric of 'aguante'. Aguante designates wider meanings than its strictly etymological reference and is linked to a rhetoric of the body and to a collective resistance against the other (other fans, the police). As Archetti (1992: 266) has noted, aguante is 'a resistance to pain and disillusion, a resistance that does not involve open rebellion, but leads through its tragic and comic elements to a series of possible transgressions'. Given the idea of violence as deriving from an asymmetrical bond (Izaguirre, 1998), aguante is a form of imaginary restoring of symmetry.

Finally, when the hinchadas provoke disorder as a response to what they consider a violation of sporting justice (or more simply, a wrong decision by the referee), they recreate the imaginary democratic spirit of sport, according to which a sporting contest is a contest between equals, without favouritism, and where only the ability of the contestants determines the winners and losers. That image comes into collision with another image: the image of a sporting world of complicities and conspiracies, where the media dominate powerful clubs. Thus, the violent action (spontaneous and often targeted at representatives of powerful groups – police and referees, but also against television, with attacks on cameras or journalists) seeks to restore that imaginary democracy. Justice, which has disappeared as a legitimate institution of the state with the political changes of recent years, is thus metonymically represented in the stadium. The spontaneity of fans thus designates, also by metonymy, a last step of scepticism, of distrust, of boredom. Not of barbarism.

Chapter 3

Australian soccer's 'ethnic' tribes: a new case for the carnivalesque

John Hughson

Introduction and background

This chapter examines contemporary soccer hooliganism in Australia and its relationship to ethnicity. A theoretical discussion of football hooliganism follows a brief historical and social contextualisation of Australian soccer. I conclude by recommending Bakhtin's notion of carnival as a theoretical means of explaining the occurrence of soccer hooliganism in Australia and perhaps elsewhere. In so doing it provides an interpretation of carnival fandom which differs from that so far found in football academe. Rather than dissociating hooligan fans from carnival fans, hooligans (so-called) are regarded as fans who test the limits of the carnivalesque in their pursuit of a collective 'expressive identity'.

During most of the time since its post-Second World War regeneration, Australian soccer has suffered a popular image associated with hooliganism. However, the image of Australian soccer hooliganism has differed from the image of football hooliganism in Britain, which is focused on subcultural groups of young males venting a deluded sense of territorial aggression. The popular image of Australian soccer hooliganism is certainly focused on aggressive masculinity, but the basis of this aggression is understood to be associated with expressions of ethnic identity and nationalistic allegiance, rather than defence of local 'turf'. This prevailing image is very much wrapped up in the post-war history of Australian soccer. Australian soccer has taken on a distinctive character that has been shaped by the influence of the non-English speaking communities which have enjoyed a high level of involvement with the sport. Many members of the range of non-English speaking ethnic groups who have migrated to Australia in the period since the war have used soccer as a means of fostering a community spirit and developing a social network for their respective diasporas (Mosely, 1995). From a functionalist viewpoint, soccer has been described as a major institutional vehicle through which non-English speaking ethnic groups have achieved 'socialisation' within Australian society (Hay, 1994).

This generous, but not unreasonable, reading is challenged by the more popular perception of soccer as an institutional arena of deviance, which has been infiltrated by hostile ethnic groups that use the soccer ground as a public forum for the settling of grievances related to long-standing political squabbles in their homelands (Hughson, 1992). This common perception places soccer in a double jeopardy. In a politically conservative country, the public venting of political protests associated with foreign lands is generally frowned upon and the opprobrium is compounded because the protest is seen as subverting the institution of sport which remains something of a 'sacred cow' in Australian popular culture. Elsewhere, I have spoken of the mythology of 'riots' at Australian soccer matches being traceable to the mass media reporting of crowd disturbances dating back to the 1970s (Hughson, 1996a). Specifically, I have referred to the creation of a 'moral panic' which arouses a fear that attendance at an Australian soccer match might expose patrons to physical harm should they find themselves trapped between warring ethnic groups on the terrace.

This characterisation of the reaction to soccer riots as a moral panic does not mean that ethnically based violence has not occurred on Australian soccer terraces, only that it has been exaggerated and amplified. Research by both Mosely (1995) and Vamplew (1994) clearly shows that sporadic crowd conflicts rooted in ethnic antagonisms have occurred at Australian soccer matches during the post-war years. A key source of conflict has been matches featuring teams linked to communities from the former Yugoslavia. Mosely (1994) has catalogued a number of violent confrontations between the Croatian and Serbian migrants respectively supporting teams such as Sydney Croatia and Avala. Although some of the reported incidents have involved the use of makeshift weapons such as fence palings, it is important to note that few injuries have been reported from crowd conflicts and few arrests are on record. Nevertheless, the pejorative image has persisted and has been used to good effect by some within the sport (including administrators, promoters and media commentators) to advance an argument for the severing of the allegiance between national league (A-League) clubs and ethnic communities. As well as being regarded as anachronistic in a modernised national league, the lingering affiliation of some A-League clubs with ethnic communities is often cited in the press as a continuing source of crowd problems (Hughson, 1996a).

The de-ethnicising agenda

The explicit association between ethnic communities and A-League soccer clubs has all but disappeared in Australian soccer. During the 1990s a number of initiatives have together represented what academic commentators have referred to as the 'de-ethnicising' of Australian soccer (Hughson, 1992). While these commentators have expressed concerns about the implications of the 'de-ethnicising' agenda for the cultural diversity promised by Australia's bi-partisan political policy of multiculturalism, soccer officialdom, under the guise of Soccer Australia (formerly the Australian Soccer Federation), has pressed ahead with directives for the A-League which include: no team in the competition may bear the name of a foreign country or related political organisation; insignias on playing strips must not bear symbols associated with a foreign country or related political organisation; and a ban on supporter flags which feature emblems associated with a foreign country or which could be construed as being associated with a foreign nationalism. A specific example of the impact that these directives have had is that the A-League team associated with the Croatian community of Sydney is no longer known as Sydney Croatia but as Sydney United; the team's playing strip no longer bears a crest featuring the Croatian national chequerboard symbol; and the fans of the team are no longer able to wave Croatian national flags on the terraces. Visible signs of Croatian ethnicity (as well as those of other groups, such as the Italians and the Greeks) have therefore been removed from national league stadia.

The 'de-ethnicising' agenda of Soccer Australia did not have an easy passage to implementation. A good deal of acrimony transpired between officials and supporters of implicated A-League clubs and the leadership of Soccer Australia before all playing logos were changed in accordance with the required specifi-cations in the latter half of 1996. But while resentments may linger between club officials and Soccer Australia, it would appear that formal organisational resistance to the 'de-ethnicising' of the A-League has been put to rest. Supporter groups now offer the only remaining prospect of resistance. However, resistance based on a brazen display of ethnic identity provokes ire among the leading figures in Soccer Australia because it contravenes that organisation's directives on supporter behaviour. Resistive fan behaviour based on ethnic identification has occurred on A-League terraces throughout the 1990s via the initiative of a number of male youth supporter groups, which have arisen partly as a reflection of international supporter trends and partly as a reaction to Soccer Australia's rather authoritarian line on ethnicity. Parochial fandom associated with ethnically affiliated teams is not new to Australian soccer, as Mosely's account of crowd conflict testifies. However, the emergence of youth supporter groups bearing some similarity to British and European football hooligans is a phenomenon of the 1990s (Warren, 1995; Hughson, 1997).

A key difference between the Australian hooligan scene, which includes groups such as the Bad Blue Boys (Sydney United, Croatian), the Mad Boys (Sydney Olympic, Greek) and the Hellas Hooligans (South Melbourne, Greek), and the British and European scenes is that, while the latter have moved to a casual supporter guise abandoning team colours and paraphernalia for designer label attire (Redhead, 1991: 77–8), the former is based very much on the display of team colours. The key reason for the adoption of a visible association with the team by Australian hooligan groups is that the team colours usually reflect those of the homeland of the ethnic community with which it is affiliated. For example, Sydney United's playing strip is red, white and blue. Team scarves are worn or carried by Bad Blue Boys (BBB) members as a sign of association with their parent culture. This rather obvious symbol of Croatian ethnicity is combined with more 'secretive' symbols which distinguish BBB members from the bulk of Sydney United supporters. Specially designed t-shirts featuring anagrams and logos of present and past Croatian political organisations are amongst the stylistic codings which identify BBB members to each other and to other members of the Croatian community. Such usage of secret symbolism also allows groups such as the BBB to defy the dictates of Soccer Australia in spirit if not in letter. While police and private security personnel are able to prevent the brandishing of national flags and other readily apparent symbols of political and ethnic identity, more obscure symbols are less likely to be detected. Accordingly, one BBB member has spoken of the endeavour to 'keep ethnicity in on the sly' (Hughson, 1997: 255).

Violence and ritual

The importance of symbolic codings typifies the ritualistic nature of contemporary soccer hooliganism in Australia. The work of Marsh (1978), though much criticised, is nevertheless of explanatory value. Marsh may have overstated the purely ritualistic nature of violence on British soccer terraces, for example in his argument that, unless there is outside interference, people do not actually suffer physical harm in hooligan confrontations. Yet his observation that hooligan behaviour, in general, involves an illusion of violence is certainly an apt description of the Australian scene. My own doctoral fieldwork which involved two years of participant observation research on the terraces at A-League matches found that while a keen rivalry – even hostility – existed between groupings such as the Bad Blue Boys and the Mad Boys, this resulted in fighting on only a few occasions (Hughson, 1996b). The main venting of hostility involves the groups exchanging taunts and imprecations from their respective positions on the terrace. On occasions when fighting has occurred, it has been quickly interrupted by police and security personnel. One member of the BBB spoke of such an outcome as the ideal hooligan episode, where groups verbally work each other into a frenzy and then come to the brink of a physical encounter before being restrained from fighting by the police. This is not to suggest that groups such as the BBB recoil from violence, but that fighting is an optional extra of the Australian soccer hooligan experience rather than an integral feature of it. This ethnographic picture of soccer hooliganism in Australia bears similarity to that recently provided by English ethnographer Gary Armstrong (1998) in his study of the Sheffield Blades. Armstrong (1998: 233) reports that fighting is not, contrary to popular opinion, the raison d'être of soccer hooligan subcultures. Rather, Armstrong highlights the rivalry between hooligan groupings as a 'ritualised procedure' which may, at times, result in violence, but which is generally conducted through routines which are 'implicitly safe'. Hooligan groups gain honour through the ritualistic humiliation of rival groups which is more likely to involve running and chasing than the 'actual physical violence' of fighting (Armstrong, 1998: 234).

Armstrong brings a fairly new approach to the study of football hooliganism by combining the findings of highly engaged ethnographic research with analytical insights from a range of sociological theory including symbolic interactionism, the cultural sociology of Bourdieu and the postmodern sociology of Maffesoli. His project stands in inverse relationship to that of the dominant British school of research on football hooliganism, located at the University of Leicester. While Armstrong's work operates with a unitary research epistemology and is theoretically eclectic, the Leicester theorists are eclectic in research (using, inter alia, ethnography and document analysis) but unitary in their approach to theory. The application of the figurational theory of Elias by Eric Dunning and his colleagues to explain the phenomenon of football hooliganism is summarised in Chapter 1 and so it will not be rehearsed here. As the dominant 'school' of theory in the field, the work of Dunning and his associates is unavoidably addressed in subsequent scholarship on football hooliganism. At times the treatment is extremely critical, and this is none more so than in the case of Armstrong. In an early paper Armstrong (and Harris, 1991: 430) criticises the 'limited nature' of the 'Leicester School's' ethnographic endeavour in contrast to his own more 'detailed' approach to fieldwork. In his recent work, the attack takes aim at figurational theory and its associated concept of the civilising process, as a general theory of society and, particularly, its utility as an overarching explanation of football-related crowd violence. Armstrong (1998: 304) is ultimately unable to accept that young men who engage in violent social practices associated with football support can be defined away as an *uncivilised* rump in a society which is generally civilised. A comparison with Australian research provides another angle from which to view the debate.

Kingsley lads Down Under

The majority of academic work on soccer hooliganism in Australia has been done by historians, and figurational theory has received only passing reference in these accounts. The most systematic application of the theory of the civilising process in Australian sports sociology is in Hutchins's and Phillips's (1997) paper on the changing culture of violence in rugby league. In relation to soccer hooliganism, my own paper (Hughson, 2000) on aggressive masculinity within the subculture of the BBB provides a comparative analysis of that group with the 'Kingsley Lads' discussed by the Leicester theorists in *Football on Trial* (Murphy et al., 1990a: 129–66). The comparison focuses on 'incorporation', a key term in Dunning et al.'s (1988) adaptation of Elias's theory of the civilising process. Underpinning the analysis is my argument that, if the term incorporation is to provide a flexible means of social analysis, then we must be able to speak of people being more or less incorporated into the ways of civilised society. Accordingly, by comparison, it was found that the young men of the BBB were more socially incorporated than those of the Kingsley Lads. To assess the degrees of incorporation of the respective groups, I considered the findings regarding violence in each of the studies. It was found that the members of the BBB had a lesser proclivity to violent behaviour than members of the Kingsley lads. The BBB subculture was certainly charac-terised by an aggressive masculinity, which included constant talk about violence but, as indicated above, there was little enactment of violent practices during the course of the research. By comparison, the subcultural life of the Kingsley Lads appeared to involve a good deal of actual violent behaviour.

The explanation for this difference is most obviously traceable to the different social circumstances of the two groups. While the Kingsley Lads have been raised and live on a Leicester housing estate in conditions of economic deprivation, the BBB have experienced no such hardship. Although living on the western outskirts of Sydney in suburbs which do not enjoy the social advantages of those close to the cities and beaches, the BBB live in very comfortable housing owned by their parents in 'respectable' working-class neighbourhoods. The Kingsley Lads come from the ranks of what the Leicester theorists describe as the 'rough' working class. Violence tends to be an ingrained part of the culture within this fraction of the working class, so the Kingsley Lads, like their fathers, take on a disposition of violence. The BBB situation is, perhaps, a little more complicated. Their class fraction in Australian society is not predisposed towards violence and they would not encounter regular displays of violence in their neighbourhood. The aggressive masculinity exhibited within the BBB subculture is related to their perception of the male Croatian peasantry (the stock from which their fathers came) as a hard form of manhood. The BBB see themselves as the heirs of this tradition, a tradition which is dying out in Australia as many young Croatians gain tertiary-level education and professional employment. The BBB have little stake in the upward mobility of their Croatian age cohorts as they themselves have only modest career aspirations that do not extend beyond manual trades. Their aggressive masculinity is largely an attempt to 'magically recover' an ethnic community tradition in decline. Importantly, though, the BBB conjure an 'imagined' community through which they negotiate a feeling of security denied them by the external social environment (Hughson, 1997).

The carnival reconsidered

Figurational sociology is used in the above-mentioned study as an analytical device which provides a framework for comparing empirical studies of football hooligans, rather than as a general theoretical explanation of football hooliganism. Soccer hooliganism in Australia has a peculiar genesis, occurring within a supporter base that is indeterminate in class composition and overridden by a complexity of ethnic relations. Given the link between hooligan behaviour in Australian soccer and the collective expression of ethnic identity, it is appropriate to look for a theoretical model which can account for hooliganism, and parochial soccer fandom in general, as a form of resistance. To this end, I propose the use of Bakhtin's notion of carnival which, although not originally proffered as a theory, has been used within recent cultural studies work to describe a variety of contexts in which carnival has been used as a means of social transgression. Bakhtin (1968) takes his notion of carnivalesque from his reading of the novels of Rabelais on the medieval carnival. The medieval carnival provided an occasion of unbridled festivity in which the routines of social order were 'turned upside down'. Forms of public officialdom were mocked during the carnival as the streets were handed over to the people for a brief but poignant period of critical expression. The carnival was certainly about fun, but serious messages were also conveyed by the caricatured visages of officialdom on display. As Bakhtin's best-known interpreters note, the carnival represents a 'symbolic inversion and transgression' of the forms of oppressive social power endured by the people engaged in it (Stallybrass and White, 1986: 18). Although carnivalesque activity might not transform society, it does provide its participants with a fleeting but meaningful experience of transgressing social authority.

A number of critics have taken issue with the optimistic interpretation of carnival implied by much contemporary cultural studies work (Hughson, 1998: 173). The basic objection is that the celebration of carnival tends to overlook its dark side. The carnival can be, inter alia, sexist, homophobic and even violent. Andrew Blake (1996: 51) has recently expressed concern about football hooliganism as a form of carnivalesque which exhibits negative social practices, violence presumably being the worst of them. Anticipating such objections Giulianotti (1991; 1995) has incorporated the notion of carnival into his studies of football fandom in a way that demarcates carnival fans from hooligans. Carnival behaviour, thus interpreted, is hedonistic and associated with activities such as excessive drinking, swearing, singing, wearing of costume and so on. Importantly, though, it is 'decidedly non-violent' behaviour and carnival fans (the Scottish fans in Giulianotti's studies) deliberately pursue relations with rival fans which are non-confrontational (Finn and Giulianotti, 1998: 190–1). This differs from the hooligan behaviour of the casual subcultures studied by Giulianotti, which are associated with Scottish Premier League teams, and whose behaviour is characterised by fighting with rival fans. Giulianotti's desire to distinguish between these two forms of fan groups is entirely reasonable, but it is questionable whether the idea of carnival provides the most appropriate means of making the distinction. My objection is based, firstly, on the restricted understanding of Bakhtin's notion of carnival which Giulianotti's usage implies and, secondly, on the implications which this usage has for an ongoing discussion of football fandom in terms of carnival.

While the Bakhtinian notion of carnival embraces a sense of camaraderie between carnival participants, it also allows for the enactment of social behaviours which can be hurtful and injurious to people. Young males were key participants in the medieval carnival and their ritualistic pranks would often involve verbal abuse and violence (Boethius, 1995: 15). The carnival is transgressive because it gives rein to the activities which people bring to it. Not all these activities – fighting being an obvious example – will be regarded as socially progressive from a humanistic standpoint. It is the unrestricted excesses of carnival which concern critics and, in regard to football support, this would relate to violent or hooligan behaviour. The potentiality of hooliganism leads Blake (1996: 51) to express concern about the football match as a modern 'occasion' of carnival. While I do not necessarily share Blake's apparent pessimism about carnival in general, I accept his implied image of the carnival as a social space. The carnival is a social space with an atmosphere of 'almost anything goes'. This is not to say that anything does go, as the carnival is always policed by agents of social control who often possess fairly arbitrary powers to stop carnival participants from going 'too far'. In studying the football viewing occasion as an example of the modern carnival, the primary focus of analysis should be on the relevant spaces (such as the stadium and its surrounds) and the way that they are physically and metaphorically occupied. Once focused on the spaces, we can then concentrate on how certain participants within the carnival push the boundaries of social authority. Football hooliganism, from this perspective, occurs within the space of carnival rather than outside it. Indeed, hooligan fans are those who take the liberties of the carnivalesque to extremes and, accordingly, unsettle social authority.

Carnival comes to the A-League

Although I have used the term carnival to describe the overall space of the football stadium, this does not mean that all fans are carnivalesque. Carnivalesque fans are expressive fans. They are fans who use football support as a means of venting a collective 'expressive identity' (Heatherington, 1998). Expressive fans enjoy the carnivalesque possibilities which the soccer supporting experience offers. Carnivalesque possibilities in this context offer the chance of transgressing or overturning the authority which attempts to proscribe behaviour within the social domain which is the football stadium. Expressive fans will seek to support their team in a manner of their own choosing. Some of the related behaviours such as waving home-made banners, barracking opposition players and drinking alcohol smuggled from outside, rather than purchased within the stadium, appear rather innocuous. Other forms of behaviour, though, such as a highly derogatory abuse of players and other fans, igniting distress flares, pitch invasions, and fighting with or physically goading rival fans, indicate a harmful hooligan excess. However, the unifying trait of expressive fans is that they are willing to defy the edicts set by bodies such as Soccer Australia which curtail their self-expression of soccer support.

While the emphasis of the Bakhtinian notion of carnival is very much on transgression and hence disorder, the lived carnival also involves the countervailing power of order. This not only suggests an order coercively imposed by agents of control, but a related order to which a good number of carnival participants willingly comply (Heatherington, 1998: 112). Accordingly, in relation to soccer fandom, we can speak of submissive fans who are happy to accept the rules as laid out for them. The submissive fan can, no doubt, be found in any context of modern sports fandom, and in relation to soccer was anticipated over twenty years ago by the Birmingham theorist John Clarke (1978: 60). At the time of heightened moral panic over soccer hooliganism in Britain, Clarke predicted a trend towards a form of soccer support which he described in terms of 'disinfected commitment' and 'contained partisanship'. Submissive fandom is evinced in the contemporary Australian soccer stadium by a colourful display from the stands and terraces of team regalia and other Soccer Australia 'official licensed products', such as flags and banners. Submissive fans may enjoy the carnival but, via such emasculated displays, they surely do not embrace the carnivalesque.

Two contrasting examples of these different types of fandom were exhibited in the A-League final series at the conclusion of the 1997 season. At the preliminary final match held at Sydney's Parramatta Stadium between Sydney United and South Melbourne, antagonism between the hooligan sections of the respective ranks of supporters led to three arrests and the subsequent gaoling of one BBB member after an alleged assault on police officers. This episode became the most notorious of Australian soccer riots, receiving front page coverage in the following day's newspapers and headline treatment on commercial television news bulletins (Hughson, 1998: 175). Much was made in media reports of the ethnic affiliations of the fans involved in the crowd disturbance and subsequent editorials took the opportunity to question once again the appropriateness of professional soccer teams in Australia's premier league bearing affiliation with ethnic communities (Wells, 1997a).

The week following the Parramatta Stadium 'riot' saw the Grand Final hosted by one of the newer 'one team city' clubs, the Brisbane Strikers. The Strikers have no particular ethnic support base, instead relying on a Brisbane-wide civic appeal. For the purposes of the Grand Final, this appeal seemed to pay off as an overwhelmingly hometown crowd exceeding 40,000 set a new record for attendance at an Australian club match. In contrast to media reports from the previous week, the Brisbane crowd was praised for its 'orderly' behaviour (Wells, 1997b). The mediated image showed a submissive crowd par excellence – a sea of blue and gold shirts, happy families waving merchandised Strikers' flags, and Mexican waves which lost sequence only when they reached the small band of travelling Sydney United supporters. The promotional success of the Grand Final was capped by a Brisbane Strikers victory. That it was scored against Sydney United added to the image of the older ethnically based clubs being overhauled by the new city based teams. It also gave view to an emergent form of fandom which is actively sought by soccer officialdom at the national organisational level as well as by a number of clubs, with the then Chairperson of Soccer Australia declaring the well-behaved crowd in Brisbane as the 'future' of soccer fandom.

Conclusion

There is certainly reason to believe that the end of the 1997 A-League season represented a watershed in the recent history of Australian soccer support. The tightening of ground security following the 'riot' at Parramatta Stadium has not only restricted hooligan activities but has also been accompanied by greater intolerance of displays of ethnic identity on the terraces. As expressive fandom in Australian soccer is almost inextricably linked to such displays, it has suffered a significant setback. Subsequent informal interviews with BBB members indicate that a number have given up on soccer support because of the curtailment of supporter behaviour. The emergence of other non-ethnically affiliated teams in the A-League such as Carlton (Melbourne), the Perth Glory and, most recently, the Northern Spirit (Sydney), also has implications for the continuation of expressive soccer fandom in Australia. However, despite appearances, the carnival is not over as I have suggested elsewhere (Hughson, 1998: 177). Even given the challenge posed by newer teams, the traditional ethnically based clubs remain strong performers in the Australian Premiership. Following the Brisbane Strikers' success of 1997, South Melbourne, the team supported by Melbourne's Greek community, claimed the title in 1998. Against the threat of the 'de-ethnicising' agenda, which has gathered force over the last ten years, the majority of ethnically based teams have held their positions in the A-League. Restrictions on explicit displays of ethnic identity notwithstanding, the continuation of these teams in the A-League keeps open the possibility of expressive identities being formed through symbolic displays of resistance.

Finally, it should be noted that the implied dichotomy of supporter types between the traditional teams and the newer 'one team city' teams cannot be drawn neatly. While the example of the Brisbane Strikers does indicate that the 'one team city' teams lend themselves to submissive support, contrary examples of expressive fandom associated with new teams have already arisen. Most prominent in this regard are the 'Boys from the Shed', a group of expatriate British males who support the Perth Glory. Although the club itself has no affiliation to an ethnic community, the team has clearly been claimed by this group of apparently non-hooligan fans as a vehicle for expressing ethnic identity. Although not involving the display of the Union Jack or other British national flags, British identity is stylistically demonstrated by the wearing of a variety of replica strips of British club teams. This poses a problem for Soccer Australia's 'de-ethnicising' agenda which, thus far, has been swept under the carpet by a refusal to recognise the Boys from the Shed as an ethnically driven supporter entity (i.e. the British do not count as an ethnic group) (Hughson, 1998: 177). The inadequacy of this response will become more apparent should groups like the Boys from the Shed emerge in support of other ostensibly non-ethnically supported teams. The culture of Australian soccer is so enmeshed with ethnicity that not only are old allegiances difficult to sever, but new and unanticipated ones threaten to emerge. That British ethnicity should appear as a new configuration of Australian soccer support at the turn of the century is ironic but, nevertheless, indicative of the power of soccer within the cultural domain to provide a collective sense of expressive identity. It also indicates that Soccer Australia may not have found its yellow brick road to a future of submissive soccer support. As long as soccer needs supporters to fill a stadium, then soccer offers an occasion of carnival. As Giulianotti (1995: 194) advises, 'the carnivalesque always threatens to transgress the authorised boundaries granted to it'. Expressive fans will find a variety of ways to 'keep ethnicity in on the sly' in Australian soccer if they so choose. It remains to be seen whether hooliganism re-emerges within and between the emergent and existing fan alignments once the dust of 1997 has settled.

Chapter 4

Bohemian rhapsody: football supporters in the Czech republic

Vic Duke and Pavel Slepička

Association football reached Central Europe in the 1890s when English expatriates introduced the game into what was then the Austro-Hungarian empire; the first recorded match was in Vienna in 1894. From there, football spread quickly to Budapest and Prague. The two leading clubs to this day in what is now the Czech Republic were formed as football sections of multi-sport clubs – Sparta Praha (Prague) in 1894 and Slavia Praha in 1896. A league for football clubs in Prague was in operation by 1896, although more broadly based Czech and Moravian leagues did not appear until 1912.

The geographical area comprising the current Czech Republic has undergone several political changes during the twentieth century and these have had important implications for the nature of football support and the history of football hooliganism. Beginning the century as part of the Austro-Hungarian empire, Bohemia played a series of international football matches between 1903 and 1908, mostly against Hungary but also against England in 1908. The redrawing of the European political map after the end of the First World War included the establishment of the first Czechoslovak Republic in 1920. This lasted until 1938. Bohemia and Moravia (the Czech lands) became a German Protectorate under German occupation in 1939, whilst Slovakia was an independent (puppet) state aligned with Germany. Czechoslovakia was reunited at the end of the Second World War, but in the sphere of influence of the Soviet Union which resulted in the imposition of a communist regime. A socialist structure of sport was imposed on football during this period (see Duke, 1990). As part of the general collapse of communist regimes in 1989, Czechoslovakia underwent the 'Velvet Revolution' which restored a demo-cratic capitalist structure. By 1993, the 'Velvet Divorce' created separate Czech and Slovak Republics. The question of national identity and regional rivalries in Czech football has been far from straightforward.

We are grateful to Petr Kavalír for his assistance with the archival part of our research.

Of the 101 incidents of football-related violence in 37 countries presented in Chapter 1, none occurred in Czechoslovakia or the Czech Republic. However, our analysis of Czech newspapers over two periods indicates that football-related violence has occurred in the Czech Republic. The next section will examine football spectator behaviour in the first Czechoslovak Republic (1920–38). Sections two and three will consider football spectator behaviour in two later periods, the communist era (1946–89) and the post-communist 1990s respectively. The fourth section will summarise evidence from two surveys into the social background of football spectators in the Czech Republic, and after that, in section five, we shall present our overall conclusions.

Football spectator behaviour in the first Czechoslovak Republic 1920–38

Football became highly popular during the period of the first Czechoslovak Republic. A national professional league was established in 1925 and attendance at matches was high, with the classic Sparta–Slavia derby matches regularly attracting in the region of 30,000 spectators. The high standard of Czech football at this time is indicated by the success of Czech clubs in the prestigious Mitropa Cup, competed for by leading clubs from Austria, Hungary, Czechoslovakia, Italy, Switzerland, Romania and Yugoslavia. Sparta Praha won the very first competition in 1927. Further Czech victories were secured, by Sparta again, in 1935, and by Slavia Praha in 1938.

Football was an important social phenomenon in the first Czechoslovak Republic, finding its way into contemporary literature as well as the newspapers. A famous humorist wrote a novel entitled *Muži v ofsajdu* (Men Who are Offside). This novel, which is read to this day, contains an excellent description of the atmosphere among fans in the football stadium. Reference is made to incidents between fans of different clubs both inside and outside the stadium.

Intense support for teams was the order of the day with wild celebration of victory and loud condemnation of defeat. Football players became idols for the first time, worshipped by the clubs' supporters, especially after a win. Spectators went to the stadium for a strong emotional experience, for the excitement of the game. Spectators felt that they could influence the game by inciting the players to a higher level of performance. Obtaining a shared experience at the match became a primary motive for attending.

Occasionally the emotional involvement of the supporters gave rise to violent incidents in the stadium. Table 1 provides examples of crowd incidents at football matches in the period 1920–37 as reported in Czech newspapers.

The first example in the table is a 1920 derby match between two leading Prague teams, Meteor Vinohrady and Nuselský SK. A fight between two players was the spark for a pitch invasion by Nuselský fans, who attacked

Table 1 **Crowd incidents at football matches in the period 1920–37**

Date	Match	Type of incident
2.9.1920	Meteor Vinohrady *v* Nuselský SK	Pitch invasion; players attacked; spectators injured.
18.3.1930	Viktoria Žižkov *v* Teplitzer FK	Pitch invasion.
7.7.1932	Slavia Praha *v* Juventus (Turin)	Pitch invasion; match interrupted.
8.7.1934	SK Kladno *v* Ferencvaros	Ferencvaros whistled off and abused.
27.4.1936	Czechoslovakia *v* Spain	Both teams whistled off by 30,000 spectators.
25.8.1936	Slavia Praha *v* SK Prostějov	Slavia whistled off.
14.9.1936	Sparta Praha *v* Austria Vienna	Overcrowded stadium barriers overrun.
12.10.1936	Slavia Praha *v* Sparta Praha	Both teams whistled off at half time and full time.

Sources: České slovo, 1920–25; České slovo večerní, 1920–37; Narodn'i listy, 1932–33.

Meteor players with sticks and knives. In the ensuing brawl one spectator was seriously injured by a knife wound to the head. Fighting continued outside the stadium and several more people were taken to hospital for treatment. According to reports at the time, some female Nuselský fans were involved in the fighting.

A further example of a pitch invasion occurred in March 1930 at the match between Viktoria Žižkov and Teplitzer FK. On this occasion, supporters attacked the players of the away team. Such attacks were facilitated by the fact that Czech football grounds at this time had no segregation of opposing supporters and there was little in the way of barriers to prevent a pitch invasion.

Aggression against referees was also common in this period, though the perpetrators were both players and spectators. Often a player's assault on the referee would in turn lead to a pitch invasion by supporters who would attack the offending player's team. This occurred, for example, in the semi-final of the Mitropa Cup between Slavia Praha and Juventus (of Turin) in July 1932. Rough play by both teams in the first half produced a tense atmosphere amongst both players and spectators. At the beginning of the second half, a Slavia player was injured by a Juventus player and had to be carried off the pitch. Immediately afterwards, a penalty was awarded to Slavia, whereupon Cesarini of Juventus attacked the referee. This action provoked a pitch invasion by Slavia fans who attacked the Italian players. Even some Slavia players came under attack as they tried to protect the Juventus players from the mob. There was a long interruption to the match, which eventually resumed after the referee had received treatment and the Juventus captain had duly apologised.

A serious crowd incident of a different kind took place in September 1936 at a Mitropa Cup match between Sparta Praha and Austria Vienna. The match took place at the new Masaryk stadium with a capacity of 48,000. When all the tickets had been sold, those who had been unable to obtain tickets broke through police barriers and stormed the stadium. It is estimated that 60,000 people got into the severely overcrowded stadium. As the crowd spilled out in front of the barriers, the referee was unsure whether to start the match. Eventually the game was played, after which the disappointed supporters of the defeated home team dispersed quietly.

The most common type of negative reaction by spectators was the shrill collective whistling of players, which was considered unsporting behaviour by the newspaper reporters. The other four examples cited in table 1 are of this kind of behaviour. It is interesting to note that, although most commonly employed against the away team (Ferencvaros at Kladno in 1934, Sparta at Slavia in 1936), sometimes the home team (Slavia *v* Prostějov, August 1936) or both teams (Czechoslovakia *v* Spain, April 1936) were whistled off the pitch.

The distinctiveness of this kind of behaviour, this time aimed at the referee, is confirmed in the autobiography of Raich Carter, a leading player of the time who visited Prague with the England team in May 1934:

> There was one point about the Czechoslovakian crowd. Whenever they didn't agree with the referee they whistled; and several times I had to put my fingers in my ears to shut out the shrill blasts (Carter, 1950: 86).

In summary, most of the crowd incidents at Czech football matches in this period were match related. Attacks on players and officials were characteristic of football spectator behaviour in the first Czechoslovak republic. Battles between groups of rival fans were not common and there were no reported examples of the police coming under attack from gangs of fans.

Football spectator behaviour in the communist era 1946–89

Most of the Czech population were liberated from German occupation by the Red Army in 1945 and came within the Soviet sphere of influence. Complete communist control was not established until 1948. The change of political system proved a turning point in football. A socialist structure of sport was imposed and many famous clubs underwent enforced name changes. Slavia Praha became Dynamo Praha and Sparta Praha were known as Spartak Sokolovo, in both cases from 1953 to 1965. However, the fans continued to call the clubs by their traditional names.

Slovak clubs came to greater prominence in the first division during the communist era, a development not without significance for national and regional football rivalries. In the early post-war years, spectator interest was maintained at the pre-war level, but thereafter a gradual decline set in. In the 1960s, the average attendance at first division matches was over 10,000, but during the 1980s the average declined to just over 5,000.

Crowd incidents and negative spectator behaviour almost disappeared following the change of political system. The communist state was repressive in nature, intolerant of anti-social behaviour and powerful enough to eradicate any form of hooliganism. At the end of the 1960s, however, crowd problems at football matches reappeared, increased gradually in the 1970s, and culminated in a serious escalation of football-related violence in the 1980s. By this time, the so called 'English disease' of football hooliganism (involving fighting between rival groups of fans) had spread to Eastern Europe, as it had to Western Europe in the 1970s (Duke and Crolley, 1996b).

Immediately after the Second World War, football spectator behaviour reverted to the patterns evident in the 1930s. In May 1946 the English FA Cup winners, Derby County, played a 'friendly' at Sparta Praha (though the English source cited below claims that Derby played a combined Sparta–Slavia team). A rough first half, blamed on the English players by the Czech reporter and on the Czech players by the English source, produced a tense atmosphere in the stadium at half-time. Three minutes into the second half (Czech version), an altercation between two players led to a mass pitch invasion in order to attack the Derby players. The match was interrupted until the police were able to restore order. Raich Carter played in this match for Derby County and described the incident thus:

> There was plenty of tension when the second half started, and after about ten minutes play the climax came. From all sides the crowd, with yells, whistles and waving arms, charged on to the pitch. I seemed isolated from the rest of the team who were scattered all over the place anyway, and I looked round for somewhere to run (Carter, 1950: 176).

Table 2 below highlights crowd incidents at football matches in the period 1980–87, during which football violence became more serious and changed in nature. Still in evidence at Hradec Králové in June 1987 was the shrill whistling behaviour of the 1930s, directed on this occasion at the home team. The most common occurrence in the table is the throwing of objects onto the pitch, of which four examples are given. By 1987, the Czechoslovak FA had introduced fines for the home team in response to such incidents, 3,000 crowns in the case of Dukla Banská Bystrica and 4,000 crowns for Sparta Praha.

Fighting between rival groups of supporters became a feature of football violence in Czechoslovakia in the 1980s. At the Slavia–Sparta derby in November 1985, the fighting began after the match and led to injuries and arrests. Another feature of this period was the tendency for football-related

Table 2 **Crowd incidents at football matches in the period 1980–87**

Date	Match	Type of incident
25.3.1983	Dukla Praha *v* Slavia Praha	Objects thrown onto pitch.
2.6.1983	Bohemians Praha *v* Dukla Praha	Players abused by fans; match interrupted.
4.4.1985	Dukla Praha *v* Slavia Praha	Windows broken, cars damaged; fans arrested.
19.6.1985	Dukla Banská Bystrica *v* Sparta Praha	Train carriages demolished; vandalism in streets; 30 fans imprisoned.
4.11.1985	Slavia Praha *v* Sparta Praha	Fighting after match; one spectator hospitalised.
3.9.1986	Sparta Praha *v* Slavia Praha	Objects thrown onto pitch.
7.6.1987	Hradec Králové *v* Teplice	Home team whistled off.
10.10.1987	Dukla Banská Bystrica *v* Dukla Praha	Glass thrown onto pitch.
30.3.1987	Sparta Praha *v* Slavia Praha	Objects thrown onto pitch.

Source: *Rudé právo*, 1980–87.

violence to take place outside the stadium and involve damage to property in the vicinity of the ground or en route home for the away fans. After the Dukla–Slavia derby in April 1985, windows were broken, cars damaged and several fans arrested.

The worst case of football-related violence in Czechoslovakia in the 1980s occurred on the last day of the 1984–85 season when Sparta Praha clinched the championship at Dukla Banská Bystrica in Slovakia. After the match, Sparta fans ran riot in the streets of Banská Bystrica, damaging property and attacking bystanders. More serious incidents followed on the long train journey back to Prague. A total of eight carriages were damaged, one of them completely demolished, and other passengers were attacked and terrorised throughout the journey. Upon arrival at the Prague terminus, 30 fans were arrested.

So concerned were the authorities that they commissioned a documentary film on Sparta fans travelling to an away match entitled *Proč?* (Why?). The film was intended not only to describe the event but also to examine the causes of such behaviour in order to educate the public. However, the film resulted in more widespread copying of violent behaviour by young people, even among crowds leaving the cinema after watching the film.

A relaxation of restrictions on Czech media coverage in the mid-1980s contributed to the dissemination of information on English football hooliganism in general and the Heysel Stadium tragedy in 1985, in particular. Sparta fans involved in the Banská Bystrica riot were heard to chant 'Liverpool, Liverpool'; the Dukla Banská Bystrica–Sparta match took place shortly after the Liverpool-Juventus game at Heysel, which was shown live on Czech TV.

The Czech media, especially television, played a pivotal role in providing young Czech football supporters with an exemplar of football hooliganism to follow. An element of 'copycat' behaviour was thus present in the escalation of Czech football hooliganism in the mid-1980s. Increased liberalisation of society can evidently have unanticipated, and what some might consider to be negative, consequences.

Fighting between rival gangs of football supporters was a new development in the Czech Republic. Participants in the fighting displayed strong hostility to those wearing symbols, such as flags and scarves, of the opposing club. Most aggressive of all were the so-called 'flag-carriers' who were at the core of the gang. Initially the fighting was spontaneous, developing from a verbal argument between two fans which then escalated into a battle between rival gangs. The defence of club territory played a part in these conflicts as did nationalist sentiments against Slovak teams/supporters and regional enmities with other cities.

There was a rapid escalation in the frequency of these brawls. Slepička (1989) has suggested that the most frequent reason for starting a fight was the motive of revenge for similar action at the last match between the two clubs. A chain of revenge reprisals developed involving a small number of common individuals at the core. These collisions were typical during matches between teams from particular regions. The most regular confrontations were Praha *v* Bratislava, Praha *v* Ostrava, Praha *v* Brno and Ostrava *v* Brno.

As football hooliganism escalated in the late 1980s a greater element of premeditated planning was involved. Revenge for the previous match was carefully planned. Certain individuals were also attracted to matches because of the prospect of fighting. Associated with the move to greater planning and organisation was a tendency for hooliganism to occur outside rather than inside the stadium. Ambushes could be better executed in the streets on the way to the ground using local knowledge to outwit both the opposing fans and the police. Brawls outside the stadium led inevitably to increased material damage to property and injury to members of the general public who happened to be in the vicinity.

For many young supporters, the game itself was not important. The football stadium became a place where, unlike most other locations in communist society, public control could be evaded. Social, political and nationalist tensions could be aired in the anonymity of a football crowd in a way that they could not in the main squares of Prague. The rapid escalation in football hooliganism led, however, to a repressive response from the authorities.

The most important measures introduced were the segregation of rival supporters in the stadium and a repressive police presence at matches. All fans were searched on entry to the ground, and hecklers in the crowd were arbitrarily ejected and sometimes arrested. On the one hand, this increased repression in the stadium accelerated the move towards fighting away from the stadium, in the streets and at the railway stations. On the other hand, ordinary supporters were discouraged from attending football matches. Average attendance in the first division fell to an all time low of around 4,000 towards the end of the 1980s. Football hooliganism was at its peak during this period.

Football spectator behaviour in the post-communist 1990s

The collapse of the communist state and its centrally planned economy in 1989 was reflected in all aspects of society, including football. Most notably, the transition period resulted in economic hardship throughout football – for clubs, players and spectators. Professional football was reintroduced to replace the socialist structure of sport which had existed under communism. Football clubs had to seek new forms of private sponsorship in order to survive. Most of the leading players migrated to Western Europe seeking higher salaries and higher status (Duke, 1994).

In the initial period of transformation, until January 1993 when Czechoslovakia split into two separate nations, interest in football and attendance at matches were relatively low. Coping with everyday life in the face of rapid economic change was paramount for most people. There was little in the way of football hooliganism during this period. Leading up to the peaceful separation into two independent states, tension was guaranteed at matches between Czech and Slovak clubs, but there were no seriously violent incidents.

Following the founding of the independent Czech Republic, a new Czech national first division was set up for the 1993–94 season. Six new teams were promoted from the former Czech second division in order to replace the Slovak teams, now in their own Slovak national first division. The overall spectator base was affected by these changes. Many of the new clubs promoted to the first division in the early years were from small towns such as Slovan Liberec and Atlantic Lázně Bohdanec, or even from villages such as Petra Drnovice and Chmel Blšany. Each of these newly promoted clubs has a stadium with a capacity of less than 10,000.

Petra Drnovice were sponsored by a wealthy entrepreneur. This enabled the village team to rise up to, and survive in, the first division. However, for many other clubs, financial problems have persisted in the new capitalist environment. Dukla Praha, formerly sponsored by the army and highly successful under communism, were relegated to the third division before reviving with the help of entrepreneurial support. The club relocated in 1997 to a provincial town and play now as Dukla Příbram. Union Cheb went bankrupt in the summer of 1996 and resigned from the first division. Even the great Sparta Praha, champions of the Czech Republic four times in five years since 1993, almost went out of business in the 1995–96 season; the club was saved by a Slovakian steel company, who also own FC Košice in Slovakia.

The best Czech players continue to leave for higher rewards elsewhere, mostly in Western Europe. A survey in 1997–98 found that 345 Czech players were playing abroad. Attendance at matches has remained relatively high considering the problems facing Czech football. In 1996–97, the average attendance was around 7,000, although this figure disguises wide variations, with Boby Brno attracting the best crowds, including a record attendance for a Czech league match of over 44,000 for a game against Slavia Praha.

In terms of hooliganism, the response to all these changes has been, on the one hand, to maintain traditional rivalries and, on the other, to develop new forms of violent behaviour. Fighting between rival groups of fans has appeared mainly during matches between clubs from rival cities such as Prague, Brno, Ostrava and Olomouc. Especially high risk are the matches between Sparta Praha and Baník Ostrava, or between Sparta and Boby Brno. Old national rivalries were revived in 1997 when the Czech Republic played Slovakia twice in World Cup qualifying games. Predictably there were violent incidents in both Bratislava and Prague.

One new development in football hooliganism in the Czech republic in the 1990s has been the formation of coalitions between two groups of fighting fans in order to attack the police, an example of which occurred at the Viktoria Žižkov–Baník Ostrava match in February 1997. Also new is the appearance of supporters of militant socio-political movements, such as skinheads and anarchists, among football spectators. They use football matches to make an impact and attack their rivals. Skinheads were involved in a battle with the police after the Boby Brno–Viktoria Žižkov match in November 1996. Evidence from survey data of broader changes in the social structure of football spectators in the 1990s will be presented in the next section.

The level of brutality associated with football-related violence has increased in the 1990s. The first death linked to football hooliganism occurred in the Czech Republic in 1997. Fans returning from the Sparta Praha–Boby Brno match attacked fellow passengers on the train. One young man, not a football supporter, was beaten up and then thrown out of the moving carriage to his death. People in the Czech Republic still face many problems relating to the transformation from communism to capitalist democracy. Amid all the social, political and economic problems, football hooliganism is not regarded by politicians and the media as a priority. However, the phenomenon itself is still alive and kicking in the Czech Republic.

The social background of football spectators: some empirical evidence

Data on the social backgrounds of football spectators are available from two surveys conducted in the Czech Republic (see Slepička, 1991). The first data set was collected between 1986 and 1989 and comprises 3,420 first division football fans. In 1995, a second sample of 2,680 first division spectators was studied. A comparison of the two samples, communist and post-communist, suggests that the social composition of football crowds is changing.

Figure 1 summarises the age distribution of football spectators in the two periods. The trend is towards a more youthful crowd. In 1995 young people (defined as 22 and under) constituted more than half the crowd. Compared with their elders, young people are generally more spontaneous, identify more strongly with the club and its players, and are more likely to be influenced by the atmosphere in the stadium. The potential for football hooliganism in such a crowd is clear.

Figure 1 **Age distribution of football spectators**

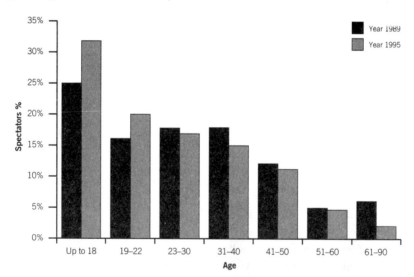

The level of education attained is an important social characteristic of football spectators which is relevant to their behaviour. Data on the educational level of Czech spectators are presented in figure 2. Given the youthfulness of the sample, many have not yet reached university age and some of these may still go on to this level. However, the trend over the two periods is for the football crowd to have received less formal education in the 1990s. Almost 70 per cent of the 1995 sample had received only elementary education, and it is this group who are more likely to take part in football-related violence.

Figure 2 **The highest level of attained education**

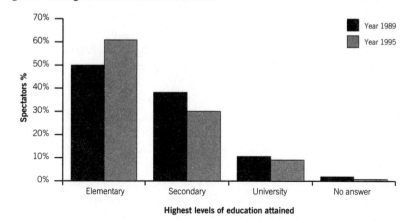

The occupational data provided in figure 3 confirm the increased youth of the 1995 sample, which shows a notable increase in the proportion of apprentices and students by comparison with the 1989 sample. A slight increase in the proportion of manual workers is discernible, too. Two distinct groups of spectators were evident in these data. The largest group consisted of young supporters (apprentices, students, manual workers), who are more prone to react to incidents both on and off the pitch. Football is more important in their lives and their commitment to their club is stronger. The second group comprised older spectators with a higher average level of education. They were more likely to be married and less likely to engage in football hooliganism.

Figure 3 **Type of occupation**

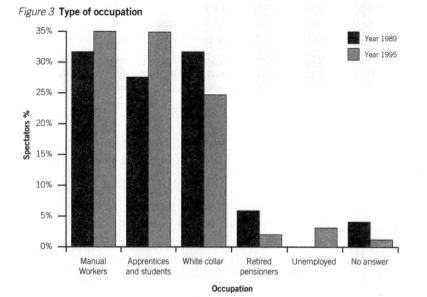

Conclusion

Analysis of football-related violence in the Czech republic indicates both similarities and differences with other countries, most particularly with reference to the archetypal English case. Unsurprisingly, some of the differences · reflect the turbulent political history of Eastern Europe in the twentieth century. What is now the Czech Republic has been the site of various nation states and has experienced radically opposed political systems. Interaction, or the lack of it, with neighbouring countries has also played a part in determining the characteristics of its people and their culture.

The most obvious similarity with most other countries is that crowd incidents at football matches in what was formerly Czechoslovakia have a long history. In the earlier period, before the communist era, incidents were overwhelmingly spontaneous and match-related, involving attacks on players and match officials. More recently, from the mid-1980s (towards the end of communist control), fighting between rival groups of fans, increasingly of a premeditated nature, became the norm.

With regard to the social structural basis of hooliganism, similar groups appear to be involved in the Czech Republic as elsewhere. Football-related violence is particularly associated with young males with low educational qualifications who are predominantly from manual working-class backgrounds. Finally, the role of the media in escalating football hooliganism is apparent in the Czech Republic, too. Czech TV played a part in advertising the potential excitement of football hooliganism, as did the film *Proč?*

Although many of the features of Czech football hooliganism are similar to those elsewhere, their evolution has taken place somewhat later. Dunning has suggested that, in England, attacks on players and officials predominated before the First World War; in the Czech case this phase continued until just after the Second World War. Dunning (1999: 144) further states that, in England, fighting between rival groups predominated after the 1960s; in the Czech Republic this has only been the case from the mid-1980s. The 'copycat' phenomenon of English football hooliganism happened later in Eastern Europe because of the relative isolation, restricted media coverage and rigorous repression under the communist regimes. Football-related violence virtually disappeared in the early period of communist rule; in a word, repression can be effective, at least in the short term.

This Czech pattern of later evolution fits well into the framework for comparative and historical analysis of football-related violence proposed by one of the current authors in an earlier article (Duke and Crolley, 1996a). Developments in the Czech Republic occurred later both in terms of the degree of organisation involved and the nature of the violence. The 1990s witnessed the first instances of attacks on the police by groups of

Czech fans. Such activity is a much more regular feature among football spectators in Argentina.

In the Czech case, the major fault lines in society on which football-related violence thrives have remained constant throughout the period examined in this chapter. Football hooliganism is most likely to take place at the Prague derby matches, as well as at games involving key inter-city rivalries. To some extent, the cities involved reflect long-standing regional enmities. In the case of Slovakia and Slovakian clubs, such conflicts have been exacerbated by nationalist fervour. During the twentieth century, Slovak clubs have joined with Czech clubs in a joint league, and twice left to play in their own independent national league: from Bohemian rhapsody to a new world.

Chapter 5

Another side to French exceptionalism: football without hooligans?

Patrick Mignon

Football is, incontestably, the most popular sport in France and has been for a long time. For many years, though, it has lacked the passion and excess that can be seen in England or Italy. There have also traditionally been fewer spectators. No city has been able to support two teams. The 'ends' occupied by the 'ultras' have seemed empty compared to the 'kops', 'curves' and 'sides' in grounds elsewhere in Europe. And the French police could once have testified that French hooligans were far easier to control than their foreign counterparts.

But French football has become increasingly popular since the beginning of the 1980s. During the 1987–88 season, attendance levels matched the best ever previous attendances, recorded during the 1950–51 season, with an average match attendance of 12,000. In 1999–2000, attendances reached new record levels with an average of 22,000 spectators per game. Although these are well below the attendance figures for Germany and England, French club teams are now playing to 50–80 per cent of capacity. The number of season ticket holders has also increased from 150,000 in 1998–99 to 211,000 in 2000–01.[1]

The transformation is also qualitative, for fans' involvement in the clubs is now much stronger. During the seventies, with the success in European competitions of Saint-Etienne, Bastia and Lens, France discovered noisy, passionate and parochial supporters, with their scarves, their chants and their banners. For most French people, this seemed to illustrate an aspect of an old France, a traditional working-class culture of miners in Saint-Etienne or Lens or the normal eccentricity of Corsican people, rather than a symptom of deep changes in French society. But it is now clear that these changes were part of a dramatic expansion of different forms of 'supporterism', including hooliganism and the style of supporting associated with the ultras. The behaviour of the French ultras and the development of hooliganism are spectacular aspects of changes in the ways in which collective and individual identities are now produced in France: personal identities, or identities linked with gender, locality or age, are now as important as political identities - whether republican or clerical, of the left or of the right – as expressions of an ideal conception of what it means to be French.[2] However, if we wish to describe French hooliganism, it is necessary to focus on football at the club level, rather than at the level of the national team.

A new social world

From a dedicated football supporter's point of view, the French are divided into two kinds of supporters: the 'hools', influenced by the first wave of British hooligans and by the Germans; and the 'ultras', influenced by Italy. Until the mid-eighties, there was a difference between the North, where the 'kops' were to be found, faithful to what was seen as the English style of supporting, flaunting their club's colours and chanting, and the South where huge flags were displayed, choreographies were set up and supporters were organised in associations. Since then, a tendency towards 'Italianisation' has occurred everywhere in France, but two patterns of supporting remain, one of which tends to be more sober, restrained and informal, and the other more outgoing and more organised. Disorderly supporters can be found in both categories, but in the two cases the mechanisms and the meanings leading to violence or disorders are different.

Hooligans

At the end of the 1970s and the beginning of the 1980s, groups of supporters who drew their inspiration from British subcultures could be seen in France organising themselves in the ends – traditionally called 'virages' (curves) – of the football stadiums, which they re-christened 'kops'. These supporters, from Paris, Lille or Le Havre, were expert in British football and pop music which they had come to know from their trips to London, where they experienced the atmosphere of the stadia, the pubs and the musical venues. This importation of British cultural goods was, of course, not new. The Beatles were popular in the sixties, but between 1975 and 1980, the importation of British culture concerned less well-known artists and other subcultures: British rhythm and blues, pub rock or punk became the musical and street styles for a significant minority of young French people, as did the skinhead and hooligan subcultures.

The development of these subcultures took place mainly in the larger cities such as Paris or Lille, which had large numbers of students and a network of 'cultural go-betweens', that is people who travelled regularly between cultural centres in different countries. It was in these two cities that the first skinhead and hooligan disturbances in France occurred, with the most dramatic scenes taking place in Paris. In describing the hooligans, I shall draw particularly on data from Paris, because the capital has been for a very long time the main centre of football hooliganism in France. The major reason for this is that the adaptation of British subcultures coincided in Paris with the establishment of Paris Saint-Germain Football Club in the football landscape. Created in 1973, the club was desperately looking for spectators to fill the stands and this situation lasted until the mid-nineties. During the 1978–79 and 1979–80 seasons, the club took a decision which has been very important for the history of supporterism in Paris. More particularly, in order to attract more supporters, the club proposed putting on sale very cheap tickets to attract young people.[3] The result was that more and more young Parisian football fans, eager to watch good football and to support a team of their own, began to come regularly to the Parc des Princes, assembling especially on the 'Boulogne curve' which they christened the 'Kop de Boulogne'. However, this pricing policy also gave those involved in the new skinhead subculture access to a new status, for they found in the stadium a way of acquiring 'street credibility' by imitating their Millwall, West Ham or Chelsea models.

Other than those provoked by English visitors, the first hooligan incidents occurred during the 1978–79 season. Thereafter, activities such as flaunting Celtic crosses, raising right arms, chanting 'France for the French' and, after matches, chasing Arabs and Blacks more often than opposing supporters became a new routine at the Parc des Princes. Very quickly, and especially after the Heysel stadium tragedy in 1985, the behaviour of these hooligans attracted media attention and led to the erection of fences around French grounds, the mobilisation of huge numbers of police and the implementation of specific laws against hooliganism. During the 1980s, the French skinheads followed their English counterparts and became 'casuals'. Subsequently, they came to call themselves 'hools' or sometimes 'independents', accusing other supporters of being under the control of the clubs. What distinguishes them from other supporters are their special mix of extreme-right ideas, their refer-ences to Fascism or Nazism and the affiliation of some of the leaders to Fascist organisations. Above all, however, they are distinguished by their taste for violence, for creating disorder and by the feeling of power which their capacity for creating disorder induces in them. That is also why some kinds of anarchists – those who think disorder must be created at every opportunity – can sometimes be found among them. Political rivalries and fights sometimes occur between these groups though they can also occasionally form an alliance against the police.

Ultras

A major difference between the hooligans and the ultras is to be found in the 'show' which the ultras organise every week with their chants throughout the game, their huge flags, their choreographed movements and their pyrotechnic show. Another difference lies in the high degree of organisation characteristic of the ultras. They have to prepare the show during the preceding week and there is a division of labour among the members. They also have an official name – the name of their association – and officers such as president and treasurer. They also negotiate with the clubs and sometimes, as in Marseilles or Saint-Etienne, with the local authorities. For them, organisation is necessary and visible. They differ both from the 'kopites', who draw upon the culture of the kop and for whom spontaneity is all important, and from the hooligans who project an image of themselves as a violent bunch or horde.

The associations and 'shows' of the ultras have developed since the mid-1980s. One of the reasons for their success is to be found in their model of action, which is spectacular, visible and emotionally arousing, but which is not usually violent. Everybody has to do something during the game or during the week and 'doing something' provides the content of a football supporter culture which, without this, could never have developed the shared meanings or common usages which define a culture. This is because there were no massive crowds during the development of French supporterism in the 1970s and 1980s, as there were in England, able to chant songs derived from a long history and several generations of football fans. Hooligan or kopite styles are in effect competitions between supporters, a way to attract attention during a game. This is also the case for the supporterism of the ultras, though in this instance supporterism has become an end in itself. As a consequence, both right and left wing supporters can be found among the ultras though political issues are not raised because to do so might threaten the unity of their association and give rise to schisms.

Ultra supporterism is not necessarily violent but may be seen as threatening for a variety of reasons: it is noisy and aggressive and uses means that might endanger the safety of others (fireworks, choreographed crowd movements). The ultras also want to be independent from their clubs, but to take part in making decisions concerning the club. And they criticise the club and other football bodies. In brief, theirs is a protest organisation. Ultras may also be seen as threatening because of the competition between the ultras of opposing clubs and between different ultra groups within a single club, and because they want to use the stadium and the surrounding streets as sites for the expression of their own particular style of supporting. As each ultra association has created a heritage of flags, scarves, memories and sometimes money, so opportunities have developed for producing tension, disorder and violence.

Of course, participation in violence or other illegal activities is also 'doing something together' and as such it produces shared memories and a sense of belonging within the group.

Thus a social world of supporterism now exists in France. Ultras, their associations, and their power to attract those who want to 'do something', have been playing a bigger and bigger role in French football. But there are others kinds of associations, ones which are not protest organisations but which attract younger or older football fans; these are often called 'official' associations because they are integrated into the clubs. All of these different groups offer a range of opportunities for expressing support for a team.

How many ultras? How much violence?

Is it possible to quantify the importance of these different kinds of supporters? There are currently at least two supporters' associations in each professional football club in France. In First Division clubs, five or six associations can often be found. In Marseilles, there are ten or eleven, and fifteen at Paris Saint-Germain. The numbers of these associations and of their members fluctuate, depending on the club's results, on splits inside the clubs and on the ageing and retirement of leaders. There are, in all, approximately 150 supporters' associations in the French Championship, consisting of identified hooligan groups, ultras and 'official' associations. Some of these associations, for example in Lens, can bring together 6,000 or 7,000 members. The big associations of ultras, in Paris, Bordeaux, Marseilles and Lyon, consist of between 500 and 2500 members. Others are relatively small, consisting of only about twenty members who have decided to create what is in effect a group of faithful friends rather than a 'bureaucratic' association. The strength of the ultras varies from one club to another. In Marseilles, several groups of ultras may together account for 20,000 people at each game, while in Paris they may account for 15,000 spectators and, because of their club's reputation, they have networks all over France. The power of these associations means that in the bigger clubs, they represent almost a quarter of the attendance and the majority of supporters travelling to away matches with their club. In total, there may be 50,000 registered supporters and 150,000 supporters who are within the sphere of influence of ultra associations. There are far fewer hooligans: about one hundred in Paris, about fifty in Lyon, Strasbourg, Lille or Saint-Etienne, and perhaps as few as ten in less successful teams such as Cannes and Nice. However, it should be noted that the development of supporters' activities has been very fast during the last five years: in 1994, for example, all of these groups were embryonic, with the exception of Marseilles, which already had large crowds and powerful ultras, and Paris with its hooligans. These recent developments mean that disorders now have more chance of occurring anywhere in France.

The level of serious violence is still for the moment comparatively low in France. Since the beginning of this new supporterism at the end of the seventies, there has been one death, caused by a missile, though this was more an accident than a deliberately violent act. There have also been some serious injuries, the most dramatic being a serious injury to a policeman during a game in the Parc des Princes in 1993 and, more recently, in October 2000, a Marseilles supporter was wounded by a broken seat thrown by a Paris St-Germain fan. Despite this situation of relative calm, new laws were passed in 1984 and 1993, and police mobilisation has become increasingly important in and around the stadia. But what is the content of the violence and disorders that take place in football-related contexts in France?

First, there are clashes between opposing supporters. These now rarely occur in the form of direct fighting between fans inside the stadium. More common are disturbances involving the throwing of missiles at opposing fans and, most often, confrontations outside the ground, around railway stations, city centres and motorways, for example at toll or resting areas. The favoured haunts of local fans are favourite targets because they allow the 'invading' group to claim that they successfully entered the enemy's territory and stole trophies (for example a banner) or painted the local walls with their slogans. There are also sometimes fights between ultras or hooligans of the same club over occupancy of the best places in the 'curves', to mark ideological differences, or to punish traitors who have collaborated with the club's officialdom in an attempt to gain some advantage.

From the beginning, clashes with police have been a marked feature of the behaviour of hooligans or ultras in France. The police, who are often present to prevent incidents between opposing supporters, have themselves become the targets of violent attacks. In this regard, it should be noted that, in France, clashes with the police are often seen as a means of expressing both opposition to society and the seriousness of one's cause. They are also a means of gaining reputation. Since 1998, stewards have taken the place of police inside the stadia and they have become the new target.

Physical attacks or harassment against passers-by of African or Maghrebian origins are still common, and in European Champions League games between Paris St-Germain and Turkish teams there have been attacks on ordinary Turkish supporters. Racism is the background of this violence which comes from the most right-wing supporters among the ultras. Racist chants and the exhibition of fascist symbols by the 'hools' at matches in Paris, Lille or Lyon, may also be directed against black players. Recently in Strasbourg, in the context of a run of poor results by the local team, a group of supporters wrote anti-Semitic slogans against the coach and mailed racist letters to the club, directed against the team's Black and Maghrebian players and the coach who was held to be responsible for recruiting foreigners.

There has also been a more general increase in both verbal attacks and vandalism. Vandalism is undoubtedly the most common offence. For example in 1998, Marseilles ultras who had travelled to Paris for an away game destroyed two buses and several compartments in a train. Frequently, parked cars and buses, or cars with number plates from the city of the opposing team, are damaged. Shops are sometimes looted. More generally, verbal insults, provocative attitudes, spitting at the police, at the club's manager or at other spectators are the new reality of French football stadia.

There is, then, a series of gradations ranging from symbolic to actual but limited physical violence. Another dimension ranges from violence or disorders which appear largely expressive in character and which may be linked to the results of matches or to the oversensitivity of young males, to instrumental violence linked to political motives with a mix of extreme-right ideology, racism, the corporate sense of the ultras and local identities. Most violence, as has been noted, is not serious in terms of the number of casualties, but this is a new phenomenon and this novelty has revealed the deep changes that are taking place in French society. This raises the question of whether those processes which have caused the development of the ultras' supporterism and hooliganism are going to have longer-term and more serious consequences.

Football disorders and the transformation of French society

The violence and disorders taking place in French football can be analysed through the emergence of a new set of actors: the supporters. Let us begin with what has been the most dramatic change in supporterism – the emergence of the ultras – for there are strong connections between the ideas and values that can be identified in the ultras' social world and the motives which explain much of the violence which takes place in French society at large.

An internal logic to violence

The ultras' world can be seen as a protest movement. They want to be considered as different from other spectators, both from traditional supporters whom they see as too 'soft' and from the hooligans, whom they see as too violent and too far from real football values. In developing their own pattern of supporterism, they have put themselves in a situation of confrontation with clubs and other football bodies.

To be an ultra, a supporter has to be a partisan, deeply committed and faithful to the club's colours and to the ultra group to which he belongs. To defend the independence of his group, he has to contribute his money, his time, his energy and his physical involvement. By taking part in a contest with other ultra groups, he demonstrates his authenticity and his solidarity with his mates. This solidarity is shown during matches by taking part actively with the tifo (committed fans) and, during the week, by working to prepare for the next game. It is also demonstrated when one's group is attacked, physically or verbally, by standing up for its honour against other supporters, the police or the club's managers. An ultra is committed to a struggle for recognition as a football actor who is equal to other actors within the world of football, and as one who stands for the traditional values of football against VIPs and sponsors.

From their point of view, the ultras' violence can be seen as the justifiable defence of these values, as an answer to all the attacks against them, or as a protest against injustice. Their actual level of violence is low and it is better to speak in their case about the threat of violence or a challenge to the existing balance of power. From a sociological point of view, this threat of violence can be seen as a means of building a group around what is perceived as a legitimate cause. It can be used to demonstrate to the club, but also to the group's members themselves, the strength of the group. Deliberate or not, violence strengthens the group; it creates a reputation, a shared memory for group members, and stories that members can repeat to each other. It thus creates a division between insiders and outsiders which is necessary for the group to exist. However, for the ultras, violence is not an end in itself.

This subjective logic of honour and group solidarity and the social process of forging a group through shared experiences, so clearly evident in the activities of the ultras, are not alien to the hooligans. In their case, however, there may be political-ideological elements which mean: (i) that the targets are not only opposing ultras or supporters but also foreigners who may be attacked simply because they are foreign; (ii) that there is no goal of achieving recognition by the club because this recognition is a path to negotiation and incorporation, and these the hooligans do not want.

Who are the new supporters? Who are the hooligans?[4]

A survey carried out in 1997 found that in the Parc des Princes 60 per cent of spectators were under the age of 35, and 40 per cent were under 25. Those who came from the suburbs of Paris constituted 75 per cent of those attending the game. Younger spectators were found mainly in the 'curves': 54 per cent of those in the 'curves' were under 25 and 36 per cent were aged between 25 and 35. The vast majority – 90 per cent – were male. This survey and several ethnographic studies carried out between 1997 and 1999 confirmed that these new supporters were primarily young males: 34 per cent were students or older secondary school children. Forty-nine per cent were employed, often in their first job. The rest were unemployed or young people scraping along in temporary jobs. When looking more specifically at the hooligans,[5] the majority were young males aged between 16 and 22, from Paris and its environs, sometimes unemployed, but more often employed (half were non-manual workers or skilled manual workers; the other half were unskilled manual workers), students or schoolchildren. Finally, though they often came from the working class or lower middle class, some came from middle-class backgrounds.[6] Some policemen and judges believe that football delinquents are among the more educated of delinquents. But because of the democratisation of education in France, obtaining a baccalaureate at 18, or even going to university, are not guarantees of middle-class origins or a middle-class destiny.

In assessing young supporters, schoolteachers describe what they see as an atmosphere of threat, the toughness and permanent restlessness of these young people. They also stress what they see as their lack of self-control and 'oversensitivity', and say that some of the convicted hooligans had problems in school before having problems in the football ground. These outcomes are the result of tensions arising from the democratisation of education in France where the official goal is to bring 80 per cent of the relevant age group to the 'bac'. This policy has transformed schools into places where young people, and especially young males, are likely to experience failure, intense competition (often with a group dimension) or boredom, which drive them to seek more satisfying and exciting experiences in their leisure lives.

Changes in the socialisation of young males

The increase in the size of crowds and in fans' involvement in football in France may be linked with several processes. The first of these relates to the development of France as an urban society. Other than Paris, all the big French cities have been really big only since the 1950s.[7] This means that new town-dwellers, who used to have neither the time nor the motive for supporting a football team, are now settled in their environment. It is also the case that living in Paris is no longer considered as being as special as it used to be in terms of links with culture, politics or opportunities for social mobility. Correspondingly, living in Marseilles, Lens or Nantes is no longer seen as a mark of social inferiority. Hand in hand with this has gone a rediscovery of local identities. Moreover, between 1962 and 1980, what can be described as the crisis years of football in Paris, the Parisian urban space underwent profound changes. The city became more densely populated, increasingly by Parisians and their descendants, and the latter increasingly lived in suburbs which were ranked in terms of the wealth of their inhabitants and the degrees of security and safety they could offer.

Processes of suburbanisation occurred elsewhere, too, and this has meant that the mechanisms of social integration have changed. What one might call the new supply of football during the seventies and eighties was a result of the efforts of the clubs' new managers and of local authorities searching to attract new investors and new inhabitants and to reinforce local pride. This development in turn met the demands for participation in a shared routine from people whose horizons were no longer defined only by upward mobility from country to city or from working class to middle class, but also by patterns of downward mobility symbolised by spatial movement within the big new metropolises.[8] This meant that: (i) because of the competition between cities for economic growth; (ii) because of the competition between social and ethnic groups; and (iii) because trades unions and political parties are no longer seen as vehicles for the expression of discontent or for sharing a vision of the future, allegiance to a club became a legitimate means of self-definition. To have one's own space in a football stadium means being able to meet, and to have a good time with, people who share the same social experiences. It also enables young people to fix regular meetings as a way of mapping out the week with activities and places to go to. Becoming a football activist brings a little more meaning to one's leisure activities and offers a new means of expressing and crystallising one's experiences in social life.

These new forms of supporterism are linked to the democratisation of the experiences of young people and to the prolongation of the period of 'post-adolescence' (Galland 1991). These two processes are also connected with the democratisation and the increasing duration of the period of study and to difficulties in finding steady jobs and becoming integrated into the wider society. 'Post-adolescence' is also linked to the loosening of social constraints which, in turn, is associated with the growing importance of relatively auto-nomous generational groups where young people are socialised increasingly independently of the adult world. Such changes in the 1970s and 1980s brought young French people closer to their British and German counterparts, that is to a model of youth founded on an experience of the emptiness of social life and participation in mass popular culture. These two decades saw young French people escaping from the tutelage of school and parents. More particularly, during the 1970s and 1980s, there was a shift away from socialisation founded on identification with the parental model and towards a model based on experimentation (Galland, 1991). For the young working-class male as for the middle-class student, to be young no longer meant adhering to a course determined by the social position of one's parents. Nor could young people be sure any longer of being able to reproduce their parents' experiences in the sense of occupying the same social position or undergoing the same process of upward mobility. Because of unemployment, the transition for young people into work and into the wider society increasingly required them to construct strategies based on the principle of trial-and-error until they were able to achieve a satisfactory definition of themselves, both in their own eyes and in the eyes of others. In ways such as these, supporters' groups have come to express the importance of peer groups in the socialisation of youth and the importance to young people of having their values recognised, not by adults, but by their peers.

Mass popular culture, music and football have thus become elements of a shared experience. They also provide a context within which new experiences can be gained. Being a supporter, and for some being a disorderly supporter, is one of the ways in which, through the adoption of anti-institutional attitudes, young people can negotiate a process of social transition. On the one hand, it offers a field of self-discovery and experimentation through a search for both differentiation and inclusion in something wider – a cause or a movement in which they can participate – with the young and the 'true' ranged against the old and the tame. Sometimes, the roles which are attributed within supporter groups may lead to the acquisition of socially useful skills such as managing groups, negotiating with others and developing enterprise. There is also the experience of travelling across France and going abroad, thereby participating in national and international networks. Football and belonging to a supporters' group provide an opportunity to acquire status and a reputation. They also offer a career to young people as members of a supporters' group. In this regard, those involved in ultra groups usually drop out of such groups between the ages of 22 and 25. They do so either when they feel they have nothing more to profit from being an ultra, or to set up home, start employment or resume their studies. The few who stay in supporterism – some beyond the age of 30 – do so because they have a position of responsibility in a supporters' club or because they have difficulty finding an established place in the wider society. For such fans, supporterism or hooliganism are among the few activities in which they feel they can find social relationships which they value. A gradation of violence parallels a gradation of commitment to the experience of being an ultra or a hooligan. Hooliganism and violence remain a minority experience. The central question is: who is that minority and how is it socially produced?

Supporterism as a new way of life[9]

Some of those involved in football disorders are political activists and are best described as instigators of disorder rather than as regular members of supporters' organisations. Leaving these people aside, we can develop an hypothesis based on career analysis[10] and elements of Elias's theory, as used by Lagrange (1995), to link careers in supporterism with 'breaks' in the process of integration or interdependence, what one sociologist has called 'disaffiliation' (Castel, 1991). For adults, this process may be associated with the consequences of unemployment, with moving house, lack of money, divorce, loss of sociability, possibly alcohol dependence and finally social exclusion. For young people, it may involve failure in school, moving house, family breakdown, or parental unemployment. It may also be associated with affective failures or low self esteem, sometimes for physical reasons. Structurally, we can refer to the experience of downward mobility, or 'the fear of falling', which may be linked to a change in the construction of self-esteem or an incomplete process of the internalisation of self esteem. The process of integration through family, school and further/higher education, work, welfare state, citizenship and familiarity with the national culture sustains the process of internalisation of constraints because people are able to develop a strong sense of their own individuality, a sense of 'fit' or 'closeness' between their inner life and their social circumstances. But large-scale unemployment, a high rate of school failure, a more general urban crisis and a culture of individualism, conveyed through a media culture which is in competition with high culture, can lead to the development of people who have a weak sense of their own identity and morality, who are more dependent upon others to define who and what they are and who may have more difficulties in coping with the problems of ordinary life. This is sometimes today described as 'oversensitivity'. For young people in this situation, peer groups in school, in a gang or in the stadium, are contexts in which they can get confirmation of who and what they are: in these groups, spontaneity rather than constraint is valorised. To be 'mad' (or more precisely, to act in a 'mad' way) is seen not as bad but rather as a way to gain a reputation. Such groups offer a means to confirm one's identity in a situation where there may be few other positive experiences. In such groups, male values are highly valorised, and this may be a means of coping with one of the most painful experiences of young people, namely the competition with girls in school and with girls and other boys in sexual relationships. An answer to the problems of low self-esteem is provided by the model of toughness, which expresses the honour and authenticity of young males.

Hooligans are not always people who come from a neighbourhood which is seen as a 'territory'. This might be true for a very deprived area where most of the young people are from immigrant backgrounds and in relation to whom others have a real or imagined rivalry. Football, and especially supporterism, is a male preserve, but also until very recently it has been a preserve of males who are young and white. For some of them, supporterism is seen as a defence of 'whiteness'. The rivalry with North African or African gangs is interpreted as a war between races, and becoming a supporter means defining oneself against what appear to be other communities by proclaiming oneself to be part of a community as well. Their presence in the stadium is the expression of the relationship between the centre and the periphery, of their appropriation of the centre in response to the appropriation of the suburbs by ethnic 'enemies'. A whole section of the 'Kop of Boulogne' bears witness to this logic: the creation of a territory in opposition to other territories. Others who are not so sensitive to the 'race' argument also go to a territory where they gather with those who are like-minded.

The other source of meaning, if one does not see non-white youth as an enemy, is a career in the ultras' organisation. A notable change in the social composition of ultra groups is that in recent years more low school or low work achievers are to be found. More Maghrebian and African youths can also be found in these groups.

With its stress on organisation and organised action, supporterism in France continues to be marked by the stamp of politics. In this way, ultra groups act as a shield against violence because they socialise people, give them a cause and a frame for dealing with their restlessness. But this is threatened by the individualist feeling which leads to the questioning of the ultra groups as substitute schools or families.

Chapter 6

Football hooliganism in Germany: a developmental sociological study

Hubert Dwertmann
Bero Rigauer

Introduction

In this chapter, we investigate the sociogenesis of football hooliganism in Germany. We do not simply take for granted the view that the hooligans are a problem. Rather, we look at the more basic question of what it is about them that causes problems for society. We consider the social actions and reactions that made it possible for a group such as football hooligans to emerge. In the mid-1960s, using the terminology of critical theory, it was said that 'sociologically more interesting than the juvenile revolt against the authority of the manipulated order is the influence which this order has on the revolt itself' (Friedeburg, 1965b: 182). Our perspective in considering topics such as 'spectator disorders' and 'sport and violence' can be described as a developmental orientation, geared especially towards explaining 'changes in figurations . . . by other, prior changes . . . , not by a "first cause" which, so to speak, set everything in motion' (Elias, 1978: 162). We therefore deal first with the development and meaning of the idea of a 'hooligan', second with the historical preconditions for fan disorders as a form of behaviour, and third with the fan disorders of the 1970s. This will then help us to discuss, fourth, the formation and development of the hooligan scene, and fifth, to investigate the changes which took place during the 1990s. We present the overall conceptual framework of our study in the first section, together with our elaboration of the sociological basis of the concept of 'hooligan'.

Translated from the original German by Eric Dunning

The social development of football hooliganism in Germany

On the meaning of the term 'hooligan'

The word 'hooligan' appears in three of the chapters in Friedeburg's (1965a) classic edited text *Jugend in der modernen Gesellschaft* (Youth in Modern Society). In all instances, the concept was used mainly to refer to the youths who were then taking part in riots in the various countries of the former Eastern bloc. The chapters shared the supposition that, while these riots were only understandable against a background of political repression, the youths themselves were distinguished by their apolitical attitude. The French sociologist Lapassade (1965: 191ff) summed them up as 'Rebels without a cause', borrowing, of course, from the title of the 1950s James Dean film. Friedeburg himself (1965b: 176ff) singled out the 'conventional socialisation process'. This can be understood, given his perspective, as implying a cause-and-effect relationship. The so-called 'teddy boy riots' (*Halbstarkenkrawalle*) of the 1950s, for their part, were attributed to factors which are still held to play a role today – family background, education, work situation, leisure time, social pressure to consume, and clothing preferences. Even the adventure motive, well known from interpretations of the 1980s and 1990s, appears in a contribution written as early as 1963, in which it is held that 'the open taking of risks is itself a guarantee of pleasure' (Friedeburg, 1965b: 182). These explanations in terms of 'compensation', together with Friedeburg's perspective, were taken up in German sports science research in the 1970s.

In 1975, the term 'hooliganism' appeared in the title of a contribution by Ian Taylor (1975) to Hammerich and Heinemann's *Texte zur Soziologie des Sports* ('Texts on the Sociology of Sport'), although only in reference to the original English title. Contrary to Taylor's intention, but in keeping with the public understanding of fan disorders in Germany at the time, the concept was translated into German as *Fussball-Vandalismus* (football vandalism). The translation was on a level with then-contemporary media reports which referred for example to *Rowdytum* ('rowdiness'), *Krawalle* ('riots') and *Fanhorden* ('fan hordes'). However, conceptualisations in social science and sports science research into 'football fans' (Hermann, 1977) or 'spectator riots' (*Zuschauerausschreitungen*, Pilz, 1979) are a clear sign that a more differentiated and objective approach than that of the media began to emerge in the mid-1970s. Then, at the end of the 1970s, the concept of *Hooliganismus* became more common and, in a 1979 article by Dunning and Sheard, the English was no longer translated. A year earlier, the psychologist Stemme had used the term in a lecture to a police management academy to characterise what he called 'the growing wildness of some spectator groups' ('Verwahrlosung einiger Zuschauergruppen', *Frankfurter Rundschau*, 12 May 1978). At the end of a talk influenced by American and British research, Stemme recommended that 'people should be sent to England in order to get advice'. However, in the summary of sports science findings on the subject edited by Gunter Pilz and published as *Sport und körperliche Gewalt* (Sport and Physical Violence) in 1982, the concept of 'hooliganism' was not even mentioned.

Since the mid-1980s, the general, synthesising concept of hooliganism in German usage has changed. This is related to the events in the Heysel Stadium, Brussels, in 1985, which were shown live on German television. The term began to be used principally to refer to a specific set of spectator behaviours that emerged in conjunction with certain structural developments then taking place among the fans. By looking at use of the concept of hooliganism in the German newspaper, *Tageszeitung* (*Taz*), we can show how its usage has changed since the mid-1980s. Until 1988, the concept was used now and then by *Taz's* London correspondent, but mostly not with reference to football. Then, in 1988, it appeared in reports on the European Championships. Usage of the term reached its high point in 1991 in reference to East–West relations. After that, its general usage declined for a while, only to reappear later in strengthened form in relation to specific events. In 1997, for example, it was used a total of 30 times but only twice in reference to the violence of German football hooligans. In 1998, there were no fewer than 128 mentions but these related overwhelmingly to the World Cup and the events in Lens in which German hooligans beat and kicked a French policeman nearly to death. A study in 1996, based on the number of mentions in *Taz*, maintained that hooliganism in Germany was changing from 'an attractive fashion-craze . . . to an increasingly peripheral phenomenon in the football realm' (Ek, 1996: 20). The number of hooligans had ranged between '7,000 to 8,000 but there was a tendency to decline after about 1994' (Ek, 1996: 137). This diagnosis will certainly have to be revised, however, because since then there have been signs, not of the problem being solved but rather of processes of physical violence changing and being displaced. There has been a reduction of the level of violence in the hooligan scene itself, which raises the question of whether the halting of processes of differentiation and the lifting of restrictions on the use of physical violence by specific groups are going hand in hand with an increase in the use of physical violence in everyday life and renewed processes of displacement.

On the development of the relationship between sport and violence in German society

Only through an investigation of the long-term development of sport and violence within the changing social formations of Germany in the twentieth century will it be possible to understand the levels of violence specific to the hooligans, and in consequence their social relevance. Since such a long-term study has yet to be carried out, only a few hints can be offered here.

Authoritarian, nihilistic and rationalistic attitudes and orientations prevailed in the German sports movement from the Wilhelmine authoritarian state (1871–1914) until the 1950s and 1960s. These attitudes and orientations were, of course, tempered somewhat by the democratic constitutions of the Weimar and Federal Republics. During the period of National Socialism, however, they were radicalised. The initial development of football in Germany and the socialisation of people into the game started in the Wilhelmine period, a fact reflected both in the use of militaristic language in the game and in the organisation of army pack marches by football clubs before 1914. In short, 'The personality structure of an ideal footballer corresponded to that of a modern soldier' (Eisenberg, 1997: 102). With the de-civilising process of German society and German sport under National Socialism, this became particularly clear towards the end of the Second World War. Sports officials and National Socialist sports officials like Diem and Halt regularly contributed to newspapers such as the *Kampfblatt der nationalsozialistischen Bewegung Grossdeutschlands* (Fighting Paper of the National Socialist Movement of Greater Germany) and the *Völkischer Beobachter* (People's Observer) at the time of Breitmayer's 'Appeal for a Bulwark of the Faithful' (*Bollwerk der Treue*, 13 September 1944). They emphasised sport as an 'inexhaustible source of military power' in the 'decisive battle for the survival of the Greater German Reich' (14 April 1945). Diem, in his speech of 18 March 1945, by drawing a parallel between the Hitler Youth – who were being sent to their deaths by then in the utterly hopeless military situation – and the Spartan training of youth for war, merely illustrated in exaggerated form the values of the German sports movement. Diem's speech, like various other statements by members of the sports movement at the end of the Second World War, points to the spectrum of violent propaganda of the National Socialist regime. This raises the question of whether and to what extent the German sports movement underwent a de-civilising process. That such a process did take place is obvious both from the massive involvement of sports officials in Germany's military propaganda, and from the parallel which was drawn between sporting and military stamina. An orientation towards the practice of violence had become anchored in German society in such a way that it led through National Socialism to a process of what Mommsen (1976) called 'cumulative radicalisation' and Elias (1992) a 'breakdown of civilisation'.

For present purposes, two references to individual stages in the development of football behaviour in Germany will suffice: one from before 1914, 'the howling, roaring mob forced their way to the playing field' (Heineken [1898] 1993: 252); the second from the 1930s, 'thousands of excited spectators pressed towards the football field' (Fritsch and Pilz, 1996: 219). Spectator behaviour has closely corresponded in its development with the practice of sport which, in turn, has been connected with (i) the regulation and level of violence in

German society at large; (ii) developments in sporting organisations; and (iii) socio-spatial changes, such as the regular use of stadia. Because there have been no historical or, more precisely, no process-sociological studies of the relations between sport and violence in Germany, we shall refer to a study of a rural sports club (Dwertmann, 1991) to illustrate the social context of the sport–spectator–violence linkage in Germany up to the 1950s and lead us on to more recent developments.

Resort to violence in German peasant villages was a regular occurrence in the 1950s and football matches were occasions when it was expressed. Fights before matches, spectators interfering with play, the abandonment of matches, and attacks on the referee were all common forms of behaviour. Such behaviour corresponded to a pattern of normatively anchored violence in village life which, as well as reaching into the game of football, found expression at church festivals, fairs, weddings, and, on more everyday occasions, in pubs. To quote a player from the 1950s: 'If an opposing player broke through, we tried, naturally, to break every bone in his body'. However, the level of violence changed as the village changed, especially as peasants became less dominant. After the mid-1960s, no more examples can be found in club records comparable to those of the 1950s in which, to cite just one example, a tribunal of the Deutscher Fußballbund (German Football Association) found a player guilty of 'punching an opposing player in the face' (1957). The change in the 1960s involved a shift in conflict management in the club, with the effect that in the 1970s there were no more attacks on referees and the authorities no longer intervened directly in the field of play. A disciplining of physical violence had taken place – a shift in the way in which conflicts were resolved.

The findings from microsociological research can be used in macrosociological explanations (see for example Elias and Scotson, 1993). Apart from the fact that figurations and regularities can be detected 'which can also be useful as a guiding thread for macrosociological investigations' (Elias and Scotson, 1993: 61), a long-term regularisation[1] of sport and violence took place from the 1950s to the 1970s in the increasingly rapid modernisation of the village. This corresponded to a shift in the level of violence then taking place in German society as a whole. That is, the changes which took place in the structural characteristics of the village have to be understood as correlative with changes then occurring more widely in German society. This can be illustrated by an example of spectator disorder which broke out at a match between Hannover 96 and Manchester United in 1965 (see Fritsch and Pilz, 1996: 220–1). Newspaper reports (for example in the *Hannoversche Allgemeine Zeitung, Neue Presse,* and the *Bild Zeitung* of 7 August 1965) claimed that 'the biggest football riots ever' took place at this match in Hanover. Such descriptions are, of course, typical examples of sensationalist reporting. However, the manner of newspaper reporting can shed light on other things. Take the following hypothetical headlines: 'Things have calmed down'; 'Let him have it, if you can'; 'Two hard leftists mown down'. On the one hand, representations of this kind can indicate uncertainty as to what precisely was going on. On the other hand, they can demonstrate what was the normal social standard regarding violence at that time. The emergence of a degree of detachment in the reporting of football disorders in the 1970s – we are departing somewhat here from the standard critique – had its basis in a societal detachment in relation to violent clashes *per se*. Put briefly, spectator disorders at a match can be understood as the clash of two different national patterns of group behaviour. The practice and intensification of violence by a specific spectator group is to be understood as a deviation from the norm in this regard.

Shifts in the societal violence level and fan disorders in the 1970s

In our portrayal of the prehistory of fan disorders and the hooligan issue in Germany, we focused first on processes of development and change, second on features of the social context, and third on the characteristics of physical violence as part of everyday social behaviour. In order to clarify the difference in social orientations towards violence still further, take the following example. In 1974, the German magazine *Der Stern*, reporting under the headline 'the stadium as battlefield', suggested that 'professional football has become a theatre of war'. Until 1945 – especially in the years before 1914 and under National Socialism – such a statement would not have been regarded as a criticism. Bearing this historical reference in mind, we should like to propose the hypothesis that the spectator disorders of the 1970s and the connected issue of hooliganism should not be understood as a sign of a rise in the level of social violence. Rather, a relational shift and displacement can be observed in the level of violence of specific groups whose members were prepared for violence. As can be seen in the quotation from *Der Stern* about 'the stadium as battlefield', the media reporting of spectator disorders 'characteristically contributes to the development of the problem' (Dunning, n.d., 127). If the mass media are seen not only as reporters of social data but also as active mediators in their production, a further fact becomes clear: insofar as physical violence did not figure as a central theme in newspaper reporting in Germany in the 1950s, the silence marked the degree of public acceptance of the level of violence in those years. The massive, extreme, disapproving and in part defamatory reporting of the 1970s thus simultaneously assumed, as part of the 'fan-problematic', a communicative function in the change that was taking place in the public discourse over violence.

Within this development, a specific and intense mode of reporting lay on the same level as the legal and political measures that were undertaken as part of the overall 'repressive climate' of the 1970s (Ek, 1996: 65). And the attribution of violence to 'deviant behaviour' was, at the time, central to an attempt at scientific explanation. The diagnosis of 'deviance' can be understood as a demarcation between fan behaviour and compulsory, normatively legitimised, generally accepted ways of behaving, a diagnosis that was reinforced by the representation of fan behaviour in the mass media through such expressions as 'stadium as battlefield', 'nightmare of terror', 'terror of the police station'. Such phrases can still be read today from time to time. Since the 1970s, however, the emergence of somewhat more discriminating viewpoints can be discerned. Some examples are Stemme's lecture in the *Frankfurter Rundschau*, and reports of scientific investigations and of conferences which paralleled the development of scientific understanding of spectator disorders (see for example reports in *Westfälische Rundschau*, 20 October 1979; *Münchener Merkur*, 11 November 1982; and *Kölner Stadtanzeiger*, 12 February 1983). A higher valuation of scientific research can be observed here, and it flowed into other social realms. At the same time, the diagnosis of 'the impossibility of critical distance' in sports journalism (Pilz, 1991) points in the direction of greater detachment in the research area.

In contrast to the sociological construction of spectator disorders as 'deviant behaviour', in the 1970s there developed explanations which can be summed up under the heading of 'compensatory behaviour'. Spectator violence was thus attributed to a 'solidary sub-group within the overall mass' (Hermann, 1977: 20), or described according to the 'typology of crowd disorders' (Pilz, 1979: 184ff) and seen as being engaged in by a rather diffuse and heterogeneous group of younger male adults. Their group memberships and boundaries were held to be socio-spatially produced and expressed on the terraces where a 'socially constructed inner order' became visible (Marsh, 1980: 129). In the 1970s, confrontations took place overwhelmingly 'between the members of such groupings – among whom there have arisen over the years historically produced rivalries and enmities' (Schulz and Weber, 1982: 61). Corresponding with this, a 'typical habitus' emerged, expressed through forms of sartorial behaviour which were specific to the hooligans and distinguished them both from other fans and the rest of the population. Such clothing choices signal 'a relation to the body the generative principle of which is bodily strength and aggressive masculinity' (Becker, 1982: 80). Alcohol consumption and emotionally laden situations during a football match were stimuli for the behaviour of such groups.

Developments from the 1960s to the 1980s can be summed up as a process of differentiation in which certain ways of practising violence became quantitatively limited to spectator groups and qualitatively strengthened. The process involved a social marginalisation of youths, or rather of young adults, a socio-spatial marginalisation of these groups in the stadium (i.e. on the terraces), the adoption of group-specific styles of behaviour and dress, and the practice of violence *per se*. Until that point, the confrontations of these groups had been directly and immediately related to football matches. In the 1970s, however, they began to become increasingly displaced from the stadium onto the surrounding streets, a fact that was documented in a report on *Sport und Gewalt* (Sport and Violence) (1982). This displacement took place in the context of a massive process of social marginalisation that was driven by the mass media and reinforced by police, judicial and political measures, and which led eventually to a situation where landlords turned football fans away from pubs simply on account of their dress (Pramann, 1980: 221). Police swoops on fans in a search for knives and cudgels, the tightening of crowd control, the socio-spatial demarcation and segregation of fans inside stadia – in other words the 'repressive measures' (Ek, 1996) of the 1970s – resulted in an increase in external social pressure (what Elias called *Fremdzwang* or external constraint), leading to an increase in the public control of sports events and the disciplining of fan behaviour.

The internal differentiation and social construction of the hooligans
Sport und Gewalt (1982), the report commissioned by the Federal Ministry of the Interior, can be seen as a sign of a change that was taking place from 'repressive' to more differentiated measures. This change can be seen in other areas of life as well, for example in the socio-pedagogic treatment of fans (that is, the involvement of social workers with fans and the application of their claimed knowledge to the hooligan problem), as well as in the application of scientific research to political action and in the critique of police measures. In the process of social stigmatisation, a polarisation of fan behaviour had begun to take place as early as the 1970s. On the one hand, the external segregation and 'moral demarcation' (Becker, 1982: 83) found its inner counterpoint in the self-understanding of the fan groups – as was later the case with the hooligans. That is, the segregation and demarcation became part of the group style and made the fan habitus 'attractive' and 'resistant to change' (Becker, 1982: 83). On the other hand, the stigmatisation contributed to contradictory forms of fan behaviour. It was in this context that an Association of German Football Fan Clubs was proposed in 1974, and established in 1977, on the basis of 'an eight-point declaration' in which, for example, 'all disorders in the stadia . . . were condemned as strongly as possible' (cited in Pramann, 1980: 67). These attempts at self-regulation and limiting disorder can be described as precursors of the fan projects of the early 1980s, the first of which was in Bremen in 1981. This kind of social work was described as 'preliminary pedagogy', and involved accompanying and supervising fans at matches and other leisure settings. Fans were also assisted with financial, family and criminal problems, as well as with their problems of co-operation with the police. What was involved was not simply a process of change in socio-pedagogic praxis marked by the establishment of the fan projects, but a shift

from and differentiation of the 'law and order' model of 1970s with its stress on repressive measures (for example, bans on entering stadia, the keeping of data files on hooligans) together with a withdrawal of police from the stadia and the use of officials who were familiar with the scene.

In order to shed light on their social significance, we shall first examine the public actions which, more than anything else, led to the violent hooligans of the 1980s. The change to a hooligan figuration was grounded in changes that took place in the overall spectator figuration and in the public control measures that had been introduced. An investigation of this figurational process leads to the question of who has the social power to define 'violence'. The hooligans do not, even though they are involved both in its social definition and production. From this, it becomes clear that the debate on the hooligans in Germany has to be stood on its head. More particularly, as well as the public action taken in the 1970s, a shift in the conflict situation and also a change in the internal and external relations of the fan groups took place. Social reactions in the 1980s to public disorder, and the evaluation of these reactions, were linked to the change, as well as police tactics and the treatment of fans. In this process of figurational change, the external constraints of public stigmatisation and repressive police action were transformed after the end of the 1970s into the pacification of public spaces inside the stadium through the use of more discriminating ways of acting and behaving. Parallel with this, scientific findings and recommendations were incorporated into the praxis of the mass media, the police, politicians and social workers. In short, an interdependent network of public actions by the media, scientists, politicians, police, lawyers, sports bodies and fans can be discerned which represented a variety of different orientations and interests, and which interacted to produce the change in and displacement of violent acts. The social groups and institutions who were 'striving for peace' (Pilz, 1994: 9), that is who were seeking to reduce the level of violence in spectator behaviour, all became participants in acts which contributed to an unintended or 'blind social process' (Elias) making them co-producers in a process of displacement together with the hooligans themselves.

The displacement of violent disorders to outside the stadium as early as 1982 can be understood as a process of distancing and differentiation. This influenced spectator behaviour and the group style of the hooligans who removed their violent acts farther and farther away from the stadium and the football match. A connection between the external relations and the internal relations of the spectator groups can be observed. The displacement of violence from football stadia was paralleled by a splintering of spectator groups and the emergence of the violence-based 'elite self conception of the hooligans' (Ek, 1996: 71). The formation of this hooligan group who distanced themselves from the rest of the fans took place in Germany in the 1980s. Let us illustrate this with an example. Among the spectators in the Hanover FC Stadium, the following distinctions can be observed. There is the now largely pacified group of fans called 'monks' (*Kuttenfans*) on account of their wearing club clothing – the hooligans call them 'monkeys' (*Kuttenaffen*). There are also the 'old rockers' (*Altrocker*), right-wing and left-wing fan groups, the 'ultras' and the 'hooligans'. These groups stand close to but are spatially separated from the pacified fan block, a fact which points to socio-historical connections and the internal differentiation processes of fan groups. And, as happens typically in such developments, fluid overlaps have arisen between the different groups, for example, the younger *Kuttenfans* form potential recruits for the hooligans. This in turn creates a central task for the social workers of preventing such a transition. The displacement of violence to outside the stadium corresponds to the internal differentiation of the fan groups as expressed, for example, in their clothing fashions, or in forswearing alcohol on sporting occasions and before fights. Their 'outer appearance' (Ek, 1996: 76ff) communicates the form of their own group style as a means simultaneously of social inclusion and exclusion. This confirms the sociological assumption that there is a connection in social developments between processes of integration and disintegration.

With regard to their fashion-conscious clothing style, taste in music, use of slang, modes of informal interaction, and social origins – according to research conducted in the mid-1990s, they are male, in the 16–25 age-group, and come from a variety of social backgrounds (Ek, 1996: 73) – the hooligans are not conspicuously different from other youth groups. But one of their central behavioural features, their relation to and profession of violence, nevertheless established their special status as a group in public opinion. This is reinforced by their self-evaluation as an elite in relation to other fan groups, as well as by the hierarchical structure of their internal organisation. Out of their socio-spatial separation and distancing from the socially permissible experience (*Rahmenereignis*) of a football match, their freely chosen practice of violence emerges during the so-called 'third half' (Farin and Hauswald, 1998). That the risks of their violent game guarantee pleasure (Friedeburg, 1965b: 182) is a taken-for-granted aspect of the hooligan scene. The risks and the pleasures produce a social dynamic in the context of which the hooligans define themselves as a group. It is accordingly understandable that violent fights between hooligans often take place outside the public gaze according to a self-determined code of honour (for example, a taboo on weapons, restricted violence once opponents are defeated) which has, however, today grown fragile. Given the structural developments we have described, the specific characteristics of hooligan figurations can no longer be adequately explained in terms of compensation theory, for example by reference to family background, or living-, work-, and leisure-situations.

Apart from the publicly relevant question of whether 'physical confrontations constitute the exception' (Ek, 1996: 76), structural factors affect both the social praxis of the hooligans and recent changes in the kinds and levels of violence in spectator disorders. On the one hand, the definition of the hooligan group by reference to violence induces a process of partial differentiation since they have to distinguish their violence from that of others. On the other hand, with the exception of their violence, all the group-constitutive characteristics of the hooligans are not only linked to a normal youth biography but are indicative – and here their violence is included – of the self-perception of an informal grouping. According to sociological findings, social movements of this kind are usually grounded in the maturation processes of their actors. This leads to their formation of groups which parallel institutions such as clubs. Precisely this possibility is closed for the hooligans, however, because of the public disapproval of their constitutive feature, the practice of violence. Either the group connection erodes because the members become integrated into other spheres of social acceptance (private relationships, family, work, age-related associations) and the hooligan scene turns out to have been a group experience of a particular biographical life-phase. Or the group produces within itself its own form of social acceptance. When this happens, the group members can no longer be described as 'hooligans'. They undergo a development comparable to that of the largely pacified fan clubs of the 1970s. Out of this, both a change in violence-related communication and the formation of another kind of group could develop. Such a process is already taking place on various levels.

Recent developments and the shift of physical violence into everyday situations

The high point of the hooligan discourse in Germany at the beginning of the 1990s coincided with the first stage of German reunification. It overlapped with the East–West discourse in the new Federal Republic and with the related critique of the legitimacy of the state monopoly of power in the former Democratic Republic (DDR). All of this now became reflected, however, in a crisis of radical social change. In the expansion of the German nation state, spectator disorders and the attitudes of young people to violence were assigned to a different normative dimension. This was revealed in a lowering of the threshold of inhibitions towards violence both in hooligan confrontations and in the radical right youth scene in the new Federal *Länder* in the East. Even though a current research project on xenophobia and right-wing extremism has established that 'young adults in Frankfurt an der Oder . . . are not as bad as they are painted' (*Frankfurter Rundschau*, 21 July 1999), there are differences between the old and the new Federal Länder regarding the violence potential of extreme right youths.

The connection of people who have extreme right and nationalistic attitudes with violent disorders is obvious, and has to be researched against the background of the society of the DDR and the processes of radical change that are now occurring in the new Federal Länder. Two points need to be made about the DDR. On the one hand, both in comparison with the Federal Republic and in marked contrast to their own internationalist propaganda, the DDR was a nationally isolated society. On the other hand, hooliganism and right-wing extremism developed there in the 1980s, especially in East Berlin. But this development, which was controlled by the two 'repressive organs of the state' (the people's police and the Stasi, the secret police), was not communicated to the public. The connection between the hooligans and the radical right is also grounded in the fact that 'opposition to the communist regime could be very simply but nevertheless effectively expressed through the open display of right-wing views' (Ek, 1996: 104–5). The result of the interaction between the authorities and violence-orientated youths was that 'football fans and skinheads in the DDR distinguished themselves by their extreme violence and brutality' (Stöss, 1999: 155). Further differences between East and West Germany were caused by the radical changes of 1989–90. The demonstrations in Leipzig during the phase of radical transition can be cited as an example. The participation- and democratisation-orientated phrase, 'We are the people' was changed into the unification-orientated phrase, 'We are one people'. This can be understood as a sign of wanting a degree of national unity which ran counter to the more individualised and 'Europeanised' ways of behaving in the West. That is, hidden in the process of German reunification are two contradictory modes of orientation and behaviour, which can be characterised in terms of the values of cultural belongingness versus those of civilisational integration. That is, the unification process involves the continuation of the intra-German East–West conflict. What is taking place on both the levels of figurations and habitus is a simultaneous process of convergence and differentiation within the old and the new Federal *Länder*.

Such a development was also observed among the East German hooligans in the 1990s. During the 1980s, hooligan groups in both the old and the new Federal *Länder* emerged in the environment of extreme right skinheads. During the subsequent phase of radical transition, the number of hooligan disorders increased correlatively with the expansion of extreme right groups and the increase of extreme right violence, such as the participation of hooligans in violent attacks on the hostels where asylum seekers were accommodated. This new dimension of uninhibited violence was evident in the use of weapons and attacks on foreigners (Ek, 1996: 115). A lowering of the violence-threshold, a brutalisation and displacement of violence into everyday life, and a use of public space for purposes of committing violent acts became discernible. This raises the question of whether or not a process of partial de-civilisation is under way.

Hooliganism and right-wing extremism are nowadays equally visible in the old and the new Federal *Länder*. They are connected with the process of reunification, the enlargement of the nation state, the increase of population and the resultant geo-political situation. All this has led to a shift in the meaning of the German nation state. The present-day problems of defining German national consciousness against the historical background of National Socialism can be understood as the expression of an ambivalent development of the enlarged nation state and as a 'paradox' of the correlative acceleration of its social dynamics. One can see in the reunification process an intra-German situation in which a conflict has arisen between the East German emphasis on nationalism and nationhood and the opposite and contradictory West German attitudes and behavioural orientations. That is, the figuration of the East German hooligans can be described as one side of the supposed 'paradox', the participation of immigrants in West German hooligan groups as the other.

A further indication of this process is observable in the violence currently taking place at the lower levels of West German football and in youth matches there. This can be traced especially to the social situation of the migrants. The disorders are reminiscent in their structure of the conflicts in German village football in the 1950s. They are, however, taking place in and around big cities with large immigrant concentrations (in Hanover, for example, immigrants constitute 15 per cent of the population). And, unlike in the 1950s, the public are aware of the disorders and they are reported by the mass media. They have also been caused by different social determinants. They are traceable to urban developments of the last thirty or forty years and depend on the differentiation of styles of group behaviour and the opportunities for affiliation with different forms of group and *mentalité*. The testimony of a football official that 'our statistics do not register a percentage increase' in violent disorders in the football grounds of Lower Saxony (*Hannoversche Allgemeine Zeitung*, 15 July 1999) clarifies the facts in relation to a typical media point regarding 'increasing violence in football'. Disorders tend to take place in situations where the differentiation of group styles produces the potential for violence. Here, there is a difference in the pattern of sports-spectator violence today and that under the National Socialists and in the 1950s and 1960s. Through their violence inside and outside the stadia, the hooligans of today have contributed to the formation of a new figuration. The related public debate is likewise a part of specific developments regarding violence in present-day Germany.

Chapter 7

Subcultures of hard-core fans in West Attica: an analysis of some central research findings

Antonios E. Astrinakis

The central object of this chapter is to describe the subcultures of hard-core fans in the western suburbs of Athens. Most of the data reported here were generated via an extensive ethnographic field research programme carried out under the title *Deviant and Delinquent Youth Subcultures in a Local Working Class Setting (Athens's Western Suburbs)*, which was authorised by the Research Council of Panteion University and financed by the Greek General Secretariat of Youth.[1] This project spanned a period of one and a half years (from September 1992 to July 1993) and was carried out in the working-class western suburbs of West Attica (Peristeri, Aigaleo and Petroupoli) in the greater Athens district. The programme set out to examine subcultural membership of youth formations and groupings associated not only with expressive forms of rock culture and music, but also with sporting culture as expressed in places of sport and entertainment and in the organisational/ institutional setting of schools. It was carried out by means of a combination of field research techniques, most notably participant and non-participant observation. A large number of in-depth interviews were also conducted, mainly with students and staff members of high schools.

The research section relating to soccer fan cultures and subcultures, as well as soccer violence, was divided into three levels of study. Level one consisted of a sociological study of the characteristics of local sport cultures, based on ethnographic field research. Level two consisted, firstly, of the study of the recorded delinquency of hard-core hooligans and, secondly, of the actions of the police, considered as a key aspect of the official system of social control. Level three was focused on the analysis of the legal context of the control of sport-related violence and fan delinquency – specifically the Greek Act 1646/86 'Prevention and Control Measures of Violence on Sport Terraces' and the 'European Convention on the Violence and Disorders of Spectators during Sports Events and particularly Football Matches' – as well as a study of the Athens Magistrates' Court records for the year 1992.

The research was focused on the youth of the working-class districts of the greater Athens area, particularly in the city of Peristeri which has a population of 250,000. The choice of city was dictated mainly by a pilot project (Astrinakis, 1991), which indicated that, in this part of Greece, sport culture in general and football fan subcultures in particular are predominantly working-class phenomena, a finding which is comparable with findings on hooliganism from British and Continental European research.

This chapter focuses on the social characteristics, types of social organisation and subcultural patterns of local hard-core soccer fans and hooligans in West Attica. In particular, I examine, firstly, the social position and origins of local hard-core fans; secondly, the forms of social organisation and the prevailing subcultural patterns of this group; and, thirdly, the dynamics of the social situations (and settings) that shape and structure the relationships between police and hard-core fans.

It should be noted that I do not examine here the forms in which hard-core soccer fan delinquency is recorded by the formal agencies of social control; neither do I examine the officially and sociologically identified extent and scope of the delinquency. It should also be noted that an important aspect which was neglected in our research was the gender dimension. This can be partly attributed to the fact that no participation of females has come to light, particularly in the hard-core fan subcultures in Greece.

The social class of the hard-core fans

Central issues in relation to social class position

In seeking in our study to define people's social class position, we were faced with two fundamental difficulties. The first derives from the inadequate stock of social science research data in Greece. In particular, there is a scarcity of empirically based sociological and historical studies with regard to the structuring of social classes, strata and groups, the cultural differences between them, and their cultural traditions and practices. The second difficulty we faced was connected with the nature of the primary statistical resources available in Greece, especially the incomplete collection and inadequate classification – and in some cases even the entire absence – of statistical data, especially with regard to the local organisations that were of central importance to our research project, such as high-schools, regional police commands, local police stations and courts. Hence the social classifications that were drawn from the available data must be seen as having only an indicative character.

In our project, we opted for a multi-dimensional conceptualisation of class. This involved locating individuals in terms of their family and community class positions as well as in terms of a combination of structural and cultural parameters. The first of these parameters consists of the individual's financial position and that of his family and community (that is, income, material conditions of life). The second parameter consists of the type of relations of production in which they are engaged (that is, their position in the economy, viz. whether they are independent/dependent or a wage labourer, and, secondly, the type of labour relations, viz. the relations of domination or subordination in which they are implicated). The third parameter consists of the cultural situation in which they are embedded (that is, their position in relation to cultural capital, education level/schooling). The last parameter is linked with the degree of political power they wield and with the influence they can exert in order to enhance their interests (in other words, their access to and influence upon the centres of decision making). This conceptualisation of class involves a synthesis of Marxian and Weberian theorising, enriched by aspects of the work of Dahrendorf and Giddens.

The working-class social background of the hard-core groups we studied was founded on two factors. The first is linked with the fact that the wider community, as well as the local neighbourhoods in which most of the fans reside or where they were born, have a clear working-class structure. The second factor is linked with important stylistic (presentation of self, styles of dress), educational (features of formal knowledge), linguistic (verbal communicative competence, speech patterns/argot) and behavioural characteristics (such as demeanour), as well as with the general cultural patterns of the hard-core fans' lifestyle.

On the basis of our observations carried out at 53 football matches and 34 basketball games over 18 months, we concluded that general spectators can be differentiated depending, firstly, upon the kind of sport (football or basketball) and, secondly, the level of the match (that is, local, interlocal, or national).[2] Thus, in the case of football matches of local or interlocal importance, working-class cultural styles, behaviour and interaction patterns were prevalent. Social differentiation was also strongly related to patterns of watching the match, as well as to the spectators' overall conduct (see Rizakos, 1996).

British and continental approaches
Our findings in relation to the social class of hard-core fans, based mainly on ethnographic accounts, indicate that football hooliganism in the suburbs of the greater area of Athens is a working-class phenomenon. Because of lack of evidence, we are unable to be more specific about the particular sections or groups within the working class in which hard-core fans are to be found.

It might be noted that in the rest of Western Europe, until the end of the 1980s, most research dealing with soccer-related violence indicated that football hooliganism was predominantly a working-class phenomenon. This is the case for most English studies (for example Taylor, 1982a, 1982b; Clarke, 1978; Dunning et al., 1986a, 1986b, 1986c; Hargreaves, 1986), as well as the most sociologically informed continental research (see Walgrave and Van Limbergen, 1989 in relation to Belgium; Horak, 1991, in relation to Austria; Roversi, 1994, in relation to Italy). Those studies in continental Europe which deny the working-class specificity and significance of soccer hooliganism (for example Dal Lago and De Biasi, 1994, with respect to Italy; Van der Brug, 1994, with respect to The Netherlands), do not provide any convincing alternative analysis of the social class origins of hard-core fans. However, by the end of the 1980s in Britain an interesting debate was developing focused upon, among other things, the issue of the specific social generation of hard-core fans and hooligans within the working class. The question that was being asked was: do hooligans come predominantly from the working class, broadly defined, or more specifically from its rougher sections? That debate was initiated by scholars of the 'third generation' of hooliganism research, comprised mainly of anthropologists and 'postmodernist' scholars, who sought to challenge the 'hegemonic' position of the Leicester research group. In the course of that debate, researchers such as Hobbs and Robins (1991), and Armstrong and Harris (1991) have argued in favour of the 'working class in general thesis', while the Leicester research group has argued that in England 'the core football hooligans come predominantly from the rougher sections of the working-class' (Dunning et al., 1991; Dunning, 1994). There was also a third position, which criticised the model of social stratification used by researchers on both sides of the debate in Britain. According to this third position, the dominant model of stratification used by researchers should be replaced by a more elaborate and refined theorisation of class structure in Britain (Moorhouse, 1991).

Hard-core fan groupings in Peristeri: types of social organisation and dominant subcultural patterns

Drawing on data gathered in Peristeri, West Attica, it is possible to describe the types of collective organisations of hard-core fans and hooligans in this part of Greece, together with their main cultural and social-psychological characteristics.

The social organisation of hard-core fans and hooligans and, more particularly, the analysis of the types of group formation they display, are central issues of debate and controversy in British and continental sociological (and criminological and anthropological) research and theorising on football hooliganism (see, inter alia, Armstrong and Harris, 1991; Hobbs and Robins, 1991; Dunning et al., 1991; Giulianotti and Williams, 1994). By analysing the Greek research findings, I hope to contribute to that debate.

In the course of our field research, we identified four youth fan groupings. Two of these can be defined as hard-core fan – or even hooligan – collectivities; these were the groups known as 'the Guerrillas' and 'the Genuines'. A third group is a street corner group without a self-designation. We called this group 'the Rainbow' after its 'turf', that is, a café of that name. The fourth was a friendship group, 'the Manowar', which gave the impression of being a hard-core fan formation, though we did not study this group exhaustively.

'The Genuines' and 'the Rainbow' were investigated by means of a combination of participant and non-participant observation, as well as interviews. 'The Guerrillas' were studied by means of a combination of non-participant observation and information collected by a number of informants who were fans of Atromitos, which is the most important local football team.

We met 'the Manowar' on the ground three times only. We identified the members of this grouping by their banner ('Manowar-Peristeri') during two of Olympiakos's soccer matches at both of which large-scale disorder took place. Our field observations, as well as the information we collected, indicate that this grouping consisted of eight to ten young males, fans of Olympiakos, who are characterised by a mixture of heavy metal and hooligan stylistic elements. The name of the grouping derives from the North American heavy metal music group, The Manowar. Finally, according to our findings, 'the Manowar' constitute a friendship grouping consisting of brothers, cousins, and neighbours.

The 'Guerrillas'

The Guerrillas' are the hard-core fan grouping of the main local football team, 'Atromitos' (in English, 'intrepid', 'dauntless'). The group has a long history in relation to the club and its social organisation is characterised by a particularly close network of interpersonal relationships. They are a socially marginal group in relation to both the management of the club and the regular supporters' organisation.

Membership of 'the Guerrillas' consists of about twenty-five people in two main age cohorts. More specifically, the Guerrillas' 'old generation' consists of about ten men aged between twenty-five and thirty years, while its 'new generation' consists of about fourteen adolescents between eighteen and twenty. Within 'the Guerrillas', a figure called 'the Comet' normally played the role of organiser and animator of the 'side'.

Because of their hard-core character, 'the Guerrillas' have controversial and sometimes conflictual relations with both the management and the official supporters' club. On the basis of our conversations with members of the management, we concluded that the management of the club was ambivalent towards 'the Guerrillas'. On the one hand, they scapegoated members of the group, blaming them for any trouble that occurred before, during or after the match but, on the other hand, they sought to derive certain benefits from the activities of 'the Guerrillas', most notably through their vigorous support of the team during crucial matches (see Rizakos, 1996). In addition, 'Guerrillas' members were rewarded with money by some people within management in order to enhance, through their use of bravado, the personal status and interests of those members of management. For their part, the supporters club accused 'the Guerrillas' of being 'mindless yobbos' and also criticised the club's administration for helping them to enter the ground where they could cause trouble (Rizakos, 1996).

Subcultural delinquency patterns

The principal subcultural patterns of this grouping involved territorial identification, aggressive inter-group rivalry and a cult of physical violence. All members of the group take an active part in matches whenever the reputation of their city is at stake, especially in matches with adjacent working-class cities. They also play a forceful and leading role in all fights with rival fans. Most episodes of disorder or fighting that we recorded at Atromitos matches were connected with 'the Guerrillas'. We were also reliably informed about their participation in particularly violent episodes (for example, stabbings) in the past, as well as about their frequent use of drugs, especially marijuana. During the research for this project, two members of the group were arrested and indicted for 'possession and employment of five improvised petrol bombs which were to be thrown at fans of Aigaleo'.[3] One of the two fans, locally famous for his bravado, was convicted and sentenced to two years in prison while the other was acquitted.

If we analyse the basic constitutive elements of the symbolic interactions of the hard-core fan groupings as well as the broader symbolic practices on which they draw we can identify, for analytical purposes, four key processes: verbal communication; non-verbal communication; individual or collective stylistic expression; and the overall theatrical or stage setting. Exploring in turn the core meanings conveyed in those processes, both explicitly and implicitly, we arrive at a fourfold typology of the substantial or elementary themes of the prevailing symbols: war, love, life, and death (see the anthropological–symbolic analysis of Stylianoudis, 1996).

In relation to the stylistic expression and overall theatrical presentation on the terraces of 'the Guerillas', it is clear that both the name of the group and their central flag (which is the emblem of the Palestine Liberation Organisation) refer to the predominance of the warrior theme within the fourfold classification mentioned above. Additional symbolic elements indicate the predominance of the war theme, namely, the slogans of their English language banners ('When the end comes we will prevail'; 'The Byzantine Empire strikes again'), their graffiti, posters and flyers. The second theme that appears is linked with death and is manifested in the motifs written on their banners and posters such as 'Welcome to Hell', 'Peristeri – The nightmare returns', and the skull and crossbones.

'The Genuines'

'The Genuines' are the informal fan organisation of AEK, a well-known team nationally and internationally. According to Rizakos (1996), the creation of this organisation was initiated by a person called George when the leadership of the official supporters' club was disrupted during the 1980s. At that time, George recognised that the needs of young supporters were not being met by the traditional associations. The organisation has no formal members and there are no membership fees, though fans do pay a small extra charge in addition to the price of a cheap ticket. This helps to fund the organisation's activities, which involve renting branch offices, producing a newspaper and a number of fanzines and renting buses to travel to away matches or to dance halls for social events. However, not all the expenses can be recouped in this way, so 'the Genuines' also organise special fund-raising events. Gradually, 'the Genuines' started to set up branches of their organisation in different cities and districts, mainly in working-class areas. At first, branches are usually directed by a 'coordinator' who manages the funds and liaises with the central organisation. It is important to emphasise that each branch is formed by a number of friendship groups or companions who do not, however, go to the terrace together. Hence, the organisation is a loose collectivity.

The young 'Genuines' have a quasi-egalitarian ideology and reject any type of formal leadership. Thus George is not defined as a leader, although our research evidence suggests that in reality he does perform such a role and exerts substantial control over the organisation. It is also clear that the young fans appreciate George; he is idolised and is acknowledged as a person who sacrifices himself for the team. George spends so much time on the work of the organisation that he is unable to engage in any other formal employment. It appears that he lives on income he receives from the organisation. In this respect he is, as another 'Genuine' put it, a 'professional fan'. A supportive closed social circle (or, perhaps, 'team') operates close to George and helps to organise the activities of 'the Genuines'.

The organisation ranges itself openly against traditional supporters' clubs which are considered as the mouthpiece of management who, in turn, are accused of insensitivity and bureaucracy. Finally, while the traditional clubs strongly renounce any kind of violence and deviant behaviour, such behaviour is accepted by 'the Genuines'. In particular, within their network there are members who take drugs and fight with rival fans, and this does not raise problems for their participation in the organisation. Even George himself has led violent attacks in the past. In summary, 'the Genuines' constitute a loose but stable network of interpersonal relations. Both centrally and locally, the organisation is formally acephalous and, hence, its membership was not subjected to any form of formal or even informal social control. For these reasons, members often drifted into delinquency (Matza, 1964).

Deviant subcultural patterns

The activities of 'the Genuines' were informed by certain central subcultural patterns, six of which we identified and analysed. The first subcultural pattern was the fanatical dedication and combative support, or even the violent defence, of the organisation and the team. These were considered by the fans to be moral obligations. The second pattern was the pursuit of excitement which was expressed, among other things, by aggressive or violent rivalry between groups and fights with the police. The third pattern was a focus on leisure and particularly on amusement. That involved an intense nightlife: night-clubbing with a preference for pop and disco music on the one hand, and Greek modern music, the so-called 'skyladika', on the other. This style of entertainment was coupled with heavy drinking and the use of drugs and corresponds to what Hobbs and Robins (1991) define as the drug and disco culture which they say characterises the third generation of British hooligans, that is, the casuals.

The fourth pattern adopted by some of 'the Genuines' can be defined as an expression of a spontaneous, grassroots and romanticised but also rough and violent anarchism. In this regard, a number of 'Genuines' defined themselves as anarchists and considered hooliganism as an expression of opposition to political authority and society at large. For this reason, they engaged actively in political demonstrations which often developed into violent public disorders, mass vandalism and fights with the police. The predominance of the quasi-egalitarianism mentioned earlier is associated with a leftish ideology that supposedly characterises AEK in general; this is considered to be a peculiar feature of 'the Genuines' in that groups of this kind, in Greece and the UK alike, are not generally egalitarian.

The fifth pattern we identified was that of violence and conflict. However, while violence – between 'the Genuines' and their rivals, as well as between 'the Genuines' and the police – frequently occurred during the period of our participant observation,[4] the importance of violence was greater in terms of its symbolic (that is to say, its mythologised, rhetorical and narrative) significance than in terms of the violent acts themselves.

The last pattern we identified is the sexist masculine style common to most hooligan groups world-wide. In the case of 'the Genuines' this is particultarly evident in their collective and individual stylistic expression and in their theatrical presentation on the terraces. This sexist masculinity is a particular form of the predominance of the love theme included in the fourfold typology of the elementary symbols presented earlier (see Stylianoudis, 1996).

Central elements of 'the Genuines'' social identity

The social identity of 'the Genuines' is made up from salient features of wider and deeply rooted social-structural and cultural demarcations (such as social-class position, community, gender, religion, and age) in conjunction with some prevailing elements of the subcultural patterns discussed earlier. This identity is at the same time collective (or shared) and personalised (or individualistic) (see Stryker, 1994).

Five salient elements structure the social identity of 'the Genuines' (see Rizakos, 1996). The first is linked to their working-class position, culture and suburban territories and/or communities of residence. The second results from their Asia Minor descent, since most of their families migrated to Greece during the years 1918–22. This feature leads to the third element of their identity, which is related to a core nationalistic ideology of some Greeks (our research indicates that this ideology is not necessarily linked to the right) concerning regaining Asia Minor from Turkey; in this regard, members of the subculture wish to 'expand' the organisation beyond the territory of the country into East Thrace (European Turkey) and into North (and de facto, also Turkish) Cyprus. The fourth feature of their social identity is connected with their aggressive masculine style and is associated with a self-conception of authenticity, which is the fifth element of their identity. Their name – 'Genuines' – expresses the conviction that they are authentic, original fans. This, in turn, means that they never leave the team without support at away matches and never stop supporting (and struggling for) the team, even if this involves them in physical danger (for example, the danger of being injured in fights with fans of other teams).

The Rockabilly street corner group, 'the Rainbow'

The group called 'the Rainbow' is connected with the Peristeri Sports Club and consists of a stable membership of 12 to 15 people aged between 20 and 35. The group in the past was totally engaged in the rockabilly subculture, and was known as the 'LA Teds', a denomination which includes a double symbolism: 'Los Angeles Teds' and 'Lofos Axiomatikon Teds' (see Astrinakis, 1991). Some adolescents still adopt the style of the rockabilly subculture.

'The Rainbow' has a 15-year tradition in Lofos (that is, the 'hill') area of Peristeri and is based in the cafeteria 'Ran' which is decorated with sports trophies and banners. 'The Rainbow' members occupy a specific area of the Peristeri basketball arena and always put up two impressive banners, one featuring the Red Indian battle-cry 'Hoka-hey Hawk', and the other the Liverpool Football Club song, 'You'll never walk alone'.

The group members are fanatical fans of the Peristeri basketball team. They are very expressive and during matches support the team by singing anthems and hurling insults against the opponents or the referee. Yet they do not conceive of themselves as hooligans; they never get involved in fights, and in some situations they have succeeded in de-escalating tension in the basketball match itself. 'The Rainbow's' role is modified according to circumstances: its members mix with the other Peristeri fans, but when the team plays away matches its fans occupy a particular area of seating and act as leaders.

'The Rainbow' group members conceive of themselves as original supporters of Peristeri, and they differ from others who, they claim, began to support Peristeri only after the club achieved First Division status and after its new basketball stadium was built. Conventional Peristeri fans do not particularly like 'the Rainbow', perhaps because of the stylistic particularity and mannerisms of the group and its introversion and also because of the stereotypes of the general public. Group members are sometimes said to be 'junkies' and trouble-makers, although our research findings do not support these beliefs. The 'anti-Rainbow' stereotypes may also be responsible for the failure of the group to establish a large club of supporters, after the club management refused to provide reduced-price tickets to club members.

In relation to its social organisation and subcultural patterns, 'the Rainbow' is a typical street corner group with a stable male membership, stratified into three age (and essentially psychological) categories (the matures, the middle group and a few newcomers/teenagers). The group is currently in decline. The former leader of the group was killed in an accident while he was riding his old, traditional rockabilly-accessory, a BMW motorbike. The bonds among its membership have now become looser, although there are some people who take the initiative in organising the group and assuming leadership roles.

One of those who sporadically plays a leading role at basketball matches is the self-proclaimed 'Old Man'. 'Old Man' is in a situation of residual deviance (he is an alcoholic). He was a leading figure in the former LA Teds, and works for the Athens Transportation Company.

Relationships between fans and the police

In the narrow sense, and for the sake of a first order analysis, the social problem of football hooliganism or soccer terrace violence can be considered as consisting of three crucial factors: the police, the fans/hard-core fans, and their interrelationships. Aspects of working-class youth and police interrelationships were first analysed by Robins and Cohen (1978). As far as specifically football hooliganism research is concerned, fan-police relationships were first analysed theoretically by the Leicester group (Dunning et al., 1986a, 1988) and later, in an ethnographic way, by Armstrong and Harris (1991). Hobbs later examined, both theoretically and ethnographically, some aspects of (mainly covert) policing (see Armstrong and Hobbs, 1994).

With the exception of the above research, fan–police interrelationships have often been either neglected or stereotyped in research on football hooliganism. For this reason – and also because of their significance and complexity – we focused central aspects of our research on these issues.

Contradictions within police–fan relationships

The first dimension that characterises police–fan relationships is contradiction. This depends on two basic variables. The first variable is defined by the complexity of the conflicting functions of the police in contemporary advanced societies; the second is defined by the social and cultural divisions and conflicts that are inherent between the groups of fans themselves.

The first contradiction is highlighted in the writings of Robins and Cohen (1978) and is related to the twofold role of the police, as agents of social control and simultaneously as agents who provide social services and protection. Specifically, the police force today is characterised by, on the one hand, repressive or penal functions and, on the other, by expressive or ethical functions. This dualism is reflected on a structural level in the organisation of the police into functionally differentiated branches or services. This situation is associated with the fact that the social perception of and experience in relation to the police may vary considerably from one social group to another (Robins and Cohen, 1978; Hobbs, 1988). This was also clear in our research, where different groups of spectators frequently perceived and interpreted police actions and initiatives in soccer grounds in different ways.

These structural contradictions within the police can be found within its ranks and various units, and were expressed in our research in the different attitudes of each police branch to the fans and in the formation and consolidation of specific types of relations between the particular groups of fans and particular groups of police. Apparently contradictory events that were recorded during the research can be understood in terms of these intra-police force divisions and contradictions, as in the following examples: (i) at the same time that a police squad of the Public Order Restoration Corps was clashing with Atromitos hard-core fans, constables belonging to the local (Peristeri) police station were talking and joking with lads of the same hooligan grouping (personal field observation); (ii) in the same social situation (and place: at the main entrance of the stadium), one of our researchers observed a traffic policeman giving money to a young supporter so that the latter could buy a ticket to enter the stadium.

It is also important to note that, until at least 1974, the police force performed overtly political functions. That is, they were required to control the political opponents of an authoritarian and conservative administration, and this led to the perception of the police for many years as an 'ideological state apparatus' (Althusser, 1969), especially by those groups traditionally found in anti-government, marginalised leftist ideological loci, residing in working-class areas.

The second contradiction, highlighted by Dunning et al. (1986a) and confirmed by our own research, is associated with the fact that football hooliganism is marked by conflict between working-class groups and that the fighting between these groups results in their clashing with social control agents and with representatives of other institutions. This suggests that, in relation to football hooliganism, intra-class conflict is more dominant than (whilst not obliterating: wider figurations must always be taken into account) inter-class conflict.

An additional element is the so-called Bedouin Syndrome ('the enemy of my enemy is my friend, the friend of my enemy is my enemy' and so on) (Dunning et al., 1986a, 1986b). We found a similar pattern of alliances among the hard-core football fans in Greece. For example, Atromitos's hard-core fans support Panathinaikos, a middle-to-upper class and central Athenian team, and join with their hard-core fans ('the Cockneys') because Panathinaikos is the greatest adversary of AEK, the Athenian working-class team, and its hard-core fans, 'the Genuines'.

Antagonistic mutuality

The second main dimension of relationships between fans and police can be defined as antagonistic mutuality. This antagonistic mutuality was expressed where hard-core fans clashed with the special police. We observed that when the two groups met, there was a clearly defined antagonism whose origins could be traced to the mutual effort of establishing and legitimising their respective social statuses, roles and prestige.

This antagonistic mutuality is affected by three interdependent factors. Firstly, by the common lower social origins or class position both of large numbers of policemen and a large part of the hard-core fans. Secondly, by the fact that both policemen and fans adhere to common patterns of values and meanings found amongst the lower social strata. Thirdly, both groups have adopted similar subcultural patterns involving masculinity and aggression; these patterns have their origins either in the wider society of which fans are a part or, in the case of policemen, especially members of the special forces, in the subcultural patterns that characterise the police as an institution.

The conflictual character of fan–police relations

In our examination of the structuring of relationships between fans and the police, we identified three analytically graduated types or conflict levels that take into account the scale, intensity and size of the conflict. The first type refers to quarrels that break out between local policemen and hard-core fans or conventional spectators. These incidents are normally resolved by the disputants themselves or through the mediation of other policemen or other fans. We defined these as interpersonal conflicts. Secondly, there are group conflicts that mostly take place between the special police forces and the hard-core fans. These conflicts are marked by displays of masculinity which serve as important means of establishing and legitimising on a mutually meaningful basis the social statuses, roles and collective identities of the two groups. We called these masculinity conflicts.

The third type refers to anonymous mass fights that usually take place between special police corps and supporters' crowds or mobs, including hard-core fan groupings, usually formed on an ad hoc basis. These conflicts might follow an unexpected, or what is considered an unfair, outcome of a football match, or an ill-timed or inappropriate intervention by the police. In such cases, it seems that fans face a suddenly emergent problem that upsets the symbolic and normative social order, and the fact that they are required to respond immediately to the situation sometimes results in a violent reaction. These conflicts may escalate to generalised fighting between fans and police, taking the form of collective behaviour, and more specifically of a mass out-break (Turner and Killian, 1987). This type we termed 'authority versus people' conflict, as the conflict between police and fans additionally takes on a political-ideological aspect due to the historical background of the Greek police.

The causation and make-up of inter-group conflicts

The second type of conflict (masculinity conflict) appears to be most significant in that it occurs more frequently and on a wider basis. Its patterns are not limited to conflicts between police and fans, but are also extended to conflicts between the fans themselves. For this reason, it requires further analysis.

Our research indicated that conflicts between members of the special police forces and hard-core fans did not involve all members of the police or all soccer fans; in most cases there are particular persons or informal groups among spectators and the police force alike, who fight each other repeatedly and presumably on an interpersonal basis. It may be suggested therefore that there are persons or groups who fight each other in a context of antagonistic mutuality and that these violent confrontations are associated with the creation of mutual excitement. Excitement is, of course, one of the starting points of the Leicester group's explanation of football hooliganism (see Elias and Dunning, 1986), as well as a continuing theme of British research on hooliganism (see, for instance, Hobbs and Robins, 1991; Armstrong and Harris, 1991).

But what are the patterned or typical constitutive elements, on a social psychological level, of inter-group conflicts conceived as processes of symbolic interaction?

In our field research, we observed that conflict often began with what Robins and Cohen (1978) called ritual insult between a policeman and a fan. Ritual insult can be initiated by either party, that is, between two individuals who share common definitions of their situations because of their common structural position and cultural situation. A set of interaction ritual chains or an emotional reaction spiral (see Collins, 1990) between the parties may then develop as a response to the ritual insult. In the context of this 'confrontation performance', both parties have to display their 'character', in Goffman's (1967) sense, in order to maintain and boost their self-esteem and to gain approval from their mates or colleagues. Consequently, there is limited room for withdrawal from the conflict which leads almost inevitably to the passage *à l'acte*, that is, to a violent display of aggressive masculinity. Moreover, colleagues and friends of the participants often rush to help their mates; for these others it is also a matter of reputation, of the maintenance of self-esteem and group-identity and solidarity (Hobbs and Robins, 1991; Rizakos, 1996). Thus interpersonal conflict is expanded and transformed into intergroup conflict.

Explaining football hooliganism

Although the amount and level of violence are frequently exaggerated in media reports, soccer-related violence is quantitatively extensive and qualitatively significant. How can we explain this phenomenon of soccer-related violence?

The first main factor derives from the social marginalisation and cultural deprivation that lead to cognitive, emotional and communicative – that is, symbolic – difficulties on the part of some groups of working-class youth, in particular in constructing and elaborating specific emotional, cognitive and linguistic modes of expressing and resolving their problems. This deprivation is associated with feelings of desperation and hopelessness which are expressed physically through violence.

The second main factor is associated with the conflicts, antagonisms and rivalries between different regions of the country and different local communities, some of which are historically deeply rooted. The most important conflicts in Greece are the following: firstly, the conflict between Northern and Southern Greece, which is expressed in the antagonism between Thessaloniki and Athens. This historical antagonism has been based upon a simplified and stereotyped 'folk social theory' of political and economic 'centre and periphery' relations, as well as upon cultural differences. Secondly, the contrast between Athens, as the capital and symbolic centre of the higher social classes, and Piraeus, as a port and industrialised town, the symbolic centre of the working classes. Thirdly, and for similar reasons, the rivalry between Athens and Nea Filadelfia, another working-class district. Fourthly, the local rivalries between Peristeri and Aigaleo, Peristeri and Nikaia, and Peristeri and Chaidary, characterised by the different levels of urbanisation, social organisation and integration and by the economic structure of each working-class area.

The third main factor explaining violence within the stadium is associated with the outcome of the game, particularly where traditional local rivalries are involved and where the result has been influenced by special factors such as disputed refereeing decisions. In addition, police control and intervention measures and the fans' reactions to these measures are also important considerations.

The historical categorisation of football hooliganism in Greece

From the typology of conflicts outlined earlier, it may be suggested that inter-group conflict is of special importance; such conflicts may involve either fighting between rival supporters or fighting between fans and the police.

Following the figurational and developmental approach of the Leicester group (see Dunning et al., 1991), football hooliganism in its contemporary, post-war natural history can be classified into three historical phases. During the first period of the post-war re-emergence of this phenomenon in the UK, that is in the 1950s and 1960s, the conflicts on the terraces were interpersonal in character, took place mainly in the soccer grounds and on trains, and were for the most part directly related to the outcome of the match. During the second phase, during the 1970s, football hooliganism was transformed into mass violence, which took place outside as well as inside the grounds and took the form of violent collective, or crowd, behaviour. Disorder was still related to a considerable extent to the outcome of the game. During the last and current phase, since the 1980s, hooligan violence has been displaced from the grounds and diffused into city centres, suburbs and even further away from the ground itself and may take place independently of the outcome of the game, for fighting can begin before or after the game and can continue for a long time (Dunning et al., 1991).

This threefold classification corresponds well with the tripartite typology which we worked out as a result of our research. With respect to its central historical feature or its developmental stage, it appears that hooliganism in Greece is in the third phase of development according to the Leicester framework. Thus dispersed, small-scale conflicts among rival groups of fanatical supporters or among supporters and the police are the most common forms of violence and these take a regular and predictable form. The mass media give most publicity to the larger-scale mass disorders though these are actually less common.

Soccer terraces as delinquency pools

The following is taken from a report by one of our researchers who accompanied 'the Genuines' to an away match:

> On the way, there was a playful atmosphere with the following characteristics: (*a*) 'the Genuines' teased women, using dirty language; (*b*) occasionally they sang about AEK and 'the Genuines', in order to get more worked up; (*c*) they were quick-tempered and looking for trouble; they insulted each other; they quarrelled and, on the way, looked for rival supporters, in particular, originating from Thessaloniki; (*d*) they abused all foreigners we met on the way, Chinese, Albanians, blacks (abusing the last ones in particular). They yelled to them: 'go back to your country . . . nigger'; (*e*) occasionally they yelled and shouted war cries.
>
> On the way we found other buses and cars and travelled with them. Some hotheads lit smoke flares and all of them were singing. The smoke flares appeared to 'turn them on'.
>
> From the Isthmus, we were guided by patrol cars through roads and small streets to the stadium, obviously in order that we should not come into contact with the Corinthians.

Soccer terraces may be regarded as institutionalised areas where deviant behaviour is to some extent accepted, and thus they attract delinquents. In this regard it should be noted that some delinquents had high social status and prestige within the wider context of the informal terrace hierarchy, as well as among the hard-core fans.

Since the 1980s, strong links have sometimes developed between hard-core fans and other delinquents, for soccer grounds have to some extent become 'delinquency pools', as has been pointed out by other researchers (see Dunning et al., 1988; Walgrave and Van Limbergen, 1989; Hobbs and Robins, 1991; Horak, 1991). This is due to the attraction of delinquents to soccer grounds, which in turn is the outcome of deviancy amplification processes, and of the emergence of hooligans as folk heroes and folk devils (see Cohen, 1980; Cohen and Young, 1981). The well-established use of drugs on the terraces is related to these developments and, specifically, to the interweaving of the club dance and drug youth culture with the networks of hard-core fans.

Football hooliganism: the current situation

Terrace violence and football hooliganism in Greece have been the subject of only two systematic academic studies. The first of these focused on the general spectatorship of Athens's three major football teams (Panathenaikos, Olympiakos, AEK) and was chiefly of criminological and legal importance (see Kourakis et al., [1988] 1991). The second project was mainly of sociological importance (Astrinakis and Stylianoudis, 1996).[5]

Despite the fact that there is a dearth of hooliganism research in Greece, there is evidence from research into youth cultures and subcultures (club dance and drug culture, dance music/rave culture, hip-hop subculture, heavy metal subculture, etc.),[6] as well as into youth group street deviance and delinquency, both in the central areas of Athens and in working-class districts (see Panayotopoulos, forthcoming).[7] This evidence indicates that collective youth deviance and delinquency, of both an expressive and conflictual kind and of an instrumental and acquisitive character, has significantly increased in recent years. Especially with respect to youth group street delinquency, a recent research project concerning social control and the management of deviance was conducted in the same working-class area, Peristeri, where our own research was conducted (see Panayotopoulos, in press). This research, which was based on a combined methodology of survey and ethnographic research techniques, suggested that the above type of delinquency has considerably increased. I would therefore hypothesise that hard-core fan or hooligan disorderly activity, at least in Greece, is strongly related to the general trends of street group delinquency, as well as to expressive fringe deviance.

In relation to hooliganism proper, two additional sources of information should be mentioned. The first consists of mass media reports; these, although hardly the most reliable source of primary empirical data for sociological analysis, can provide some useful information. The second source of information can be defined as 'phenomenological knowledge' ('news from the streets', police accounts). Both sources suggest that football hooliganism in general, and hard-core fan violence in particular, have not decreased at all; on the contrary, they are continuously latent within local working-class settings, and periodically escalate into large-scale violence and collective disorders. If this is indeed the case, it suggests that this type of deviance has gradually been transformed into a structural, endemic feature of Greek society.

Chapter 8

Football's fighting fans: the Hungarian case

Orsolya Pintér and Jan Van Gestel

In this chapter, we examine a number of issues directly and indirectly related to the phenomenon of football hooliganism in Hungary. Sociological research on football hooliganism began to appear on the Hungarian academic map principally after the radical change of the political system in 1989–1990. We set out to do several things in this chapter. Firstly, we briefly outline the way in which football was introduced into Hungary. Following this, we provide an historical-sociological account of the development of football hooliganism in Hungary and of sociological research in this area. Special attention is given to the last five years, covering the 1995–2000 football seasons. A small selection of football-related violent incidents will be discussed in greater detail. Finally, in our conclusion, we draw upon existing sociological studies and seek to apply them to the phenomenon of football hooliganism in Hungary.

The development of football in Hungary

The roots of modern sport in Hungary can be traced back to the nineteenth century when aristocrats who had travelled abroad introduced the sports of Western Europe back home. As a result, two different trends of sporting activities met and developed in sport in Hungary: the 'club system' of the English, characterised by athletics, and the system of 'sport unions' based on German gymnastics. These two main sporting trends gave rise to two basic sports organisations: the NTE (National Gymnastic Union), founded in 1840 and the MAC (Hungarian Athletics Club), founded in 1875 (Hadas and Karády, 1995: 9).

Since its introduction into Hungary, football has been the country's most popular sport. Yet László Siklóssy, writing in 1928, noted that there was no accurate equivalent for 'association football' in the Hungarian language (Siklóssy, 1928: 366–75). The English term football was translated into

Hungarian as *Labdarúgás* (literally, ball-kicking) but *futball* and the abbreviation *foci* continue to be used in the Hungarian language.

From the 1890s, several football sections were established by the sports organisations. Siklóssy (1928: 371–5) indicates that the first football – that is the ball itself – was imported into Hungary from England in November 1896. He noted that a game with some similarities to football already existed in Hungary in 1881. However, like the earlier forms of folk football in England (Dunning and Sheard, 1979), the rules were not written and tended to vary from one place to another. Siklóssy also documents the establishment of the first Hungarian football team, the BTC (Budapest Gymnastic Club) in 1896 (Siklóssy, 1928: 374–5). The first public football match between the BTC and the Vienna Cricket and Football Club was played on 31 October 1897. The Hungarian Football Association (MLSZ) was established a few years later in 1901, and the national league has been organised regularly ever since that time (Hadas and Karády, 1995: 95).

Three main periods can be identified in the development of Hungarian football teams. The first period extends from their establishment until the Second World War; the second covers the approximately forty years of socialism in Hungary after the War; and the third covers the recent period since the major political changes of 1989–90. The development of football clubs may be defined in terms of these three periods primarily because of the impact which political changes have had on Hungarian football. Prior to 1945, clubs were predominantly privately owned but, following the establishment of state socialism, most clubs became, in effect, state owned and were linked to ministries or different economic areas. As part of this change, the financial and symbolic resources (logos, team colours, etc.) of the teams also changed (Hadas and Karády, 1995). The radical political changes which have taken place since the fall of state socialism in 1989–90 have been associated with the gradual attempt to return all state-owned clubs to private ownership once more. A detailed discussion of the development of football during these periods will not be provided here, however, since for present purposes an introduction to Hungarian football's 'fighting fans' is of more central concern.

The history of football hooliganism in Hungary

Before examining the history of football-related violence in Hungary, it will be useful briefly to outline the major socio-political changes which have taken place in Hungary since 1989, for these changes have had a major impact on the ways in which football hooliganism has been reported and studied by academics.

The collapse of the system of centralised state socialism in Hungary in 1989–90 was associated with rapid and radical changes. As Krausz has pointed out, 'this transformation swept away the single-party system and brought with it new power conditions in various forms' (Krausz, 1996: 147–8). Since the collapse of the old regime, some major changes have taken place in Hungarian stadia and in the wider structure of social life and, as part of these changes, those involved in the administration of Hungarian sport have had to face several challenges and problems.

During the forty years of state socialism in Hungary, sociology was a neglected science. As a consequence, only limited numbers of sociological studies of sport were conducted in this period. There was very little scientific knowledge about the behaviour of football spectators during these years since it was, for political reasons, a problematic area of study. As a result, there was a shortage of information on football hooliganism from official reports, and also a lack of systematic research using data from other sources such as local or national sports newspapers and sports magazines.

For the pre-socialist period in Hungary, a wide range of evidence on football-related violence can be found in newspapers and in the football yearbooks which were published from the beginning of the twentieth century until the Second World War. Földesi has claimed that, under the socialist regime, football-related violence was a taboo subject which could not be investigated or even reported by the media (Földesi, 1996: 196) but it is nevertheless the case that some reflections on these violent acts can be found in the national sports newspaper, *Népsport*. Although football-related violence was rarely accurately reported in newspapers during the socialist era, the newspapers did not deny that Hungarian football was faced with a football hooligan problem. The existence of violent behaviour at sports events, and especially at football matches, was admitted. It was a phenomenon which, according to the socialist leadership, could be solved through public educational programmes among spectators. The following incidents illustrate the history of football hooliganism in Hungary.

Football fighting in Hungary in 1908

Soccer hooliganism is routinely referred to as a modern phenomenon. However, the data on the worldwide incidence of football-related violence as reported by Williams et al. (1989) include an incident in Hungary from 1908 (Dunning, 1999: 131.). This incident was also reported in the Hungarian newspaper *Sport Világ* (1908.XV/22: 182–3). The newspaper reported that during a match between Manchester United and the Ferenczvárosi Torna Club, missiles were thrown and there was a pitch invasion. In a later edition of the same newspaper, some reflections on how other contemporary newspapers covered this incident are also to be found (*Sport Világ*, 1908. 23/XV: 192–3.). *Sport Világ* claimed that these other newspapers mystified the incidents and did not provide an authentic view of the match. However, it is clear that football-related incidents were already topics of debate in newspapers at that time.

Demonstration following World Cup defeat in Berne, 1954

In 1954, Berne (Switzerland) hosted the World Cup Finals. According to *Népsport* (5 June 1954, X/133, p.1), Hungary were favourites to win this event but they were eventually beaten 3–2 by West Germany in the final. On the team's arrival back home in Budapest, large crowds, disappointed and angry at Hungary's defeat, gathered at the Keleti train station (the central station of Budapest) for the team's return. The team was informed about this large angry crowd and got off the train one stop earlier at Kelenföldi station, from where they made their own way home. Much of the crowd's anger was directed at the coach, Gusztáv Sebes, who had previously been regarded as a national hero. When the train arrived at the central station without the players, the crowd were unsure what to do and eventually hundreds of people gathered in front of the radio station. At this point, the event turned into a demonstration against the Socialist Party dictatorship, for the crowd could not accept the defeat, and were convinced that the party leadership had 'sold' the game. This was the first demonstration against the Government since the Socialist regime had been established in Hungary and took place just two years before the 1956 Hungarian Revolution (Ember, 2001). Given the way in which this event turned into a political demonstration, it is not surprising that it was not reported by the national newspapers at the time. However, the events surrounding the team's return have recently been recorded by Ember (2001) in her memoirs.

Other football-related articles in newspapers in that year referred to the unacceptable behaviour of football crowds on the terraces, and also discussed the pedagogical methods with which, it was held, these problems could be solved (*Népsport*, 7 January and 7 March, 1954). The publication of these articles implicitly suggests an awareness of the social problems associated with football-related violence in Hungary at that time.

Disorder at Romania–Hungary matches, 1958

On 25 October 1958, the Hungarian and the Romanian national teams played a friendly game in the Augustus 23 Stadium in Bucharest, Romania. The countries' junior national sides also played each other. In a violent match between the national juniors, the Romanians lost 4–1. In the full international match, the Hungarian team also won, 2–1. During the games, Romanian supporters attacked Hungarian supporters and threw missiles at and verbally abused the Hungarian team (Vincze, 1999). The following day, the national sport newspaper *Népsport*, mentioned the violence but provided few details about what had happened in the stadium (*Népsport*, 26 October 1958, cited in Vincze, 1999). The Hungarian Ambassador to Romania, Keleti Ferenc, did, however, provide a report to the Hungarian Government and after this incident there were no national football matches between the two nations for 12 years (Vincze, 1999).

These events indicate that football-related violence was not confined to Hungary but that it occurred in the whole socialist block. However, it is difficult (though not impossible) to find documentation of these events in contemporary newspapers because they had only limited freedom to report them.

Football-related violence in Hungary after the Heysel tragedy

Horror at the deaths of 39 fans in the Heysel Stadium, Brussels, at the 1985 European Cup Final between Liverpool and Juventus was felt in Hungary, too. Several articles dealing with the tragedy appeared in the national sport newspaper, *Népsport*, and four days after this disaster in Belgium, *Népsport* reported an incident on the Budapest underground in which one of the carriages of a train was destroyed by hooligans after a match between Tatabánya and Ferencváros. The article emphasised the need to educate and warn Hungarian fans about violent hooligan behaviour (*Népsport*, 2 June 1985, p. 5).

The transformation of the Hungarian regime in 1989–90 offered increasing possibilities for studying violence among spectators inside and outside football stadia. Yet although football was – and still is – one of the favourite sports in Hungary, systematic research on football-related violence is still lacking for, even after the change of the political system, little research has been carried out in this area. More systematic research into the historical development of football-related violence in Hungary could yield significant data, as could interviews with football officials from earlier periods. Such research is still awaited.

Selected football hooligan incidents in Hungary: September 1995–June 2000

Football hooliganism is alive in Hungary and presents a problem which the football and police authorities have to face every season. Today, football-related violence may be witnessed inside and outside Hungarian stadia, and before as well as after matches. These violent disturbances are increasingly covered by the media and this coverage sometimes creates the impression, quite wrongly, that football-related violence is a new phenomenon which hardly existed until the last few years.

One of the main purposes of this chapter is to describe football-related hooligan acts in Hungary during the past five years (September 1995–June 2000). For this study, several sources of data were used. These included: the national sports newspaper, *Nemzeti Sport*; annual police reports; several football-related Hungarian magazines; the Hungarian Sports Yearbook, *Magyar Sportévköny*; and the records of the Hungarian Football Association.

Table 1 lists some of the most significant violent incidents reported at First Division Football League and other matches from September 1995 until the end of the 1999–2000 season. The table is incomplete, since only the more important football-related hooligan acts in Hungary within this period have been included. Nevertheless it does help to provide some indication of the type and frequency of football-related violence in Hungary.

Table 1 highlights 28 violent incidents associated with football matches in Hungary between 1995 and 2000. The table is incomplete because it is impossible to record with precision the total number of incidents of football hooliganism on a national scale; nevertheless the incidents listed above do help to provide a rough picture of the scale and seriousness of football-related violence in Hungary during the past five seasons. What is clear is that the problem of football hooliganism in Hungary has become a subject of frequent debate and that, as the data in table 1 show, the problem itself has certainly not been resolved.

Selected incidents of football hooliganism

From among a large number of hooligan incidents in recent years, two examples are described in greater detail below. These examples have been selected because they indicate: (i) some of the unintended consequences of football-related violence; and (ii) how football hooliganism has developed in ways which have created new problems for those responsible for maintaining public order at football matches.

Samsung sponsorship of the Hungarian Cup

On 27 June 1996, the Samsung Electronics Company (Hungary) and the Hungarian Football Association signed an agreement for a three-year sponsorship of the Hungarian Cup (the contract was to be renewed each year). The contract involved the renaming of the Hungarian Cup as the 'Samsung Hungarian Cup' for the duration of the contract. However, in October 1998, after the Cup Final between MTK Hungaria and Újpest FC in May of that

Table 1 **Selected hooligan incidents at or in conjunction with First Division, international, pre-season friendly and other football matches in Hungary, 1995–2000**

Date	Match/fans involved	Type of incidents
25 October 1995	Magyar Testgyakorlók Köre v Újpesti Torna Egylet	Fans attacked a tram and its passengers.
12 June 1996	Budapesti Vasutas Sport Club v Ferencvárosi Torna Club	Pitch invasion; vandalism; missiles thrown.
4 August 1996	Diósgyöri Vasutas Sport Club v Újpesti Torna Egylet	Vandalism; missiles thrown outside before and after the match; abusive language inside the stadium.
10 September 1996	Ferencvárosi Torna Club v Olympiakos	Missiles thrown at the visitors' bus before the match; missiles thrown and use of rocket inside the stadium.
26 September 1996	Kispest-Honvéd Football Club v Limes KEK	Pitch invasion.
15 October 1996	Ferencvárosi Torna Club v Newcastle	Vandalism; missile throwing.
10 May 1997	Újpesti Torna Egylet v Ferencvárosi Torna Club	Vandalism in the stadium; use of rockets; missiles thrown; pitch invasion after the match.
27 July 1997	Tiszakécske Football Club v Diósgyör Vasutas Sport Club	Fight inside the stadium.
13 May 1998	Magyar Testgyakorlók Köre v Újpesti Torna Egylet	Missiles thrown; pitch invasion after the match; attack on police.
17 May 1998	Ferencvárosi Torna Club v Újpesti Torna Egylet	Fight and missiles thrown outside the stadium before the match.
23 May 1998	Kispest-Honvéd Football Club v Zalaegerszegi TE Football Club	Vandalism outside before the match; bystander aimed shot at hooligans in self-defence (no injuries).
15 August 1998	Újpesti Torna Egylet v Diósgyöri Vasutas Sport Club	Fights inside and outside the stadium after the match.
19 September 1998	Újpesti Torna Egylet v Ferencvárosi Torna Club	Fights; missiles thrown and vandalism inside and outside the stadium, before and after the match; vandalism on the street and the underground.

3 October 1998	Győri Rába ETO *v* Videoton Futball Club Fehérvár	Fights outside the stadium before the match.
14 October 1998	Hungary *v* Romania	Missiles thrown at the visitors' bus after the match.
11 November 1998	Újpesti Torna Egylet *v* Ferencvárosi Torna Club	one day before the match Vandalism inside the stadium (holes were dug on the pitch) and outside the stadium.
17 March 1999	Tatabánya *v* Újpesti Torna Egylet	Train wrecked after the match.
3 April 1999	Kispest-Honvéd Football Club *v* Diósgyőri Vasutas Sport Club	Attack and missiles thrown at the visitors' bus before the match.
17 April 1999	Ferencvárosi Torna Club *v* Újpesti Torna Egylet	Fights and missiles thrown at police outside the stadium before the match.
28 April 1999	Hungary *v* England (friendly)	Smoke bomb thrown into the underground after the match.
29 August 1999	Pécsi Mecsek Futball Club *v* Videoton Futball Club Fehérvár	Fights after the match – young males were waiting for visiting fans.
25 October 1999	Újpesti Torna Egylet *v* Ferencvárosi Torna Club	Fight in a pub before the match.
28 February 2000	Vasas Sport Club *v* Ferencvárosi Torna Club	Vandalism outside the stadium after the match.
3 March 2000	Újpesti Torna Egylet *v* Dunaferr Sport Club	Match stopped; missiles thrown inside stadium (UTE stadium was closed until the end of the season).
16 April 2000	Ferencvárosi Torna Club *v* Újpesti Torna Egylet	Fight, missiles thrown on the street, vandalism in the underground and inside the stadium before the match.
22 April 2000	Újpesti Torna Egylet *v* Kispest-Honvéd Football Club	Pitch invasion and fight after the match.
21 May 2000	Zalaegerszegi TE Football Club *v* Újpesti Torna Egylet	Vandalism before the match.
28 May 2000	Diósgyőri Vasutas Sport Club *v* Dunaferr Sport Club	Match halted by pitch invasion; missiles thrown; vandalism.

Sources: *Magyar Sportévkönyv*, 1999 – Ladányi László (ed.), *Szurkolj ne háborúzz!* Home page, Rendőri Jelentés az 1996–97 évi labdarúgó szezon őszi sportrendezvényeinek rendőri biztosításának tapasztalatairól, *Nemzeti Sport*, February–May, 2000.

year, Samsung announced that they would not renew the contract when the then-existing contract expired. There were two major reasons why Samsung took this action: firstly, they objected to the fact that the Hungarian Cup Finals were not broadcast on TV during the period of the Samsung sponsorship; and secondly, and more relevant for our current concerns, they did not wish to continue to have their name linked with a football event in which matches were frequently associated with scenes of vandalism and riots (*Nemzeti Sport*, 24 October 1998, p. 7).

The final incident which directly led Samsung to cancel the agreement with the Hungarian Football Association was the Cup Final between MTK Hungaria and Újpest FC on 13 May 1998. At the end of the game, which MTK won by one goal to nil, an enthusiastic crowd of supporters from the winning team invaded the pitch to celebrate their team's victory. However, they clashed with police who had been instructed to prevent supporters from running onto the pitch and a fight took place between police and fans.

Damage to the pitch of Újpest TE before the clash with Ferencváros TC
Újpest TE and Ferencváros TC are great rivals and there is generally apprehension concerning the possibility of riots involving rival groups of fans before, during and after matches between these teams. In November 1998, because the police did not want to take the risk of fighting breaking out inside the stadium, the match between the two rival teams was played 'behind closed doors', that is without the presence of spectators. This happened even though the fan clubs had sought to reassure police that no violence would take place if they were allowed to attend (*Nemzeti Sport*, 10 November 1998, p. 3). The game went ahead at the ground of Újpest TE on 11 November 1998. During the night before the match, however, hooligans dug two large holes in the pitch, tore down the net from one of the goals, and wrote offensive graffiti on press boxes. The damage to the pitch of the Újpest TE stadium was not the first case of this kind, since a similar incident had occurred during the summer of 1998 (*Nemzeti Sport*, 12 November 1998, p. 3).

The damage to the pitch at the Újpest TE stadium appears to have been inflicted in an attempt to prevent the game going ahead without spectators. This particular event caused considerable consternation in the Hungarian sport community since it pointed to a new dimension of football hooliganism. Hooligan incidents, it was now clear, could take place not only during or immediately before or after matches but, on occasions, long before or after the game, thus creating additional problems for the football and other authorities.

Although other examples of football hooligan acts in Hungary could be cited, the incidents described above and those included in table 1 must suffice for present purposes as an indication of the extent to which the Hungarian football community is faced with the problems associated with football hooliganism.

Anti-hooligan campaigns and laws

The Hungarian government has taken a number of actions which are aimed directly at reducing the incidence of football-related disorders. Especially after the match between Ferencváros TC and Újpest TE on 17 April 1999, which was preceded by a major riot, awareness was increasing of the need for greater regulation of sports events in general and football matches in particular. Before this incident, there had been little attempt to formulate regulations for the establishment of order at sports events. However, in March 2000, the Government brought in new regulations relating to the 'Safety of Sports Grounds and Sports Events' (28/2000. [III.8.] Governmental Regulation). These assign specific duties and tasks to the individuals and institutions involved (the organisers, police, security companies, stewards) in the organisation and/or safety of sporting events.

Apart from these government regulations, another important step relating to safety at football matches in Hungary was made during the spring of 2000. The Hungarian Ministry of Youth and Sport introduced an anti-hooligan campaign called 'Szurkolj ne háborúzz' (Cheer, don't fight!). This campaign is aimed at reducing the incidence of football hooliganism by means of the creation of channels of communication between the different groups within the Hungarian football community. For example, a conference was held for the leaders of the hard supporter groups (so-called 'ultras') and a special website (www.foci.orig.hu) was created, containing important data concerning football-related violence. It was the first time that a data source of this kind had been made readily available.

Conclusion

With the notable exception of the work of Földesi, there has been relatively little systematic sociological study of football hooliganism in Hungary. In part, this reflects the fact that, for many years under the state socialist regime, sociology as an academic discipline was marginalised since it was seen as constituting a threat to the political system (Andorka, 1997). From the 1960s onwards, a relaxation of political tension was associated with some development of sociology as a discipline, though it continued to occupy a marginal status and throughout the 1970s research on sensitive topics such as poverty and delinquency was prohibited. It is within this broader context that one has to understand the relative lack of detailed sociological studies of football hooliganism in Hungary. Given this situation, it might be appropriate to ask what a more developed research agenda for the study of football hooliganism in Hungary might look like and, more specifically, what kind of theoretical frameworks might inform such a research agenda.

Describing the situation in England, Dunning, Murphy and Waddington (see chapter 1) have identified five popular 'explanations' of football hooliganism, each of which has been espoused by politicians and people in the media. These 'explanations' – some of which they note are partly contradictory of the others – are that soccer hooliganism is 'caused' by: excessive alcohol consumption; violent incidents on the field of play or biased or incompetent refereeing; unemployment; affluence; and 'permissiveness'. They go on to note that, in England, none of these popular explanations is supported by the available evidence, at least as far as playing a deeper, more enduring role in the generation of soccer hooliganism is concerned. A situation not very dissimilar to that which exists in England may also be found in Hungary.

The very limited amount of systematic sociological research into football hooliganism in Hungary has meant that most of the 'explanations' which are offered for hooliganism are of the same general type as the popular 'explanations' which the Leicester group has identified in England. However, like the English data, such Hungarian data as are available do not lend support to any of these popular explanations. For example, of the 28 cases of soccer-related violence described in table 1, only eight took place inside stadia. This fact, together with the occurrence of riots and vandalism before as well as after matches, lends no support to the idea that either violent incidents on the field of play or incompetent refereeing can be considered as prime causes of hooliganism. In addition, explanations of hooliganism in terms of unemployment make little sense, at least in relation to the socialist era, when it was more or less obligatory for all able-bodied people to work, and unemployment was almost non-existent. Explanations in terms of affluence, besides being, as the Leicester group note, almost directly contradictory to explanations in terms of unemployment, also make little sense in the Hungarian context for, during the socialist period (and to some extent still today) there were – and still are – only relatively small numbers of people who would be considered affluent by the standards of most Western societies. In this sense, 'affluence' as it is understood in the West has not been an issue for the great majority of the Hungarian population.

In commenting on football-related violence in Hungary, Steavenson (1997) has recognised the importance of linking the patterns of behaviour of hooligans with their social class. This linkage is of central importance to the Leicester group's figurational or process sociological approach to football hooliganism and it is precisely an exploration of this linkage – between hooligan behaviour and the characteristics of the social class from which most hooligans are drawn – which seems to be missing in sociological explanations of football hooliganism in Hungarian research. This point may perhaps be illustrated by reference to the work of the leading Hungarian sport sociologist in this area, Gyöngyi Földesi. There can be no doubt that Földesi has made important contributions to our understanding of football hooliganism, particularly in relation to racism, group identities and xenophobia in Hungarian society. In particular, Földesi (1996) provides excellent descriptions of several aspects of the behaviour of football hooligans, most notably their fighting, drinking and swearing. However, she does not explore the possibility that all these aspects of behaviour may be parts of a more general pattern of class-linked conduct. In this regard, the Leicester group have persuasively argued, on the basis of their own research data and that of others, that football hooligans are drawn primarily from the ranks of manual workers and, more particularly, from the ranks of what they call the 'rougher sections' of the working class, amongst whom shared norms legitimate a greater willingness to resort to violence and aggressiveness in everyday social relations than is normatively permitted in society at large. This linking of football hooligan behaviour with the cultural patterns and socialisation processes within particular social groups – in this case, with particular sections of the working class – has received substantial support not just from English studies but from studies in Scotland, Belgium, Italy and the Netherlands (see chapter 1). It is important to emphasise, however, that the Leicester group do not suggest that football hooliganism is always and everywhere simply a function of social class, for they clearly indicate that football hooliganism is also likely to be related to other 'fault-lines' which may include regional, subnational, generation-based, religious, city-based and other differences and inequalities.

Given the fact that studies of football hooliganism in Hungary are very much in their infancy and that, as a consequence, there is no established theoretical framework for studying the phenomenon, it may be that an attempt to relate football hooliganism to the key fault lines within the wider structure of Hungarian society would provide a useful framework for future research. As a research strategy, this would have a number of advantages: firstly, it would enable Hungarian researchers to draw upon a theoretical framework which is generally, if not universally, acknowledged to have con-siderable theoretical purchase and which has already been used with some success in empirical study; secondly, it would facilitate comparison between Hungarian studies and studies from other countries which have also focused on the relationship between hooliganism and major 'fault-lines' within the wider society; and thirdly, it would throw into sharper relief whatever distinctive characteristics football hooliganism in Hungary may have. It would also be likely to raise important theoretical and empirical questions in relation to civilising processes outside Western Europe and, in so doing, might serve as a useful basis for testing, criticising and refining a central aspect of the work of Norbert Elias which has been widely used in the interpretation not just of football hooliganism, but of several other major aspects of the development of modern sport.

Chapter 9

The dog that didn't bark? Football hooliganism in Ireland

Alan Bairner

Introduction

This chapter examines links between hooliganism and sport, especially association football, in Ireland. For reasons that will become quickly apparent, the main emphasis is on Northern Ireland and special attention is paid to one particular football rivalry – that between the Belfast clubs, Glentoran and Linfield – and the fact that the genuine hooligan problem which has attached itself to games between these clubs is seldom replicated elsewhere in Irish sport. In addition to describing and commenting on football hooliganism in Northern Ireland, the chapter also seeks to test existing approaches to the problem, particularly that associated with Eric Dunning and his fellow researchers at the University of Leicester.

As recently as 31 August 1999, the Irish League match at the Oval in Belfast between Glentoran and Linfield was marred by crowd trouble which resulted in, amongst other unsavoury incidents, the referee being struck by a missile thrown from the terraces. This was by no means the first time that hooliganism has affected games involving these Belfast rivals. Nevertheless it was a salutary reminder to the wider public that Northern Ireland is not immune to a problem which many have attributed primarily to the English. On the other hand, as this chapter will argue, either the problem has never been particularly serious in this offshore region of the United Kingdom or, as is more likely to be the case, it has simply not been widely perceived as being particularly significant. Indeed the relative infrequency of disorder is paradoxically what makes football hooliganism in Ireland interesting.

In his *The End of the Terraces: The Transformation of English Football in the 1990s*, Anthony King (1998: 3) argues that 'it may be the case that legitimate concerns about hooliganism have unreasonably biased research into football, so that issues such as the administration of the game and its political economy have been wrongly relegated to a secondary position'. There may be an element of truth in King's claim. On the other hand, the dangers inherent in throwing out the baby with the bath water should also be recognised. The importance of hooliganism lies in the fact that its impact extends well beyond the football community itself. The very large incomes of players such as David Beckham and Michael Owen have wider implications, of course, but these are not felt so immediately by people outside the game as are acts of violence which periodically threaten to engulf elderly people, children and other citizens as they go about their non-football-related business. To imply that the transformation of football's political economy has as much direct importance for society as a whole as does hooliganism is to contribute to that very process through which the game's social significance has been elevated to ludicrous levels.

If the hooligan problem were to become a thing of the past, then a very different perspective would need to emerge. However, Dunning (1999: 133), commenting on football hooligans in words uncannily reminiscent of Gerry Adams's much quoted remark about the IRA, observes that hooligans 'have never gone away'. Dunning is correct although, in the context of Ireland and in spite of problems associated with the Glentoran–Linfield rivalry, one can legitimately ask to what extent they were ever here in the first place. Certainly in the Irish Republic, hooliganism at football games and other sporting events has been relatively low on the list of social problems in a rapidly changing society. Furthermore, football hooliganism has never assumed the significance which it has in other countries. This is also the case in Northern Ireland, where the potential for violence has been a constant feature of social life at least since the late 1960s and sport has reflected and at times served to deepen the conflict (Bairner and Darby, 1999; Sugden and Bairner, 1993; Sugden and Harvie, 1995).

Leicester revisited

In *Sport Matters*, Dunning (1999: 142) revisits the main 'discoveries' of the Leicester research on soccer hooliganism 'carried out within the framework of the "figurational" paradigm advocated by Norbert Elias'. These were: (i) 'soccer hooliganism is not and never has been a solely English or British phenomenon'; (ii) 'forms of crowd violence occur in sports other than soccer'; (iii) 'in Britain, there is a history of hooligan behaviour at soccer which was not labelled as such but stretches back beyond the 1960s, the period when the problem is popularly thought to have started'; and (iv) 'soccer hooliganism is predominantly an expression of a pattern of male aggressiveness characteristically [though not solely] found, in the English case at least, in the "rougher" sections of the working class and that one of the principal ways in which it is produced and reproduced is by the experience of living towards the bottom of the social scale' (p. 143). The form of association which is thought to bind young men together in social settings of this type is described as 'ordered segmentation' (p. 158). In addition to these four specific observations, Dunning (1999: 154–5) points to two universally constant factors in the persistence of football hooliganism. These are, firstly, that 'soccer everywhere . . . is, for spectators, a leisure pursuit, one of the principal raisons d'être of which is the generation of excitement' and that, despite an increase of female power in the more 'advanced' societies, for example as a result of feminist interventions, all societies in the world today are characterised by a type of social organisation commonly known as patriarchy.

A central aim of this chapter is to examine the Leicester findings in the context of Northern Ireland and the Irish Republic. Dunning himself recognises the importance of local variations even within England. But studies of these, he contends, must be tied to some general theory. Furthermore, he argues that 'what is true of the need for a balance between particularizing and generalizing studies in a single country is multiply compounded when the focus of attention is turned to the world-wide aspects of a phenomenon' (Dunning, 1999: 154). This chapter discusses not only the relevance of specific Leicester 'discoveries' to the Irish case but also the general claim that an all-encompassing theoretical approach is possible.

In support of one of the Leicester group's findings, namely the relative longevity of the problem, it will soon become apparent that hooliganism has certainly affected football games in Ireland over a long period and not just in the modern era. However, insofar as it has been more prevalent in that part of Ireland which has remained within the United Kingdom, the view that the problem is essentially a British one is not entirely discredited. Furthermore, other sports played in Ireland have scarcely been affected by the hooligan phenomenon, which prompts further concern about the applicability of the Leicester findings to the Irish case. In any case, it is arguable whether football hooliganism in Ireland has ever been as serious a problem as in Britain and elsewhere. This chapter considers why this should have been so. It also seeks to identify the causes of the limited amount of hooliganism which has occurred in Irish football and where the problem is best located both in terms of other social issues and in terms of theoretical debate. For example, most discussions on the problem evade the central question of what actually constitutes football hooliganism. Does the concept describe any form of anti-social behaviour which occurs within a football stadium? Or does it include violence between fans in other locations and, in some instances, on days when matches are not even taking place? Furthermore, in the case of societies characterised by major conflicts, such as Northern Ireland, there is a problem concerning the relationship between football-related anti-social acts, including violent ones, and other forms of violent behaviour (Bairner, 1997; Bairner, 1999a). Much of the existing analysis, including that of Dunning, appears to be based on the premise that we know what football hooliganism is for the simple reason that certain activities are categorised as such by the media. Examining the subject in the context of Northern Ireland, however, forces us to be clearer about the precise nature of football hooliganism as opposed to other forms of hooligan conduct. In addition, this chapter specifically assesses the relevance of the Leicester School's analysis as regards the identification of those sections of society which are most likely to produce the football hooligans, defined more precisely and regardless of local nuances. To what extent does that analysis, which focused on hooliganism in England, help us to understand football-related violence in Ireland?

The Irish crowd

In the past, leisure activities in Ireland were commonly associated with violence. Traditional Irish fairs, the most notorious of them being Donnybrook which has become a byword in Ireland and beyond for unruly assembly, were similar to European carnivals and, as such, were given over to food, sex and violence. As Malcolm (1983: 43) has commented, 'such occasions seem from the beginning to have been recognised as times of special licence'. In the modern era, however, violence linked to popular recreation has been more closely associated with the particularities of Irish political life and it has been difficult at times to disaggregate football hooliganism in Ireland from other forms of anti-social, particularly politically inspired, violent behaviour. For example, shots were fired at soccer matches involving Belfast teams and Dublin-based rivals in the 1920s, but any suggestion that these were simply extreme manifestations of football hooliganism would be impossible to sustain (Brodie, 1985; Coyle, 1999; Kennedy, 1989). Most incidents were prompted by a sudden change in the wider political atmosphere or even by specific external events. The same holds true for the present period. Thus, when in 1984 fans fought with policemen at a friendly game between Cliftonville, a club based in north Belfast which has had a predominantly nationalist following since the 1970s, and (Glasgow) Celtic, whose supporters in Northern Ireland come from precisely the same community, football hooliganism was not the problem. Rather, the ethno-sectarian conflict in society as a whole was simply being reproduced at a football ground. In this instance, a few days earlier a young nationalist man had died after being hit by a plastic bullet fired at close range by a Royal Ulster Constabulary officer. Inevitably feelings were running high at the match with almost predictable consequences. Similarly, followers of Cliftonville Football Club were prevented from gaining access to two separate grounds in 1996, not for reasons rooted in the game itself but because they were regarded as nationalists seeking to enter loyalist areas (Bairner and Shirlow, 1998).

This is not to take the easy way out with reference to the problem of football hooliganism by simply claiming that it is not football's fault. However, in a conflictual society like Northern Ireland, and specifically in a divided city such as Belfast, it is impossible to prevent inter- and even intra-community tensions from spilling over into a variety of different public spheres. That football grounds are amongst the most commonly used spaces in this respect tells us much about their location and also about the sort of people who follow the game in Northern Ireland. But this is insufficient reason for categorising such incidents as examples of football hooliganism. In any case, John Sugden and I were only partly correct when we argued that 'while divisions based on class, region, age and opportunity are important, the most potent force of group solidarity is religious labelling and it is this, more than anything else, which determines the pattern of football support and crowd trouble in the province' (Sugden and Bairner, 1988: 577–8). Ethno-sectarian identity is certainly a major factor in determining the affiliation of football fans in Northern Ireland. However, despite outbreaks of trouble at matches between 'loyalist' Linfield and 'nationalist' or 'republican' Cliftonville or Donegal Celtic, the fact remains that such incidents are only tangentially connected with football hooliganism as such and, in any case, the clearest examples of true hooliganism are increasingly centred on games between clubs with fans who, for the most part, share the same ethno-political identity.

Indeed, even the events surrounding the European Cup tie in 1979 between Linfield and Dundalk – arguably the most serious outbreak of football-related violence at a game in Ireland, with the possible exception of the havoc caused by England fans at a friendly international match against the Irish Republic at Lansdowne Road, Dublin, in 1995 – cannot be explained without reference to the political context within which the match took place. As Brodie (1985: 115) recalls, when it was announced that Dundalk had been drawn to play against Linfield 'officials feared the worst but it proved to be a disaster on a more monumental scale than anyone had imagined'. The first leg game was played on 29 August 1979 at Oriel Park, Dundalk, a border town in the Irish Republic. The visiting team, Linfield, are a Belfast club with an almost exclusively Protestant support and a reputation for being the true football representatives of loyalist Ulster (Bairner and Shirlow, 1998; Bairner and Shirlow, 1999; Bairner and Shirlow, 2000). Protestants in Northern Ireland had long been suspicious of the Irish Republic with its political designs aimed at the unification of Ireland. They were particularly preoccupied with the image of Dundalk as a frontier town which, it was widely believed, provided a safe haven for members of the Irish Republican Army, an organisation that had been responsible, a few days before the Oriel Park game was due to be played, for the assassination of Lord Mountbatten, an uncle and close friend of the Prince of Wales. Against this background, the likelihood of violence was very real from the outset. Television footage of fighting and stone throwing inside the ground would suggest the replication of hooliganism throughout the soccer world. But whether the people who engaged in the unruly behaviour can be categorised as football hooligans is again questionable. One might argue that similar events surrounding games between the (traditionally Catholic) Celtic and the (traditionally Protestant) Rangers teams in Scotland share identical roots in the politics of ethno-sectarian conflict. Against this, however, it needs to be said that, in Scotland, the age-old rivalry between the two sets of 'Old Firm' (Celtic and Rangers) fans has virtually assumed a life of its own which is largely independent of contemporary political disputes, either real or imagined.

Overall despite, or arguably because of, the more overtly conflictual character of Irish society, hooligan incidents, no matter how they are construed, have been relatively rare in the history of football in Ireland. Nevertheless, the violent rhetoric with which football hooliganism has at times been associated is relatively common, particularly in Northern Ireland. But, as with more overtly violent incidents, the relationship between the terrace chants and the wider political context must be taken into account. Indeed, it can be argued that sectarian abuse at soccer games lies at one end of a continuum at the opposite extreme of which is located paramilitary violence (Bairner, 1997; Bairner, 1999a). For many people, however, this may overstate the social significance of the actions of football fans. Certainly far from being the cause of intense moral panic, as has often been the case in other countries, anti-social behaviour at soccer games in Northern Ireland has tended to be seen as relatively innocuous by the standards established in other areas of civil society. Attendance figures at most Irish League games are generally low with even 'Big Two' (Glentoran–Linfield) matches normally attracting crowds of only around 10,000 fans. The police have arguably been less concerned with this issue than their English counterparts, given the greater demands on their time created by widespread civil disorder. Nevertheless the large-scale security operations which accompany high profile games – although neither implemented with the immediate objective of curtailing hooliganism nor, unlike in the rest of the United Kingdom, paid for by the clubs – have clearly impacted on the behaviour of supporters.

It is also worth considering the argument that sectarian invective – or worse – at soccer games has tended to have a cathartic effect on many of those who engage in it and who might otherwise be more likely to become involved in explicit sectarian violence. In that regard, manifestations of football hooliganism might actually be considered beneficial in a society where other, more deadly, forms of violence have for so long been the norm. One rivalry, however, which can be more securely located in the realm of football hooliganism is that between the two Belfast clubs, Linfield and Glentoran.

The 'Big Two'

Arguably, the rivalry between the so-called 'Big Two' reached its lowest point during the Irish Cup Final of 1983. During the game at Windsor Park, play was stopped for four minutes when bottles and other missiles were thrown at the Glentoran goalkeeper and, at the end of the game, fans fought on the pitch and 16 people were arrested.

However, there are signs that this local rivalry has assumed more sinister and persistent proportions during the 1990s. Both clubs draw their support mainly from the Protestant community and, in that respect, the inter-community divisions in the wider society are rendered irrelevant. Tension between the two sets of fans may owe something to intra-community division with the right to be the main champions of loyalism at stake. In general, however, the rivalry is rooted in factors which are common to intense competition between soccer fans in most societies.

As the nickname 'The Big Two' suggests, these clubs have been by far the most successful in the history of Irish League football, at least since the demise of Belfast Celtic at the end of the 1940s. They attract the largest crowds in local football and are based in different parts of Northern Ireland's largest city. The rivalry on the field of play is thus exacerbated by territorial affiliations. The end result has been a series of violent incidents involving fans and also, on occasions, club officials and players. While many of the outbreaks of hooliganism have taken place at matches, violence linked to this intense club rivalry has also occurred in other social settings, including hotels where players' dinners have been held. It is possible to argue that aspects of the rivalry between Glentoran and Linfield fans are linked to the circumstances which prevail in a divided society in which certain forms of violence have been valorised. Furthermore, it is not entirely surprising that hooliganism has increased or, at the very least, has been given greater publicity during the most peaceful decade experienced by Northern Ireland since the 1960s. As opportunities for paramilitary violence have declined, so young men have sought other avenues through which to engage in combat. Again, the explanation for hooliganism is linked to the particularity of the social formation under discussion.

In general, however, the explanations offered by Dunning and his Leicester colleagues for the social roots of football hooliganism are adequate in this context. With reference to their linkage of the problem to the prevalence of segmental bonding in particular sections of society, it has been argued elsewhere that 'it is clear that many Protestant working-class communities in Northern Ireland, particularly in Belfast, are characterized by this segmental type of attachment' (Bairner, 1999a: 294). In the case of those Linfield and Glentoran fans who are responsible for the violence – as opposed to those who limit their anti-social behaviour to forms of sectarian rhetoric which are linked at least in part to a specific parental culture – we are speaking of young, working-class men, relatively free from adult control, with low levels of formal educational attainment and a largely fatalistic approach to life. Many of them appear lacking in self-consciousness as regards the norms of civilised behaviour. They remain relatively unincorporated into the wider society, although they are by no means marginalised within their own immediate communities.

As an example it is worth noting that, although since the 1970s intermittent attempts have been made by British based neo-Nazi groups to embrace the hooligan element at clubs like Linfield and Glentoran as well as Crusaders and Coleraine, this has met with little success. This is also largely true of similar attempts to promote a neo-Nazi agenda at football grounds elsewhere in the UK, but the failure of groups such as the British National Party to recruit loyalist soccer fans in Northern Ireland is specifically linked to the lack of success which the British extreme right has experienced in associating itself with the cause of loyalist paramilitarism. This is not to deny that some high profile loyalists are, or have been, linked to the British National Party and Combat 18. In general, however, it would seem that the parental culture, which has increasingly contained elements of anti-Englishness, has been sufficient for Ulster loyalists both on and off the terraces. Explanations of the Glentoran–Linfield rivalry are also relevant to our understanding of crowd behaviour in the Irish Republic and specifically to the fact that hooliganism has been even less of an issue in the Republic than in Northern Ireland.

Other people's troubles

Most readings of the behaviour of soccer fans in the Irish Republic have tended to focus on a propensity for the carnivalesque (Free, 1998; Giulianotti, 1996). This is essentially true as regards support for the national team although it would be dangerous to ignore completely other elements of fan culture, including anti-Englishness, or to suggest that forms of behaviour associated with the carnival are of recent origin. As far as support for domestic soccer is concerned, it is worth noting that the kind of communities which have been the source of football hooliganism in England, Northern Ireland and elsewhere have traditionally been less common in the Republic of Ireland. As Curtin et al. (1993: 2) observe, 'seen in the context of the island as a whole, Irish urban growth has developed along two distinct trajectories, each now clearly marked by the fracture of the political border which separates Northern Ireland's six counties "in the north" from the twenty-six county Republic "in the south"'. Modern urban industrial life was established much earlier in Northern Ireland, and particularly rapid development took place at roughly the same time as football was becoming established as a mass spectator sport, that is to say in the last two decades of the nineteenth century. In the Irish Republic, on the other hand, urbanisation has increased dramatically only since the 1950s. As a result, according to Curtin et al. (1993: 2), 'north and south have each been characterised by a set of urban "problems" distinct in certain but not all respects'.

The problems which most affect towns and cities in the Republic of Ireland tend to be those most closely linked to social isolation. The decline of organised religion (in this case the Catholic Church), which is arguably slightly less apparent in working-class communities in Northern Ireland, has been an important contributory factor. People are obliged to come to terms with urban life with little community support, either formal or informal. Drug abuse has become a popular form of escapism in the bleak housing estates of north Dublin, Limerick and similar areas. For a variety of reasons this particular problem has to some extent been resisted in Northern Ireland. One significant factor is a greater degree of community spirit, inspired ironically in part by inter-community strife; a related factor is informal community-based policing conducted largely by members of paramilitary organisations. The type of solidarity which the Leicester research found amongst football hooligans is more likely to be found, therefore, in the working-class communities of Northern Ireland, with young men still believing that their locality and its football team are worth fighting for as opposed to abandoning in a quest for drug-induced instant gratification. It is no accident that the only time hooliganism was regarded as a potentially significant issue for domestic football in the Irish Republic was when Derry City, a club based in a long-established urban community in Northern Ireland, entered the League of Ireland. In addition, incidents occur from time to time in connection with games between Dublin clubs, notably Shamrock Rovers and Bohemians, but these are relatively insignificant compared with other forms of urban crime in the city and they attract little comment from those sections of the media which are normally in search of material with which they can promote moral outrage.

The shared gender of the hooligans who attach themselves to Linfield and Glentoran provides us with crucial insights into their behaviour. The use of the concept of 'masculinity', particularly with reference to crime, is undeniably problematic (Collier, 1998). Nevertheless, although by no means all men are football hooligans in Northern Ireland any more than is the case in any other society, the overwhelming majority of football hooligans, wherever one chooses to look, are men. Armstrong (1998: 7) points to 'the symbiosis between the game and local male cultural mores'. Football, he writes, 'is *the* arena wherein men can hold opinions on everything, enact various levels of emotional turmoil and shout at the TV with mates'. In football, 'masculinity, muscle and fantasy are combined with location' (Armstrong, 1998: 13). According to Dunning (1999: 147), 'for the young men involved, football hooligan fighting is basically about masculinity, territorial struggle and excitement'. Of course, football is not the only arena in which this construction of a certain form of masculinity occurs. Dunning (1999: 147–8) refers to patriarchy as being the setting 'in which males generally are expected under certain circumstances to fight, and high status is legitimately conferred on good fighters in particular occupational contexts, for example the military and the police'. Football fandom is simply another such site.

In Northern Ireland, football grounds are dominated by men. These men may differ markedly in various respects. The overwhelming majority of them, however, are Protestant and come from working-class and lower middle-class sections of society. The prevailing atmosphere created by these fans is sexist as well as sectarian. This is not to suggest that all the fans, or even a majority of them, actively contribute to this atmosphere. But all are certainly exposed to a hegemonic masculine culture in which making sexist comments and engaging in sectarian, and on occasion racist, rhetoric is presented as acceptable (Bairner, 1997; Bairner, 1999a).

In the case of Northern Ireland, some of the men who are involved in football-related violence are unemployed and therefore lacking in masculine self-esteem in communities in which the manual labour of the shipyard and the factory was traditionally a key source of identity and pride. Many of those who are employed tend to find themselves in settings in which macho representations of manliness are constructed and reproduced. Others, however, have jobs which could be and often are performed by women; this has further implications as to how their personal masculinity is to be asserted. In the specific context of Northern Ireland, furthermore, the fact that members of the loyalist community as a whole feel besieged, their union with Britain threatened by what they regard as the combined forces of pan-nationalism and successive perfidious British governments, is highly significant. This has particular implications for those men who regard themselves as the legitimate defenders of the parental loyalist culture (Bairner, 2001a).

It has been argued that, for many young men in Protestant working-class communities, an involvement with loyalist marching bands and, in some instances of course, with loyalist paramilitarism, have offered appropriate channels for the reassertion of their masculinity (Bell, 1990). Segmental bonding coupled with a range of challenges to their male self-respect can also help to explain the anti-social behaviour of young men at football matches (Bairner, 1999a). It should be added that the close relationship between paramilitarism, parental culture as embodied in the marching bands and the attitudes and behaviour of some football fans is highlighted by the fact that members of paramilitary organisations and, to a lesser extent, bandsmen have acted as role models and, in some instances, proxy warriors in the eyes of those working-class youths in certain parts of the city who are most likely to be attracted to football hooliganism. In some cases, indeed, they may be the same people.

Allowing for local particularities, the analysis offered by the Leicester approach provides us with valuable insights into what is arguably the main manifestation of genuine football hooliganism in Ireland. It is also the case that in Ireland, as in Britain, football hooliganism is by no means exclusively a modern phenomenon but that it has a long history. However, other aspects of the Leicester research are perhaps less relevant in the Irish context. What, for example, do the Irish data allow us to say about two other 'discoveries' of the Leicester group, namely their claim that soccer hooliganism is not an exclusively English or British phenomenon, and that forms of crowd violence occur in sports other than football? In relation to the first point, while football hooliganism may not be exclusively English or British, it is nevertheless the case that hooliganism has certainly been more significant in 'British' Ireland (i.e. Northern Ireland) than in the Republic of Ireland while, in relation to the second claim, hooliganism in Ireland has seldom been linked to sports other than soccer.

Undeniably there have been occasional outbursts of ill temper at rugby matches in Ireland, particularly since the all-Ireland league competition and the subsequent professionalisation of the game gave added significance to club rivalries. In general, however, there has been no evidence of a hooligan problem. Indeed, when Ulster won the European Cup in 1998, beating the French club Colomiers in the final which was played in Dublin, huge numbers of fans travelled south carrying Northern Irish flags in scenes superficially reminiscent of the arrival of Linfield fans in Dundalk in 1979 but with none of the attendant violence. Although some might argue that the greater physical contact involved in rugby acts as a safety valve for the fans, the main explanation for the absence of violence at rugby games in Ireland, as in many other countries, can be traced to the middle-class character of the fans. Even where cross-border rivalry is involved, rugby followers do not share with their soccer counterparts any sense that it is up to them to fight for the 'cause'. This does not mean that they are politically neutered but rather that their politics are customarily channelled through the constitutional process and additional sites for cultural resistance are less likely to be required.

Similar observations can be made about many of the fans at Gaelic games (football and hurling) in Ireland although, since these attract working-class as well as middle-class followers, alternative explanations for the relative lack of trouble must also be sought. Fans do fight. They do so, however, in a relatively spontaneous fashion prompted by on-field events combined with the passion of local rivalry. Core hooliganism is not involved. The main reason for the absence of hooliganism at Gaelic games – despite the gender, age and social class of a certain section of the support which would locate them socially alongside football hooligans – is that crowds have traditionally been far more mixed, including more women and family groups, than would be present at most soccer games, with the result that particular forms of hegemonic masculinity have been easier to resist. In addition, the fact that the overwhelming majority of Gaelic fans in Ireland either live in rural areas or have a recent rural background may mean that they are less likely to have experienced the kind of segmental bonding which Dunning et al. have associated with core hooligans. It is also reasonable to argue that there is a form of cultural bonding which unites the entire crowd at any Gaelic event and serves to transcend parochial or county rivalries. The common enemy, the 'other', consists of those who do not follow Gaelic games, in particular members of the unionist community. It is they who are ultimately being resisted by virtue of attendance at a Gaelic football or hurling match. For Gaelic fans to fight amongst themselves would be to weaken this greater, transcendent sense of cultural resistance.

Conclusion

As Dunning (1999: 158) observes, 'it is important by way of conclusion to stress that it is unlikely that the phenomenon of soccer hooliganism will be found everywhere to derive from the same roots'. It is important to recognise the significance of the specific fault lines which prevail in particular societies. Dunning correctly argues, however, that all fault lines create structural approximations of 'ordered segmentation'. Armstrong (1998) disputes the validity of this concept in the Sheffield case. But in Northern Ireland, it is undeniably a feature not only of the ethno-sectarian conflict between nationalist and loyalist fans but also in the intra-community, territorial disputation which characterises the Linfield–Glentoran rivalry.

As regards the observations which Dunning believes to be universally applicable, it is apparent that football is certainly a source of excitement in Ireland although it should be noted that some of this arousal is increasingly secured away from Irish soccer grounds and is more frequently to be found in the course of trips to England or Scotland and, even more commonly, in front of a television set. The relevance of Dunning's other universally applicable observation – namely the impact of patriarchy on the behaviour of football fans – is even more clearly identifiable. According to Dunning (1999: 155), 'all societies in the world today are characterised by general forms of male dominance, especially in the public sphere, and hence are permeated by patriarchal values and institutions'. Indeed, the arguments presented in this chapter and elsewhere indicate that Ireland, or more specifically Northern Ireland, is characterised to a far greater extent than most European societies by the influence of patriarchy (Bairner, 1999a; Bairner, 1999b). Although no single factor can ever be held exclusively responsible for football hooliganism, at least in the case of Northern Ireland the masculinity of its perpetrators is of decisive importance (Bairner, 2001b). The reasons for this, as has been shown, are both general and specific. According to Armstrong (1998: 317), 'men . . . will always seek out some classifiable "higher purpose" to fight and die for, and there will always be young men who, when honour has been felt to be transgressed, take a punch and give two in return'. No doubt this somewhat gloomy prognosis contains a degree of correctness. But it should not negate the need to search for the reasons why some men will do so and, perhaps as importantly, why many others will not. Put simply, it is important to take account of the fact that many men (and women) attend football matches as well as other sporting events in Ireland and reveal by their behaviour that civilising processes do occur.

It should be noted, for example, that despite widespread fears about possible crowd trouble, the 2001 Irish Cup Final between Linfield and Glentoran passed off amidst considerable drunkenness but with no reports of violence. On the other hand, the impact of local politics on the behaviour of fans was clearly apparent when, during a friendly international against Norway at Windsor Park on 28 February 2001, a section of the Northern Ireland supporters turned on one of their own team members, Neil Lennon, following his move from Leicester City to (the historically Catholic) Glasgow Celtic. Although the Irish Football Association took measures to ensure that the abuse to which Lennon had been subjected would not be repeated during the two World Cup qualifying games that followed the Norway match, the booing that rang out on that February evening was indicative of the fact that, although numerous factors come into play when crowd trouble occurs in the Irish context, ethno-sectarian division remains the most potent.

Chapter 10

Italian ultras today: change or decline?

Antonio Roversi and Carlo Balestri

Introduction

In this chapter, we seek to outline certain aspects of the current situation of football hooliganism in Italy. However, before starting, a caveat is necessary. In the international academic literature on soccer-related violence, the term 'football hooliganism' is not infrequently used to indicate two distinct phenomena. The first of these has to do with what we may call 'spectator disorderliness'. This term denotes acts of wild behaviour by fans, the character of which is not programmed; such acts are not aimed at the fans of the opposing team but can be primarily traced to the emotional climate of excitement aroused by the match. Such disturbances usually occur within the stadium, during or after the match, and are aimed at the protagonists of the game (players, referees and linesmen, managers, trainers). They may also involve various types of spectator (ranging from the regulars at the stadium ends, to the supporters in the 'distinti' area, to the enthusiasts on the stands).[1] The most frequent disorderly behaviours of these fans involve throwing objects such as bottles, stones and coins onto the field at the referee, linesmen and players; assault on the referee outside the stadium; and attacks on the coach of the away team.

The second, rather different, phenomenon concerns behaviour that can be described as football hooliganism in the strict sense, i.e. acts of vandalism and systematic aggression carried out in the context of football matches by particular groups of young fans – in Italy, the 'ultras' – to the detriment of similar opposing groups both within and, above all, outside the stadia.

The first form of soccer-related violence has, on the whole, always been an integral part of the stadium atmosphere (Dunning et al., 1988) and represents a stable social behaviour in the sense that its phenomenology displays no major variations in time. Looking at the most recent data, taken from some daily papers regarding incidents of this type occurring from February 1995 to the present,[2] we note that these behaviours are now more frequent in southern Italy, where football support still entails a high degree of involvement and passion; they are also an important feature even in the lower league divisions.[3]

The situation is quite different as regards episodes of football hooliganism. In Italy, this phenomenon emerged between the late 1960s and early 1970s and spread through the stadia of the principal cities in the north, subsequently reaching the south and the provinces. During the 1980s, it expanded and took root also in the smaller amateur divisions. This chapter will deal with this second phenomenon – football hooliganism in the strict sense – and will try to explain the current situation and recent changes. We shall draw upon knowledge accumulated during ten years of participant observation carried out among several groups of Italian ultras. The study of football hooliganism has been further facilitated by the establishment, in 1995, of the Archive-Observatory for football support in Europe which combines the collection of documentary material with ethnographic research in Italian soccer stadia.[4]

An overview

We begin with some statistical data. In the absence of other reliable data,[5] the statistics on episodes of football hooliganism can only be based on newspaper reports. We know, of course, that doubts have been expressed concerning the reliability of these sources (Murphy et al., 1990b) and it has been claimed that the newspapers 'are not simply passive reflectors of events such as football hooliganism, but play both an intentional and unintentional part in their construction' (Murphy et al., 1990b: 96). As regards Britain, for example, Eric Dunning argues that the widespread myth of the disappearance of football hooliganism as a social problem has been strongly supported by the British mass media which 'depoliticised the issue of soccer hooliganism' (Dunning, 1999: 132–9).

The Italian case shows a similar problem, as can be seen from table 1. After reaching a peak in the 1990–91 season, the number of incidents involving Italian ultras groups appears to diminish and to show a marked reduction, particularly from the 1994–95 season onwards. We think that, in contrast to the English situation described by Dunning, the fall in 'recorded' episodes of football hooliganism in Italy does not stem from the reduced attention focused on this phenomenon by the press.

It is, of course, possible that decades of sometimes obsessive attention to the phenomenon by the press, sporting or otherwise, have given way to a loss of interest in the face of new topics that have burst into the headlines in these last few years (such as the Bosman ruling, or the strong drive towards commercialisation in football clubs). At the same time, however, analysis of the

Table 1 **Incidents related to League matches in Serie A and B. Seasons 1980/81–1997/98**

Season	Number of incidents	Number of matches	%
1980–81	17	620	2.7
1981–82	25	620	4.0
1982–83	41	620	6.6
1983–84	37	620	5.9
1984–85	45	620	7.2
1985–86	55	620	8.8
1986–87	59	620	9.5
1987–88	61	620	9.8
1988–89	65	686	9.4
1989–90	66	686	9.6
1990–91	73	686	10.6
1991–92	56	686	8.1
1992–93	58	686	8.6
1993–94	64	686	9.3
1994–95	40	686	5.8
1995–96	34	686	4.9
1996–97	27	686	3.9
1997–98	23	686	3.6

Sources: Corriere della Sera, Resto del Carlino, Stadio/Corriere dello Sport.

changes occurring within the world of the ultras in recent years suggests that, although the figures inevitably underestimate the number of incidents that actually happened, their drop does nevertheless mark a real trend. Can we then say that episodes of football hooliganism are about to vanish from the Italian soccer scene, as some authors claim has already happened in Britain? This is not the argument we put forward in this essay. Rather, we are convinced that traditional-type episodes of football hooliganism have diminished and have been partly replaced by new forms of stadium conflict which have still largely to be identified and studied. Before discussing this point, however, it will be as well briefly to recall the salient and special features by which this world has been, and in great part continues to be, characterised and by which it is distinguished from the British and northern European hooligan model.

Firstly, the contexts in which the two phenomena are contained differ greatly. In Britain, the birthplace of soccer, the enthusiasm for this sports spectacle has until recently mainly involved the working class. To get some idea of the meld between football and working-class culture in Britain, one need think only of the architecture of the stadia whose forms closely recall the typical structures of factories; or again, as Taylor reminds us, the working-class origin of many British teams.[6] And precisely by virtue of these origins and this link, as the studies by British scholars have taught us, the model of British football hooliganism manifests as a sort of extension of the traditional behaviour scheme of the rough working class. The hooligan group usually stems from the lowest strata of society;[7] it assumes what has been called a 'violent masculine style' (Dunning et al., 1986c); it tends to assemble mainly to give support during the match and to attack the away fans; and it reveals an absence of developed and lasting forms of coordination, organisation and promotion of stadium end activities. In Italy, on the contrary, the link between football and the working class has from the outset been more tenuous, and soccer enthusiasm has always involved a large number of persons from all social classes. Hence, although the ultras group was originally influenced by the British hooligan model, its social composition tends to be more cross-class (it also comprises an important female component) and marries typical youth protest with a political slant against the system, which was shared by the extremist political groups who, in the Italy of the 1960s and 1970s, were engaged in demonstrations and provided an excellent example of group spirit, toughness and compactness.[8] This special characteristic helped the ultras movement to borrow modes of action and forms of organisation from the political sphere, and to endow itself with stable, complex organisational structures able to mobilise towards internal activities (choruses, production of banners and flags) and external ones (production and sale of gadgets, membership cards, subscriptions, relations with the club, etc.).

These differences have been responsible for two diverse systems of support. The British model hinges on a set of activities that exalt the group sense but with no particular suggestion of a durable and consistent commitment outside the match itself or during the week, and does not involve working groups or sector leaders for the various activities. In contrast is the Italian model, in which the ultras group is more outward orientated and able, due to its organisational structures, to arrange carnival-type demonstrations of support involving the whole stadium end and requiring considerable outlay in money, labour and coordination. In view of the different characteristics, it is clear how violence, too, differs in importance from one model to the other: for the British hooligans it is the main device for aggregation and union; whereas for the Italian ultras, influenced by the political view of violence as a means rather than an end, it has represented just one of the group's options. For the ultras groups also based their own sense of community on other manifestations that eventually took on a highly symbolic value (organising choruses, producing their own material, taking part as militants in weekday organisation meetings). By virtue of its complex associative nature, the repertory of unwritten rules governing the behaviours of members of the ultras groups with respect to violence was much more complex and precise than that described by Marsh and co-workers in their book, *The Rules of Disorder*, on the behaviour of the hooligans in Oxford (Marsh et al., 1978). For instance, violence was not perpetrated indiscriminately but only in specific cases and against certain defined groups of ultras seen as enemies; it was up to the members of the directorate (those coordinating and managing the group's activities) who decided whether and how to inflict violence; the youngest were allowed to take part in fights only after giving ample proof of reliability not only in the 'military' field but also in the organisational one; it was forbidden to involve people alien to the ultras logic, as it was to commit gratuitous vandalism.

At the same time, however, the self-reproducing mechanism of the Italian ultras groups displayed some traits in common with the English hooligan groups. For the ultras, too, saw the stadium as the final stage of a process of socialising the group life that went on elsewhere – in city districts, bars and youth centres, or with groups of friends or political groups – and that culminated in the stadium, with the admission of some of them into the football end groups. In other words, for many the path to becoming ultras, until quite recently, commenced in social spaces other than the terraces. This mechanism recalls the way in which, according to Dunning and his Leicester colleagues, some British football ends were formed.[9]

It was in these places that youths learnt the 'normative ethical grammar' (Salvini, 1988: 141), consisting of displaying the qualities of reliability, courage, solidarity and toughness, as a result of which they came ultimately to be considered as members of the group. Frequently, therefore, this passage was preparatory to full membership of the life of the football end and the ultras group. At this stage, the fans become involved in the process of adapting and perfecting the learnt code specific to the football end, where hierarchies and competences were far more structured, formalised and binding. Thus the experience gathered outside the confines of the stadium was reabsorbed by the classic ultras group in recurring thematic schemes – the all-involving choruses, the obsessive slogans, the 'militarisation' of the group, and a reassuring manichean vision 'friends v enemies' – while the imagination of the young fan was constantly replenished with new mythical figures and new symbolic contents drawn from the specific context of soccer.

For this reason, it must be acknowledged that for a long time the ultras culture of the historic groups was a 'strong' culture, since it was capable of turning the football end into a territory where, over and above social origins, motivations and subjective stimuli, and different lifestyles, the same rules and norms were valid for all the young fans. And this culture imposed a sort of monopoly on the use of violence, orientating it towards external enemies alone, while within the football end personal opinions were silenced in the name of common group faith. Substantially, it succeeded in endowing each individual reality of the Italian ultras movement with all the features of a self-sufficient and totalising microcosm, capable of emotionally integrating each member in their own role, their own duties and a sense of belonging to a collective dimension. Thus in the words of an ultra: 'As I see it, being an ultra is a way of life: on Monday you do the post-mortem of Sunday's match, and right through the week you do your utmost for finances, coaches, banners, smoke bombs. At nine o'clock on Sunday morning you're at the stadium for preparations . . . That's how strong bonds have come about . . . The ultras phenomenon is a collective one, a strong group one' (Roversi, 1992: 123).

Death of an ultra

At the close of the 1980s, the structure described above moved towards crisis, a crisis which is still ongoing and which is productive of various transformations. In trying to analyse the reasons for this crisis, it may be appropriate to begin with an incident that, perhaps, attained and coincided with the high point of the crisis of the rules by which the Italian ultras movement is governed: the killing of Genoa fan, Vincenzo Spagnolo.

On 29 January 1995, on the occasion of the league match between Genoa and Milan, a young Genoa fan died after being knifed by a Milan supporter. The incident produced not only a wave of alarm in public opinion and a demand for tougher repressive measures, but also a symbolic response: all the soccer championship matches were suspended for one Sunday.

But why did that young fan die? The facts are briefly as follows. As in many other Italian stadia, the Milan end no longer had the features once typical of Italian football ends, characterised by a few large ultras groups internally organised and coordinated with each other, and above all capable of exercising a kind of hegemony over the behaviour of the fans at the ends. By 1995, the Milan end had lost this unitary character and the large groups had partly lost their hegemony. Most importantly, small formations sprang up acting autonomously according to the logic of the moment, which is often unpredictable. Among these new small, spontaneous formations was a group of youths – known as 'Barbour' from the jacket then in fashion with many young Italians – who wanted to become members of the Brigate Rossonere 2, a new ultras formation born out of the split in one of the major Milan fan groups, the Brigate Rossonere. The members of this new group decided to put on a show in order to advertise themselves and earn respect both within and outside the Milan end. They also involved youths of the Barbour group and determined to organise a punitive raid, some of them armed with knives, against the Genoans.

The decision was clearly taken independently of the other end groups (which would itself have been unthinkable some years previously). Rather than using the special train for Milan fans, the group travelled by ordinary scheduled train in order to escape police control. To avoid identification, they wore no Milan badges. Arriving at the Marassi stadium in Genoa, they were spotted by a group of home fans and fighting broke out. Young Vincenzo Spagnolo faced eighteen-year-old Simone Barbaglia bare-fisted, in line with ultras logic, and Barbaglia reacted by stabbing him close to the heart. Spagnolo died in hospital shortly after.

The news of Spagnolo's death was broadcast by radio five minutes before the end of the first half. At that moment, the Genoa fans, who already knew that one of their members had been wounded, responded by trying to interrupt the match. Managers and players of both teams acceded to the request of the football end by leaving the field empty to grief in the second half. But, with the match over, the anger of the Genoa fans still smouldered. Desperate and furious, they tried to reach the sector of the Milan fans in order to avenge their comrade. Urban guerilla warfare, fought according to the ultras code of behaviour, raged throughout the night with seven people beaten up and large-scale damage. In contrast, a mere four seconds of unregulated violence had sufficed to cause the irreparable damage that was the death of Vincenzo Spagnolo.

Seven days after his death, on the soccer-less Sunday and following an initiative by the leaders of Genoa's two fan clubs (Genoa and Sampdoria), a national meeting of ultras was organised. They met to reflect – on their world and on the changes that had turned it upside down – in an attempt to set limits on violence and to reshape the rules for a world that seemed to have lost them altogether.

But before examining the content of the Genoa meeting, let us attempt to outline the objective reasons underlying the crisis. We have already mentioned how the tight bond involved in being an ultra no longer holds at the stadium ends. The example of the Milan end is paradigmatic of the loss of unity and compactness experienced by the original ultras world over the last few years; nowadays, it is all too easy for a few kids with no history behind them to set up individual groups and act independently. Within such groups sharp frictions can often be found and these may threaten their relative unity. Relations among the large end groups have become anything but idyllic.

In the 1980s, when the movement expanded rapidly even in minor and provincial stadia, it underwent important structural changes. These changes were associated with: the broad generational turnover, above all of the leadership (some historic leaders died of drug abuse); the general reaction in the political movements (whose influence had been responsible for a further element of identification and unity in a large part of the ultras movement); and the disintegration of many places of assembly and socialisation outside the stadium (which, as we noted earlier, marked the first step in identification for young future ultras). Within the ultras movement, a tendency developed for giving greater importance to the local sense of belonging and making systematic use of parochial rivalry in identifying ultras who could be considered as enemies. An ever stronger tendency to use violence, not just in an instrumental way but also as a mode of expression in its own right, developed in parallel. All this explains why the group spirit, based on the cult of toughness and paramilitary organisation, together with the morbid attachment to one's own little homeland, prepared a fertile seedbed for racist and xenophobic attitudes. Some of these groups, who in the early 1990s were to make no secret of their right-wing opinions, began trying to evict the historic groups from the leadership of the stadium end. They flaunted a dangerous attraction with military/heroic feats and the expressive use of violence and attempted to break down the end consensus of the other groups, settling accounts by physical conflict.

But the dynamics involving the stadium ends in those years and the conflicts they engendered also had implications for other aspects, including economic aspects, of fan groups. In order for the ultras group to engage in all its many activities, it has always needed substantial funds which it has sought partly through forms of self-financing (membership cards, sale of literature etc.) and, in some instances, partly through relationships with the football clubs which have not always been clearly defined. This has enabled some members of the ultras groups unashamedly to exploit their position to obtain free tickets from the club which they resell for personal gain while others, with the club's approval, have started up sales points with ultras merchandising. This situation degenerated from the late 1980s onwards and has aroused controversies and conflicts, which are still continuing, between those who favour a 'business' approach to funding, those who favour a tough line that eschews even the minimum sponsorship, and those who favour a third, classic middle path.

More generally, however, the ends ultimately became the mirror of a society more and more atomised, less and less able to produce reasons for and values of togetherness. If, up to the 1980s, the stadium was a point of arrival on an aggregative path beginning in the town district, the bar or the political meeting places and capable of producing real bonds and involving large numbers, what we now see is a fragmented structure unable to reproduce the conditions of common identity and sociality. And the stadium, even while it remains the privileged place of sociality, cannot but suffer the repercussions of these processes.[10]

There was thus a waning of interest and participation in the life of the group, a falling-off of that militancy that made the ultras existence into an involving, all-embracing style of life. As a direct result, the group's directives became fewer and they lost control and hegemony over the end as a whole. Respect for the elders weakened, as did the need to serve an 'apprenticeship'. There was a proliferation of 'stray dogs', young people who did not identify with any of the end groups and who often took a leading part in gratuitous, dangerous acts of vandalism, with no consideration or even awareness of the history and rules of the ultras movement. Even the twinning arrangements between fan groups – formerly symbolic of respect and friendship among different ends (and their chiefs) – have tended to break up or not to be renewed. At a fragmented end, the attack on a twin fan group by a single opposed group or a handful of 'stray dogs' is enough to destroy the twinning alliance.

To the internal problems of the ultras' world, were then added those concerning repression from outside. Some serious incidents in 1989 led the Italian government to adopt extraordinary measures against violence connected with sporting occasions. This produced Law 401 which introduced, as a preventive measure, banning anyone reported for violent offences in the sports context from entering stadia. This law, together with the spread, during the World Cup tournament of 1990, of closed circuit TV cameras in order to film the behaviour of the ultras in the Italian stadia and of fans travelling to the matches, began to hit some of the group organisers, thus helping to exacerbate the crisis.

A new stage begins

The killing of Spagnolo, then, took its place in the above-described context. The ultras' meeting held the week following his death thus marked both the official and the subjective awareness by the ultras movement of the deep ongoing crisis. To Genoa came the leaders of nearly all the ultras groups in Italy, thus revealing the contradictions and profound divergences between them. They included those who enjoyed excellent relations with their clubs and were adept at exploiting the circulation of money linked with the sale of tickets, for their own personal interests. There were those who used racism and right-wing politics in the stadium to keep the group united. Others, a much smaller number, were openly left-wing. Some older ones (35 and upwards) continued to maintain control over certain groups. There were young people aged 24 years who, without much experience, had acquired strong powers of decision making within their own group. The meeting produced an important result, a communiqué signed by most of those present, entitled 'No more knives, no more thugs'. The document stated, among other things: 'Enough of these ultras who are not ultras, who seek, at the expense of the ultras world, to make the headlines, to aspire to greatness, while ignoring the evil done (as in this irreparable case). Enough of the fashion of 20 versus 2, molotovs and knives'.

This communiqué was savagely criticised by the majority of public opinion, the press, and Italian politicians. And nobody caught the important element of novelty it contained. For it manifested a worried, if belated, acknowledgement of the crisis in the ultras' world, and the fear that the entire movement might crumble under attack by those whose cowardly and irresponsible behaviour – as in the case of Spagnolo's killer and his group – negated the traditional values of the ultras' world, betrayed its original spirit and thus furnished the pretext for an even tougher crackdown by magistrates and police. With a severe act of self-criticism for not having perceived in time that the escalation of the unregulated violence threatened to undermine the very foundations of the movement, the ultras decided there and then to redraw the codes and rules concerning the use of violence. They also branded as a 'thug' – that is one outside the movement – not merely anyone who betrayed a comrade or his group but also anyone disregarding the rules.

Starting immediately from the Genoa meeting, certain effects could be noted. Most groups conformed to the rules laid down in the document, with some even repudiating violence as a permissible method of action. But other groups, in a more or less covert fashion, did not accept the ban on weapons. In general, however, acts of violence have diminished, even though between February 1995 and June 1997 the number of those injured by cutting weapons remained very high (14 people injured, all with thigh wounds except for a young Moroccan who was severely wounded in the back by a group of Bologna ultras on a punitive expedition). There were, however, no stabbings during the 1997–98 season. Equally significant is the fact that many perpetrators of stabbings come, not from organised groups but from among the 'stray dogs'.

Nonetheless, the real fall in violent incidents should not lead us to under-estimate a shift of violent incidents towards the minor football divisions as well as the high level of violence in stadia in southern Italy. Most importantly, we must be aware of what appears to be a quite new element in recent years – namely, the very large number of incidents involving ultras and police. We refer here not to incidents where the police intervene in order to prevent fighting between two rival factions, but to direct fights between ultras and the police. Between February 1995 and 1998, there were 28 such incidents out of an overall total of 82 recorded for the two top divisions alone. In other words, relations between ultras and the police have notably worsened over the last few years. The climate has certainly been exacerbated by a new law passed by Parliament after the killing of Spagnolo which has made the rule about banning entry to the stadia even more restrictive. Armed with this law, the police have aimed – sometimes in a rather too explicit way – at neutralising those responsible for ultras' directives (in other words, the only ones able to exercise even partial control over violence at the ends), while neglecting the 'stray dogs' who are often responsible for violent incidents.

The very presence of the police inside and around the stadium, often bordering on a militarisation of the territory, has produced an increase in repression which is at times exaggerated and unreasonable. Police behaviour has not infrequently provoked a violent response from the ultras groups, or turned into large-scale, unwarranted and indiscriminate baton charges against the fans as a whole; in this context, we might note the harsh criticisms made by the British government of the violent and aggressive behaviour of the Italian police at the expense of British fans before, during and after the Italy–England match played in Rome in October 1997.

More generally, however, the Genoa meeting can be said to have opened a new phase of development. Since that meeting, many ultras groups have been trying hard to present themselves once again as agencies for sociality, rather than as groups noted for their use of violence. They have become more closely engaged in organising charity initiatives, almost as if to emphasise the movement's more 'solidaristic' aspects (ranging from the nationwide initiative in support of a helpline for battered children, to the humanitarian aid collected for former Yugoslavia by several Italian ultras groups). But, most important of all, they have decided to continue with meetings of ultras groups. For, in spite of the profound differences and contrasts – in social class, birth, cultural and political backgrounds – a new awareness has been taking root among the groups: namely that, differences notwithstanding, there is for all of them an essential unity of a higher entity – that of their common belonging as ultras.[11] It is no accident that, precisely at their moment of greatest internal weakness, the traditionally rival ultras groups have found themselves able to discover points of contact and common action among themselves. Hence the most important outcome of the Genoa meeting – where, for the first time, ultras from all over Italy met, became acquainted with and confronted one another – has been the ever more intensive search for further grounds for dialogue among the ultras.[12]

The search for encounter and confrontation within the movement has thus become a way of ultras protecting themselves from violent internal degeneration. It is also a means of standing solidly, firstly against a public opinion that views them simply as savage criminals; secondly, against an institutional apparatus that, especially after the killing of Spagnolo, has further sharpened its repressive weapons; and thirdly, against a football industry that tends to reduce the significance of being a fan so that those who attend matches are reduced to the role of mere consumers of a sports event.

Thus, being an ultra takes on some characteristics almost akin to membership of a resistance movement, involving a struggle not against bourgeoisification, as has been suggested (Taylor, 1969: 204–6) but against the attempt to bourgeoisify the phenomenon of football support, and to destroy the popular culture of which the ultras feel themselves the legitimate repositories.

Conclusions

In conclusion, we should like to stress two points. Firstly, even though the self-producing mechanism of the ultras groups closely resembles the principle of ordered segmentation proposed by Dunning, the social basis of the ultras does not consist predominantly of the lowest and roughest strata of society. The only two studies describing the social origins of the ultras, carried out in Bologna and Pisa (Roversi, 1992 and Francia, 1994), indicate that there was, in Bologna, a large element of working-class extraction (but of the more integrated, less marginal sort), while in Pisa the majority of the ultras originated from the town's petite bourgeoisie.

Moreover, the mechanisms by which the ultras groups reproduced themselves — through alliances of young groups that were independent but which belonged to the same community — moved into crisis towards the end of the 1980s with the break-up of spaces for young people to gather in the cities. Hence, an inverse process is nowadays much more likely — namely, that the stadium will take on the configuration of a place of primary sociability and that, within it, a community will assume form and structure, able to affirm itself and to act even outside the stadium, in other places in the city. For, despite the signs of atomisation and disintegration that we have described, the stadium ends continue to represent one of the strong places of sociality.

The second point relates to violence in the world of football support. In Italy, despite the recent reduction in the number of incidents, this is a problem which has yet to be solved. Up to now, Italy's sole reaction to the problem of violence by fans has been to adopt law and order measures and to exert ever greater social control; the task of containing, suppressing and punishing football violence has in effect been shifted to the police forces alone. The result has been continued serious tension around the stadiums and exacerbated conflict, not so much among rival fan groups but rather between ultras and police.

In order to control violent behaviour more effectively, repressive measures need to be accompanied by social intervention. What is required are not so much policies aimed at control and repression, but policies designed to analyse the reasons for this violence and, by long-term action, to change the mentality underlying certain attitudes and behaviours. In-depth knowledge of the stadium-end phenomenon reveals a variegated, contradictory universe, a social gathering place for youth that also features positive values and powerful energies, of which the violence that is expressed on occasions is only one aspect. Moreover, applying a policy of social intervention would facilitate a dialogue between self-organised fans and institutions on the lines established in other countries, for example the German Fanprojekte, the Belgian Fancoaching and the Football Supporters Association in Britain. This is an indispensable premise not only for creating a less tense atmosphere in stadiums, but also for avoiding the marginalisation of self-organised groups.

Chapter 11

Barras bravas: representation and crowd violence in Peruvian football

Aldo Panfichi and Jorge Thieroldt

This chapter contains the preliminary findings of a study that seeks, through the reconstruction of the histories of various local or district fan clubs or 'barras bravas', to understand the phenomenon of crowd violence in Peruvian football, the main protagonists of which are thousands of children and teenagers who are known in Peru as 'barristas'. We put forward the general hypothesis that a combination of two factors gives meaning and reason to the involvement of large numbers of youths in football-related violence. On the one hand, a series of conditions associated with many years of extreme economic hardship, together with weak and precarious experiences of socialisation, prompt certain youths from depressed areas of Lima to form peer groups or gangs bonded together by their common loyalty to a given football team and neighbourhood ties. These are strong emotional bonds. On the other hand, years of exposure to a period of political violence (1979–92), and the attendant impact on the attitudes of Peruvians, has instilled in these young barristas a belligerent style and a culture of confrontation. This is, above all, a style not of ideological or political beliefs but of physical and symbolic violence. We argue that the convergence of these experiences provides the explanation for the current phenomenon of football violence in Peru.

Football and society

Over the past few years football has come to be seen not just as a sporting passion, but also as a privileged setting for the study of society. Sociologists, anthropologists and communicators from different parts of the world have discovered that football is not just about a group of men running around after a ball, but that represented in it are human relationships, collective forms of behaviour and aspirations which emanate from experiences that have had a strong impact on the daily lives of people within a given society. We suggest that there is a close connection between the historical experiences that a country has undergone and the particular social and cultural aspects that football expresses and accentuates in that country.

In Peru, as in other Latin American countries like Argentina, the interest of the academic world in football centres on the behaviour and violent culture of barristas, most of whom are young males belonging to supporters' clubs. In countries like Chile, which have in the past been governed by authoritarian regimes, studies have been done of the political use of football as a tool of social control (dictators such as Pinochet in Chile and Franco in Spain professed their support for the clubs Colo Colo and Real Madrid respectively), or of support for particular clubs as a source of popular resistance to authoritarianism.

Football's capacity to represent key aspects of people's lives hinges on the fact that football is in itself a ritual representation, devoid of any specific historical significance, of non-violent confrontation between two tightly knit communities with a strong sense of identity. As Dunning et al. (1988) have pointed out, this tribal and at the same universal 'nature', turns into a metaphor where 'forms of co-operation, interdependence and conflict are subtly intertwined', leading to the formation of antagonistic groups or communities. Moreover confrontation awakens emotions of both pleasure and pain, satisfying both individual needs and the urge to achieve social status and recognition.

In this way, two teams of eleven players are ranged against each other, distributed around the field in positions of attack and defence. Each team is identified by its own distinct colours and emblems that provide a focus for the feeling of belonging to something, of 'us against them', the victory going to the side that manages to pierce the heart of the rival team's territory and humiliate them by scoring a goal. After that, they must defend their advantage in order to leave the field as victors. This symbolic representation, furthermore, takes place in a public space built exclusively for this purpose, namely a stadium. And this ritual is presided over by a referee who enforces a set of rules that all are required to observe in a 'civilised' manner.

Football is, in addition, a phenomenon of mass and multi-class appeal that creates irreducible forms of identity. Accordingly, it forges emotional ties of loyalty and group identity among people of different strata, races, classes, occupations and sexual preferences. These loyalties cut across every form of organisation and institutional structure, making it one of the dominant mechanisms of social differentiation in contemporary societies. Loyalties are structured around values and meanings that shape the aura and symbols that distinguish a given football club (Panfichi, 1995). Football is a ritual representation of a confrontation between two communities without being the direct cause of the violent behaviour of certain fans. On the contrary, it is these individuals themselves and the way in which they process past experiences in their lives that specifically define what is at stake in this representation.

In Peru, the aspect of football that most captures people's attention is the violence generated by various organised groups of young male fans. What kind of local and national experiences are behind this behaviour? To answer this question properly, we need to examine long-term historical processes together with factors originating from more recent periods or episodes in the country's history. In this chapter, we shall place particular emphasis on the latter factors, because they seem to us to be crucial in explaining the problem. We shall leave the attempt to provide an interpretation based on longer-term processes for another occasion.

We start from the premise that it is not by chance that violence in Peruvian football became a conspicuous 'problem' immediately following the period of confrontation, death and destruction that culminated in the Peruvian state's political and military victory over subversive groups which had mounted an armed revolt. Various international human rights organisations calculated that, from 1980 to 1992, nearly 30,000 Peruvian citizens, most of them young people, died as a result of this confrontation, while the costs of the material damage caused by this violence are estimated at approximately US$27,000 million (*Revista del Instituto de Defensa Legal*, 1995). The experience of this military confrontation had an impact on every segment of Peruvian society – although on some more than others – and, as we shall see, nobody in Peru can claim to have emerged unscathed from those difficult years. Moreover, an entire generation of today's young people was born and evolved socially against this backdrop of confrontation, which could be followed almost live on a daily basis thanks to mass media coverage.

The high significance we attach to this internal conflict does not mean that we think that violence had been absent from Peruvian football before this period. In reality, this is a theme that has yet to be studied in depth and constitutes a major gap in our knowledge of our social and cultural history. We will, however, mention a number of events that do deserve reflection. For instance, the first derby match in Peruvian football, that is the first ever game between Alianza Lima and Universitario de Deportes which gave rise to or 'invented' Peruvian football's longest-standing rivalry, was played in September 1928, ending before the full-time whistle when the game degenerated into a generalised brawl involving not only the players but also the fans who streamed onto the pitch from the stands. That game became known as the 'Baton Derby', in reference to the weapons used in the fighting. From this game began the so-called 'classic of classics' (El Clasico) of Peruvian football.

Years later, on 24 May 1964, a match between the national teams of Peru and Argentina ended in the worst tragedy ever seen at a football game when hundreds of fans, furious at what they considered an unfair refereeing decision, invaded the pitch only to be beaten back vigorously by the police. In the ensuing stampede, as the crowd turned back on itself and tried to get away from the police batons only to find the stadium doors locked, 328 people died and nearly 500 were wounded.

Notwithstanding these events, and recognising the lack of historical research, we believe that there is sufficient evidence to assert that, from the 1980s onwards, and especially during the 1990s, football in Peru gradually but increasingly provided an opportunity for the representation and expression of violence by increasingly large numbers of youths. Indeed, it was during this period that a significant change occurred in the composition and social organisation of football fan clubs, most notably in their forms of collective behaviour, in their chanting and verbal expression, and in their transformation of stadia into spaces for constructing radical and aggressive forms of masculinity. All of the above have turned these fan clubs or barras bravas into new social actors who are feared and often vilified, but about whom little is actually known.

Several analysts agree that, among Peru's more popular clubs in the early 1970s, class criteria dictated the places that supporters occupied at football grounds. For example, in whichever ground their team was playing, the fans of Alianza Lima, seen as the archetypal working man's team, would always occupy the cheaper stand, whereas the supporters of Universitario would always take their seats in the more expensive, middle-class stand. Both groups of supporters were loosely organised groups of 'civilised' fans who would gather at matches to urge on their respective teams, enjoying the official recognition of their clubs. This recognition included courtesy tickets to games and other privileges, and was a source of power and very often the basis for clientelistic and paternalist relationships. Several 'traditional' organisers of these fan clubs even went on to become employees of the clubs or of businesses owned by successful club directors. During those years, football clubs kept tight control over the organisation and behaviour of their followers.

In the 1980s and early 1990s, the situation slowly changed. This period was characterised by deepening economic recession, a breakdown of law and order, widespread unemployment and, above all, indiscriminate violence and terrorism. In this context, the fan clubs began to slip away from the control of their 'traditional' leaders and, at the same time, began to exert a strong pull on thousands of young boys and adolescents from Lima's depressed districts and neighbourhoods. A behavioural attitude centring on confrontation and the breaking of socially accepted rules of conduct became one of the defining characteristics of these youths. At the same time, fan clubs became more complex by uniting groups of youths organised territorially into neighbourhood or local clubs under a central leadership.

These local fan clubs, known in the 1990s as barras bravas, are made up of groups of boys and adolescents from the same neighbourhood. They are united by feelings of a common identity and loyalty to a given football club. Most of the young men who are active in barras come from economically and socially deprived families that engage in illicit or informal economic activities and are prone to high levels of drug and alcohol abuse. Our field research with several of these local barras in Lima revealed very clearly that the barristas tend overwhelmingly to be young people who live in extreme situations treading a narrow path between the right and wrong sides of the law. They distinguish themselves collectively by belonging to a given neighbourhood of Lima, which enables them to stand out in the stadium and in other public spaces.

Local barras emerged when football loyalties turned the neighbourhood gangs or pandillas from mobs of vandals and delinquents into veritable battalions waging a symbolic war with the aim of obtaining victory and triumph. However, although they might engage in similar types of activities and their members come from much the same background, gangs and local barras are not always and everywhere one and the same. Local barras are territorial groups that emerged more recently in the 1990s, loyalty to the club being the irreducible identifying criterion, which also dictates how they spend much of their time, in preparing to spur on and follow their team every week around the country. However, the reality is more complex than this simple classification might suggest since barristas, like gang members, may also engage in unlawful activities, cause damage to property, belong or have belonged in the past to other local gangs, clash violently with other barras and, most importantly, share the same codes.

From barrio to barra and vice versa

Based on our analysis of the lives of young barristas, we propose that a dual social process has taken place in recent years, consisting of the arrival at football matches of local gang members who engage in delinquent activities, and the parallel influence of football loyalties on local configurations in the neighbourhoods where street violence seems to hold sway. We believe that, by bearing in mind this dual process, we will reach a better understanding of the juvenile behaviour in question.

Our argument is thus that the ranks of the barras were swelled with gang members, which brought changes to behaviour in the stands, while local youth conflicts became tinged with local football loyalties in contexts of extreme poverty. In Peru, it would be true to say that the 'barrio' or neighbourhood as a social unit finds expression through the local barra, but the barra also feeds back into the neighbourhood, rearranging its tensions and internal conflicts. In this process, the two intertwine and exchange codes of behaviour and symbolism. First, the barra contains gang members, most of whom engage in petty crime and model their behaviour on the conduct displayed by criminal elements. This is reflected in the prison slang, codes of behaviour and role models they have adopted. Second, the neighbourhood stops being the sole stamping ground of *achorado* (local thugs), since these traditional street leaders now have a team jersey and a shared football identity to defend.

In the case of Universitario de Deportes football club, this process has been aptly summed up by Raúl Castro who says that the Trinchera Norte ('Northern Trench') fan club was founded in 1988 as a breakaway unit from the official fan club whose members traditionally sit in the East Stand. In moving to the more popular North Stand, the Trinchera claimed a new identity, but above all it affirmed the need to defend the club's emblem from attack by their arch enemies, Alianza Lima's Comando Sur ('Southern Command') fan club, and to organise their 'army' with a view to launching a 'counteroffensive'. These are tasks that the official fan club would never have contemplated, which purportedly gave rise to their being branded 'chickens' (*gallinas*) and more recently 'queers' (*cabros*) (Castro, 1995). Bit by bit, Trinchera Norte began to gain legitimacy and authority on the streets.

In organisational terms, the barras went from being a single organisation centred on a nucleus of longstanding leaders, to becoming a network of neighbourhood-based groups extending throughout the city. Strictly speaking, the Comando Sur of Alianza Lima and Trinchera Norte of Universitario are extensive networks of local barras from different neighbourhoods. In this way, the disputes and confrontations represented in football were transferred from the playing field and the stands to the local setting of the barrios or neighbourhoods. The entire city thus became the battleground for real and symbolic conflicts. District barras became embroiled in 'turf wars' for social supremacy in the local sphere, hence the importance of graffiti as a mark of territorial domination. In this way, football loyalties create and reproduce new lines of social differentiation, in addition to such criteria as class origin, age, gender, and occupation. Furthermore, the fact of belonging to a local barra provides a form of differentiated local identity within the greater football club identity.

In the case of Universitario, this process accelerated from 1994 onwards when the Trinchera organised a decentralised system for the distribution of free tickets to up-and-coming neighbourhood fan clubs. As Espinosa has pointed out, until that time fan club organisers had been in charge of distributing tickets in a centralised manner, and would do so in the vicinity of the stadium where Universitario was due to play. Under the new system, the neighbourhood fan clubs acquired greater importance as channels for the distribution of benefits and, at the same time, new leaders emerged who soon claimed their place in the senior leadership of the fan club (Espinosa, 1999). These new leaders, furthermore, sought to renegotiate their links with the football club's directors, thus emphasising a greater autonomy than their predecessors.

Benavides has described a similar process in the case of Alianza Lima's Comando Sur. In this fan club, which had always been working class, the internal hierarchy had always been strongly family- and community-orientated. The old leaders imposed their authority in the name of loyalty to a tradition which held that this community was an extended family or spiritual brotherhood. Hence the cohesive power of the notion of being a tight-knit community. However, as the legitimacy of Comando Sur began to be accepted by more and more neighbourhood or local barras, so a similar process to that which had occurred with the Trinchera Norte began to take place. That is, the authority and legitimacy of the old leaders began to be challenged by belligerent groups of youths and adolescents (Benavides, 1997).

Responses to such challenges tended to be violent. This is why, after a group of youths formed in 1993 a dissident Alianza Lima faction called Cabezas Azules ('Blue Heads'), they were forced to leave the South Stand and take up a position in the North Stand, until then the exclusive territory of the Universitario fan club. Despite repeated efforts, the Cabezas Azules were unable to attract other local barras because of the symbolic power that the South Stand held for any Alianza Lima fan and, also, because they did not have access to the free tickets over which Comando Sur held a monopoly.

Our data indicate that the Cabezas Azules were not a local barra in the strict sense, but were made up of youths from various parts of Lima, who chose to rally together under that name and dispute the leadership of Comando Sur. The dissidence of the Cabezas Azules stemmed from issues such as disagreements over the handling of free tickets and the secrecy with which the Comando Sur leaders took decisions, as well as criticisms of style regarding the repetitive and unchanging nature of their chants and activities in support of the team.

At one point, the Cabezas Azules included youths and adults from tough or 'dangerous' barrios, who resorted to street violence during the dispute. These dissidents were violently crushed by Comando Sur, which also counted among its ranks youths from other barrios that were equally 'dangerous'. Both factions called on the support of various local barras. Thus, for example, the Cabezas Azules had the backing of Los de Surco ('The Guys from Surco district', and Los Sicarios ('The Hitmen'), while Comando Sur called on Barraca Rebelde ('Rebel Shack') of Lima's La Victoria district. The result was one of the first confrontations over the official leadership of the fans between different local or neighbourhood barras that supported the same team.

Just as illustrative is the story of Barraca Rebelde. Initially, Barraca was not a local barra either but made up of youths from various parts of the district of La Victoria. Following the defeat of the Cabezas Azules, this group began to become more powerful inside Comando Sur on the strength of the respect and fear inspired by the well-known physical and fighting prowess of its members, several of whom were at the time of writing detained in juvenile penitentiaries. However, the constant abuses committed by this faction at stadia, such as robbing other fans and smashing up meeting places, prompted the other local barras to throw their support behind two young leaders from the feared 'Mendocita' neighbourhood who launched an internal takeover bid, seizing control of Barraca Rebelde and ejecting the faction's more violent members. In this way, the faction became a local barra, strongly identified with the new leaders' home neighbourhood of 'Mendocita', but one which remains prone to violent clashes and which is accustomed to taking part in gang street-fighting.

The way the fans distribute themselves in the South Stand and the hierarchical use of its space reflect the changes that have occurred. For instance, the centre of the stand is occupied by the old leadership of Comando Sur, that is, its leaders before the rise of the local barras. These are known as 'Los Antiguos' ('The Old Guard') and they have inherited the Alianza Lima tradition and still hold symbolic power; they are the ones who decide what chants are to be sung by the entire body of Alianza Lima fans in the South Stand. They are also the ones who bring the bass drum to the stadium and beat out the rhythm of the chanting. The Antiguos are a handful of adults who allow no one to occupy the central space in the stand around which they form a kind of human wall. The only ones they will permit in this place are the youth leaders of Barraca Rebelde.

There seems to be a pact between these two factions. The Antiguos retain symbolic power, which nobody questions, but have relinquished control over the organisation of the local barras. In exchange, they are granted security against possible attack from another barrio or neighbourhood faction. The leaders of Barraca Rebelde, for their part, are in charge of organising the fans, have a monopoly on the free tickets, and direct any violence that occurs in the stands and streets around the stadium. Local barras appear spontaneously, adopting gang-type organisational structures and codes. They arrive at the stadium carrying their banners and identifying themselves as fighters from a barrio or neighbourhood whose loyalty to a given football club, as we shall see later, they themselves have built up.

Football and violence

We believe that there has been a transfer of names, forms, symbols, teachings and emblems from the political violence that gripped the country in the 1980s and early 1990s to other social and cultural practices, included among which are the behaviour and iconography of young barristas. We suggest that what is involved is not a transfer of ideological or political beliefs but, above all, of forms, symbols and modes of behaviour.

The names of the various local barras supporting the leading football teams in the country, which are seen as the local battalions of a supporters' army, seem clearly rooted in the experience of political violence. On the one hand, in the case of Alianza Lima, the general army is Comando Sur and its principal battalions include Barraca Rebelde (La Victoria district), Guerrilla (Breña district), Artillería Sur (San Juan de Lurigancho district), Rebeldes (Comas district), Cabezas Azules (San Martín de Porras district), Radicales (Independencia district), Genocidas (Breña district), Sicarios (Villa el Salvador district), Malditos (Surquillo district), Apocalipsis (Rímac district), La Coalición (Magdalena district), Pueblo Grone (Pueblo Libre district), La Calle (Los Olivos district), Infierno (Vitarte district), El Cartel (San Borja district), Los Cardenales (Santa Anita district). On the other hand, in the case of Universitario de Deportes, its army is Trinchera Norte, and its main local battalions include Holocausto (Rímac district), La Turba (Magdalena district), La Tropa (San Juan de Lurigancho district), Artillería (La Molina district), Falange (San Martín de Porres district), Saigón (Vitarte district), La Brigada (Surco district), Agustinorte (El Agustino district), La Causa (San Borja district), Los Fugitivos (Independencia district), Chicago Chico (Surquillo district).

The symbolic transfer of political violence to social violence associated with football is filtered through the hard life experienced by the young people actively involved in that violence. Their lives are not only tinged by the fact that they engage in a daily struggle to survive in conditions of acute need, but also by constant confrontations with other local gangs with whom they dispute control of a territory, together with a 'street' prestige founded on the exercise of violence. With respect to symbols, the leaders of two recently founded local barras, Los Pistachos of San Martín de Porras district and Lealtad ('Loyalty') in San Juan de Lurigancho district, both use images in their club emblems borrowed from the political iconography of armed subversive groups of the radical left. For these leaders, this iconography is not synonymous with ideological adherence but is representative of the level of violence of which they, too, are capable; above all, however, it is a symbol of discontent.

Another group of barristas from Barraca Rebelde indicated in interviews with us that, among their role models, were the revolutionary leaders Che Guevara and Fidel Castro, with whom they identified most for their use of violence as a legitimate means for accomplishing their ends (Panfichi and Thieroldt, 1998). In other words, there is a positive appreciation of the use of force when, according to them, there is no other alternative, particularly when violence is one of the few weapons that these youths have in their arsenal for achieving their objectives.

The same applies to the chants, slogans and conversations of football fans. In an interesting article, Chueca analysed conversations he recorded with members of Comando Sur and narrowed their subject matter down to four basic issues: war, crime, catastrophe and territoriality. Chueca suggests that these tales constitute a verbal 'mirror' (or what we may term a 'representation') of society in which the main actors of the national unrest are present. Clearly it is a partial and fragmented representation of society, but it is the one used by a group of youths and adolescents who, generally speaking, are excluded from mechanisms of social integration and who resort to violence to make themselves heard individually and collectively (Chueca, 1998).

The criteria governing status and seniority within barras also reveal the impact of the political violence of the 1980s and early 1990s. For instance, the top positions are no longer held by the 'old guard' or 'traditional' adult leaders and cronies of club directors, but by new young leaders born on the hard streets of depressed barrios who have risen to their positions of leadership based on the ability they have shown in physical confrontation or 'warring' with 'enemies', whether these be other fan clubs or the police.

'Warring' is a constant activity for barristas, a characteristic of the street-gang ways they have adopted. These are group confrontations in which the combatants throw rocks, sticks, and Molotov cocktails at each other. Both sides employ army infantry tactics, doubtless picked up during their military service, such as how to divide into groups and attack in scissors-formation, lay ambushes, send in reinforcements, barricade streets, storm buildings and block off roads and avenues to cut off the enemy. Such attacks are not spontaneous outbreaks of violence but involve a great deal of preparation; requests are sent out to other barristas or groups of neighbours for backup and even firearms are used on occasions.

Warring has turned into something necessary and inevitable for these youths and there is a whole mystique associated with it that gives them excitement and a sense of prestige. Confrontations tend to take place between barras or local groups of youths who may or may not support the same team or be from the same district. The leader is always at the head and the rest try to ensure that he does not fall into enemy hands. They must also protect their banners and shirts, which denote their affiliation. Every local barra makes its own t-shirt, displaying the name of the group, the district from which they come and emblems and slogans avowing their wholehearted, passionate commitment to the football team they support and of which they consider themselves warriors.

Warring has become a way of life, a kind of survival requirement which is associated with a craving for intense excitement, since the latent threat of attack and defence is ever-present. Warring has also become a rite of passage for testing the courage of barras members (leaders and followers alike) and their loyalty to the team, their leaders, and their barrios. Conflicts generally stem from a combination of causes. Thus, for instance, old neighbourhood enmities and disputes become mixed up with the violence generated by loyalty to a particular football team and manifest themselves in gang fighting. We were able to group the causes of these conflicts into three categories.

First, there may be old rivalries with other barrios in the same district, the history of which is so old that even the barristas do not know their origin. Such confrontation has simply always been there as they grew up and for them it is normal that they should participate. Moreover they feel it is an obligation they cannot avoid since their 'turf' is under threat. Second, struggles may take place between local barras for domination in the stands, something they refer to as a 'fan matter' (*cuestión de grupos*), where the prestige of leading the fans, the monopoly on free tickets, and control over street violence are at stake. The fans themselves use the analogy of an orchestra conductor, the aim being to try 'to grab the baton' (*chapar la batuta*), which in street slang means to take control of a situation and direct the others. And third, confrontations may occur between fans of opposing teams, where the idea is to see which side can yell louder, filling the stadium with their chants and songs, and to defend their banners, shirts and friends. We should stress that it is the first of these three kinds of confrontations – that is, confrontations involving old rivalries with other barrios in the same district – which least concern the barras and they are also the least frequent. They occur only if a local enemy injures one of their number or represents an imminent threat, in which case an attack is organised to undermine their reputation as a strong group and to prevent them from getting stronger.

Warring among the fans divides Lima according to football club affiliations into 'grone' (an anagram of 'negro', the Spanish word for 'black', in reference to Alianza Lima) and 'crema' (cream, in reference to the colour of the Universitario jersey) neighbourhoods.[1] In addition, certain areas are said to be in dispute, while others are recognised as being more neutral. Fans imagine their colours and club loyalties as extending over the entire neighbourhood or district. 'Turf' loyalty is a crucially important element in this process. Neighbours and locals in general are expected to defend the neighbourhood when another neighbourhood attacks, regardless of whether the football team they support differs from that of the majority.

This was the case in the 'Mendocita' barrio in La Victoria district, the headquarters of the Barraca Rebelde faction, where, in time of crisis, the leaders can rely on the armed support of a certain hardened criminal famous for his involvement in acts of violence when his barrio comes under attack, in spite of the fact that he personally supports the team Barraca consider their historic enemy. Espinosa observed the same phenomenon in an attack carried out by La Coalición, an Alianza Lima local barra of Magdalena district, on 'La Huaca', the barrio of La Turba, a Universitario local barra of the same district. During the confrontation, La Coalición took the headquarters of La Turba, who called on the aid of a former boxer and well-known criminal, even though he is a widely acknowledged supporter of Alianza Lima.

The peculiar thing about football hooliganism in Peru is this twin process of exchange between gang-related violence and football loyalties built up in an imaginary fashion. Behind the violence of the warring between fans is the defence not only of an identity but also of the prestige founded on the strength and security of one's home neighbourhood. Neighbours and parents who have nothing at all to do with sports-related violence usually become involved in the defence of their territories, since, generally speaking, at stake are their houses, possessions, women and children and not just loyalty to a football team.

In addition to street-fighting prowess, the leaders of local barras must also be able to establish and maintain their roles as intermediaries between the club and the body of fans. The object of this is to obtain certain benefits, such as free or cheap tickets and financial support for travelling around the country to support the team. Leaders are only known by their nicknames as a way of withholding their identities at all times, especially where the police or the media are concerned. Anyone daring to commit an indiscretion can expect a physical reprimand. It is important for leaders to have the backing of their followers and neighbourhood, these being the only ready resources at their disposal. It would seem that, for these youths of limited (economic and social) means and job opportunities, having the monopoly on tickets and managing supporters' funds provides a temporary source of considerable income which they defend in the same way as they obtained it: using violence learned on the streets.

The barristas

Who are these youths that form the barras bravas? According to reports prepared by the Peruvian police, they come from the social sectors with the highest rates of slum housing conditions and poverty in the city of Lima (Policia Nacional del Peru, 1996a). In the opinion of the police, these conditions, combined with broken family backgrounds, explain the frustration and resentment that, the police say, barristas feel towards society. This resentment is allegedly the reason for the vandalistic behaviour of fans. As a result, almost all the complaints filed with the police refer to damage to property that symbolises social division: cars, windows of houses and smarter shops, and jewellery and the stealing of wallets.

Another police report presents the family backgrounds and psychological profiles of a group of 40 barristas arrested after a confrontation between rival fans outside the National Stadium in October 1996. This report indicated that the hooligans had many siblings. For example, of the 40 barristas, ten per cent said they had ten siblings, 30 per cent had between six and nine, and 25 per cent had five. The data show that youths come from large, poor families and, consequently, had few possessions and resources. According to the same report, the fans were also highly aggressive, a trait internalised in their family and neighbourhood environments, where they use aggression to survive. It is interesting that these youths showed themselves to be extremely mutually supportive within the circle of fans, but indifferent to the rest of the world. It was also found that they had little or no feelings of guilt as individuals since their actions are committed collectively. As a result, they took the view that either they were all guilty or none of them were (Policia Nacional del Peru, 1996b).

The survey showed that these youths did not eat at regular times, which was associated with irregularity in their bodily functions and sleeping patterns. This leads us to believe that these youths live in a constant state of bewilderment and struggle for survival, a situation that apparently prevents most of them from planning their activities or organising basic routines and regular habits. The lack of a basic routine is one of several factors that explains the high school drop-out rate among the barristas who were arrested, most of whom had finished primary school but failed to complete their secondary education.

This report also confirmed what we found in our interviews with leaders of Barraca Rebelde in terms of the high respect that these youths have for traits and behaviour generally associated with the criminal or underworld culture. It is true that, mixed in with this, is their admiration for charitable figures like Mother Teresa of Calcutta, and for revolutionary characters like Che Guevara, Fidel Castro and Nelson Mandela. For the most part, though, these young barristas are strongly drawn to anti-heroes or criminals they know in their neighbourhoods or the immediate vicinity. For example, 'Tío Ñeco' ('Uncle Ñeco') is a figure respected by the members of La Turba because he was the leader of his cellblock in prison. The same is true of 'Tío Champán' and the Demencia faction, and of 'Tio Tribilin' and Barraca Rebelde. The exact role that these individuals play in the way local barras function is a subject for further research.

The questions that still remain are: where do these youths come from? And why are they attracted to these collective forms of organisation and behaviour?

One exceptionally valuable source of information is a survey of the most active Alianza Lima local fan clubs conducted by the leaders of those clubs in 1998. This revealed that not all the fan clubs go to the stadium; those who do go are those with the resources to get there. The majority of poorer local barras stay in their barrios to watch the game on television or listen to it on the radio, after which they go out into the streets to fight with rival local barras. A look at the districts from which they come shows that 60 per cent of the fans come from depressed areas in Lima's 'Northern Cone' and 30 per cent from the Peruvian capital's oldest inner city districts (slums). According to Peru's

National Statistics Institute, the Northern Cone has the highest concentration of deprived households in Lima (34.7 per cent), while the inner-city districts are home to 12 per cent of Lima's poor population.[2] Based on the information available to date it would be accurate to say that these areas of Lima (Northern Cone and inner city) are where the violence involving neighbourhood gangs has become intensely mixed up with antagonistic football club loyalties.

The recent ethnographic studies and empirical evidence to which we have access indicate that the militant hardcore of the local barras is composed of male youths and adolescents under the age of 20 who have left school, are unemployed, and come from deprived homes characterised by urgent material need and serious domestic strife. Many youngsters go, or are pushed, out into the street to 'make a living' for themselves; in other words to face a daily existence plagued by obstacles, uncertainty and unknown 'enemies' all around. These youngsters have no personal recourse to fall back on other than the violence they have picked up at home, at school, in their barrios and from football barristas. This paucity of resources, combined with the fact that their experience of the world is overwhelmingly confined to the local sphere, leads them to perceive other neighbourhoods or territories as potential threats and enemies. Like their English counterparts (hooligans) (Dunning et al., 1986a, 1986b, 1986c), these young barristas feel secure only in the company of their peers or people they have known all their lives. This is especially true when they feel that their power is strongest as a group warring with enemy barras.

However, football-related violence in Peru has a strong sense of symbolism, of the theatrical, of putting on a performance and of representation. Although an exhaustive review of newspapers between 1994 and 1998 revealed that violence associated with football has directly or indirectly cost nearly twenty people their lives, it should be noted that unlike some groups of hooligans in Argentina, Peruvian fan clubs do not offer their services as hired muscle in local disputes. The important thing for these youths is to jump around, shout, throw stones, scaring their elders and trying to appear as bad as possible. It is all the better if the television cameras are there, enabling them to emerge from their anonymity and invade the homes of millions of viewers. The aim of this behaviour is to proclaim their 'manhood', in other words to construct an image of aggressive, radical masculinity.

According to a study commissioned by the Professional Football Sporting Association (ADFP), the body that groups together Peru's leading football clubs, violence in and around the stadia is one of the reasons for the decline in crowd attendance. It is not, however, the main reason, which is the standard of football and the convenience of being able to watch a game in comfort at home (APOYO, 1996). The violent symbolism and verbal expressions that the fans aim at the other side – and occasionally at their own – are not seen by spectators as a problem since stadia are considered spaces where giving vent to one's emotions and fury is acceptable. However, the violence outside the stadium, the looting and rioting, is regarded as a problem. That said, a household survey on victimisation conducted by the National Statistics Institute in 1998 found that youth gangs are responsible for 12.3 per cent of the robberies reported to police in the city of Lima, compared to the barely significant 0.6 per cent recorded for local barras *per se.*[3]

In conclusion, we should like to say that, like their counterparts in neighbouring countries such as Chile, Peruvian barras bravas are forms of local youth organisation that use football to provide a common identity and objectives to groups of young people who are otherwise excluded from the benefits of the mainstream economic and social system (Metifogo and Martinez, 1996). With such organisations, these youths are no longer dispersed and isolated in small groups involved in vandalism and theft, but instead build up emotional ties of identification with youths living in other neighbourhoods, cities and regions of the country, thus forming broad networks of local fan clubs and groups.

Another singular thing about football-related violence in Peru is the transfer of symbols and contents that occurs from neighbourhood streets to football grounds and vice versa. The key players in this transfer are the thousands of deprived young fan club members. Reflected in this process is the violence experienced both in the brutal struggle to survive and in years of political violence and terrorism. Peruvian barristas have borrowed styles and emblems from this political violence without adopting the rhetoric or ideology associated with it. Finally, while football appeals to all social groups in Peru, the most active members of the barras bravas do not reflect the entire class range in this country. Nor do they come from a specific organised or self-identified social group, such as the working class in England. Instead, these youths come from the most impoverished and marginalised sectors of the urban economy, those who are excluded from most educational and employment opportunities and other potential avenues of social mobility. Their main identities, therefore, lie precisely in their neighbourhoods or barrios, and in their football clubs.

Chapter 12

Violent disturbances in Portuguese football

Salomé Marivoet

Introduction

The central object of this chapter is to use the theoretical framework developed by Eric Dunning for the understanding of football hooliganism in order to examine the pattern of football-related violence in Portugal. I shall focus in particular on the specificity of violence in Portuguese football. I shall also outline the control and preventive measures developed by the Portuguese government.

A major source of data for this chapter consists of police statistics, published annually since 1978, relating to violent incidents in sport. Newspaper reports of football-related violence have been used as an additional source of information. I also draw upon data published by the Instituto do Desporto (1993) as part of a comparative multinational investigation into hooliganism in football, carried out by the European Council. The purpose of this multinational investigation was to identify the specific character of football hooliganism in each member state. Finally, I have drawn upon (i) data gathered from participant observation of the fan groups associated with the major clubs in the Premier League; and (ii) information obtained by interviewing the leaders of these groups.

Violence in football as a worldwide social problem

In many areas of social life, we are currently witnessing a process of globalisation. Sport in general, and football in particular, are areas in which, throughout the twentieth century, these transnational, intercontinental and worldwide processes have been evident.

As Norbert Elias and Eric Dunning (1992) have pointed out, the socio-genesis of modern sport can be traced to British society in the eighteenth and nineteenth centuries. The diffusion of sports from Britain to the rest of the world in the second half of the nineteenth and first half of the twentieth centuries arose from people in many countries developing leisure needs in that period comparable to those which had developed earlier in Britain and which had contributed to the sociogenesis of sport. To understand patterns of sport in different countries, it is necessary to locate these patterns within the context of broader civilising processes, while at the same time recognising the specificity of the culture, economics, traditions and socio-political patterns of each individual country.

If hooliganism in sports, and particularly in football, is indeed a worldwide phenomenon, then a general theoretical framework is needed, which allows us to identify aspects of the phenomenon that are shared cross-culturally, but which also allows us to focus on the particularities of any given country.

Dunning's essay on soccer hooliganism as a world social problem (Dunning 1999: 130–58) offers a useful framework for understanding the phenomenon of violence in Portuguese football. Nonetheless, there are certain details of that framework which do not apply to the Portuguese situation. More specifically, there are differences in three particulars from the theoretical framework outlined by Dunning.

i) The youth groups which support football teams in Portugal are formally organised and institutionalised. They are known as 'claques'. However, although they engage in various forms of violence, they do not have a predisposition for engaging in organised and pre-meditated fighting in football contexts. It should also be noted that Portuguese football supporters in general go to matches to share in the pleasurable excitement that is generated but, even though they are in an environment where a general lowering of self-controls takes place, most supporters do not mix with the youths who belong to the fan groups.

ii) Given the importance of football in the Portuguese cultural context where the affirmation of regional and sub-cultural identities is at stake, emotional involvement and the affective consequences of defeat are experienced by a large majority of supporters, regardless of differences of social background and educational level.

iii) Although there is a traditional code of masculinity in Portuguese culture in which fighting under specific conditions becomes a question of honour, the social and political conditions of Portuguese society in recent years have led to cultural restrictions on resorting to violence for pleasure, and these restrictions have been a determining factor in the socialisation of the male supporters who go to Portuguese football stadia today.[1] The following social and political conditions have been of central importance: a dictatorial régime which lasted for 45 years; a colonial war that for 14 years (1961–74) meant that Portuguese youth were drafted into the army; the weight of the

Catholic religion; the experience of democracy for 25 years but with strong memories of the dictatorial past; and a slow rate of industrialisation compared with other West European countries.

Running counter to these factors, however, a pleasure in fighting and enjoyment of the excitement of confrontation can be detected in some strata of the younger generation of Portuguese males (Pais, 1996, Ferreira de Almeida, 1990 and Figueiredo, 1988). That is, faint traces of what in other countries are called 'core football hooligans' can be found in Portugal, too. However, the organised claques have the capacity to control to a significant degree the behaviour of these groups of 'hard men'.

Statistics of football violence

Before the establishment of the democratic regime in Portugal in 1974, violent incidents at football matches received very little coverage in sports periodicals. This lack of data makes it difficult to reconstruct the history of football-related violence in Portugal in detail. However, it is clear that, despite the Government's authoritarian posture, disturbances at football matches did occur with some frequency prior to 1974. One example was an incident in the Benfica–Belenenses derby match at Luz Stadium in Lisbon on 25 January 1970. The sending-off of a Benfica player, followed by a second sending-off after 43 minutes of the match, unleashed the anger of Benfica supporters, about two to three thousand of whom invaded the pitch with the intention of attacking the referee. The referee took refuge in the showers and suspended the match. Two Belenenses players and some police officers were severely injured while trying to stop the crowd and were taken to hospital. The Benfica players, including the great Portuguese player Eusebio – whose birthday it was and who was reported to have been desolated by the incident – remained on the pitch trying to calm down the supporters.[2] In its front page headline, a sports periodical at the time described the events as 'INCREDIBLE'. The extract below indicates how the incident was seen at the time:

> For a long time, there has been an outcry from those who feel that it is necessary to put a stop to the . . . violence (physical and moral) . . . The notion of sportsmanship is drowned and corrupted by many of our sports managers, coaches, players and supporters, without any . . . effort being made by the supreme authority to put things and men in their place. Nonetheless we refuse to accept, regardless of whether the referee has made a mistake or not, that football pitches should become Roman arenas (*A BOLA*, 26 January 1970).

The nature of this report suggests that similar incidents must have occurred with some frequency. After the establishment of the democratic regime, violent incidents started to make news in the sporting press more regularly. Since 1979, the National Guard (GNR) has published on an annual basis statistics of match-related incidents. In a press statement relating to the first release of these statistics in 1979, a police official argued that:

> There has to be a campaign for the civic training of referees and especially coaches, so that they can dissuade players and managers from making matters worse . . . in order to stop sport from becoming a battlefield. Despite the financial difficulties facing our country, funds are necessary for this training (*ANOP*, 20 July 79).

From the 1980s, with increasing media coverage of violent incidents occurring during the football season, the theme of football-related violence became commonplace. References to attacks on referees were not uncommon. This is illustrated by the following declaration made by a referee to the newspaper *Diario de Notícias* (14 April 1981): 'The closer we get to the end of the football season, the more serious the problems become'. This would seem to suggest that issues of promotion and relegation coming to a climax may have been a spur to crowd troubles.

The following extract from another newspaper article published just one week later illustrates the problems which could by faced by referees who, as the article indicates, could be subject to violence from several different quarters:

> 'If you show a yellow card, I'll bash your face'; was a threat made by an Amiense player. The referee reprimanded the player by showing him the card and immediately was surrounded by players and beaten up. After the referee had withdrawn to the showers and suspended the match, the club manager threatened to kill him. Fearing the consequences, he restarted the match. . . . The score was a 2–all draw. The worst came at the end of the match when he was beaten up by a crowd of about a hundred people, which resulted in him sustaining a fractured leg and a bruised eye (*Portugal Hoje*, 24 April 1981).

Data on football-related violence for the period from 1978–79 to 1986–87 are shown in table 1. The sharpest increase in the number of matches in which violent incidents occurred came in the period 1978–79 to 1981–82. During the latter season, incidents were recorded at 30 per cent of all matches played.

The most serious incident recorded during this period occurred in the Luz Stadium in Lisbon in May 1981 when, following police intervention, a hundred fans were injured, one critically. A great deal of controversy surrounded the causes of and responsibility for the violence that took place. The police claimed that the manager of one of the clubs had asked for police intervention

Table 1 **Football matches with violent incidents**

Football Season	Matches with incidents	Total number of matches	(%)
1978–79	462	3329	14
1979–80	506	3092	16
1980–81	676	3292	21
1981–82	1007	3340	30
1982–83	623	3403	18
1983–84	912	3382	27
1984–85	700	3381	21
1985–86	686	3694	19
1986–87	726	3702	20
Total	6299	30615	21

Source: Marivoet (1989)

to disperse fans from the pitch. The manager in question, however, denied making any such request and the football club issued a press release rejecting any responsibility for the 'brutality exerted by the police' (Diário de Lisboa, 29 May 1981).

As the data in table 1 indicate, the number of matches at which violent incidents were recorded decreased after the 1981–82 season. This decrease may have been related to government legislative and other action designed to punish, control and prevent violence in sports, especially football.[3]

The GNR reports included data on types of violence and the different parties involved in violent incidents at sports events. These are illustrated in table 2.

Table 2 **Missiles thrown and aggression directed at:**

Referees	32%
Police	18%
Managers	5%
Players	12%
The public	33%

Source: Report from GNR (1978 to 1986)

Referees are the major targets. They may be targets of violence by fans, by players and by managers. In 1984, Portuguese referees went on strike in order to draw the attention of the football authorities to the frequency of these attacks and the seriousness of the situation.

After 1987, when the Portuguese government signed the 1985 European Convention on Spectator Violence and Misbehaviour at Sports Events and in particular at Football Matches, new legal measures were introduced in order to try to prevent and control violence at sporting venues. These measures included stronger policing and more severe sentences for violent offenders.

Since 1987, the Public Security Police (PSP) have produced annual reports containing statistics of violent incidents occurring during matches at which the police were present. For the period since 1987, therefore, information has been available from both police forces (the GNR and the PSP), making it possible to analyse in more detail the phenomenon of sport-related, and more specifically football-related, violence in Portugal.

Data relating to the number of sports events at which incidents of violence were recorded during the period 1987 to 1998 are shown in graph 1. These data indicate that there was a general decrease in the number of events at which violent incidents occurred between 1987 and 1993, though increases were recorded in 1990 and, more significantly, in 1992. From 1993, there has been a general increase in the number of sporting events at which violent incidents were recorded, though there was a decrease in 1996. It should also be noted that, although the number of sporting events at which violence has occurred has tended to increase since 1993, the number of such events recorded annually since 1993 has generally been lower than the number recorded annually from 1987 to 1992.

Graph 1 **Sports events with incidents of violence**

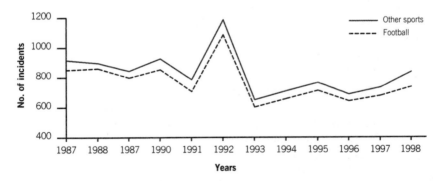

Source: Reports from the Police Forces: PSP and GNR

Football matches accounted for 92 per cent of all the violent incidents which occurred in sport between 1987 and 1998, with just eight per cent of violent incidents occurring in other types of sports.[4] District league matches accounted for more violent incidents (55 per cent of recorded incidents) than did national league matches (45 per cent) over this period.

In policed events in all sports in Portugal between 1994 and 1998, incidents took place at only 1.35 per cent of events, and in these cases there was an average of two incidents per event. Although these statistics provide some indication of the number of violent incidents reported in Portugal in that period, they give no indication of the seriousness of the incidents which occurred. For example, it is possible that at football matches with large crowds, larger numbers of people may have been involved in the reported incidents than at matches where there were smaller crowds.

The police data also indicate that many incidents are related to the match itself (table 3). That is, 44 per cent of incidents appear to relate to fans' reactions to events in the match, while 18 per cent of incidents take place on or close to the pitch itself. The data also reveal that referees are the most common targets, accounting for about 34 per cent of the recorded incidents. Moreover, 312 referees' cars and other vehicles were damaged between 1987 and 1998.

Table 3 **Types and locations of violent incidents reported by the police (1987–98)**

	% & N
On the pitch	*18%*
	N=3642
Among players	3
Among players and referees	2
Provoked by referees	0.37
Provoked by managers	4
Provoked by players	8
Spectators	*24%*
	N=4874
Among the Public	24
Arrests	0.48
Fan reactions to match incidents	*44%*
	N=8788
Attacks on referees	30
Damage done to referees' vehicles	2
Attacks on players	2
Attacks on clubs/managers	3
Pitch invasions	7
Missiles thrown and damage caused	*11%*
	N=2113
Attacks on and insults/ injuries to the police	*3%*
	N=669
Total	*100%*
	N=20086

Source: Reports from Public Security Police (PSP) and the National Guard (GNR).

Analysis of the social background of offenders arrested by the police in connection with football-related violence between 1987 and 1992 (the only period for which we have systematic information) indicates that 96 per cent are in employment, the bulk of them being employed in working-class occupations (see table 4).

Table 4 **The socio-professional profile of offenders arrested by the police (1987–92)**

Professions	(%)
Farmers and fishermen	2
Unskilled manual workers	34
Skilled manual workers	33
White collar workers	7
Highly qualified technicians and management	11
Entrepreneurs	8
Students	1
Inactive (unemployed, retired and housewives)	4
Total	100
	N=142

Between 1987 and 1993, then, there was a general decline in the number of matches at which violent incidents occurred though there were two years – 1990 and 1992 – in which increases were recorded. The increase in 1990 consisted largely of an increase in the number of pitch invasions. 1992 saw the highest number of matches at which violence was recorded in any one year. There was an increase in 1992 in all forms of violence, including an increase of 60 per cent in the number of pitch invasions and a 47 per cent increase compared with 1991 in violence among spectators.

Of the many incidents recorded by the Portuguese police in the 1990s, four stand out because of the seriousness of the violence involved. As a result of these incidents, hundreds of people were injured and four killed. These four more violent incidents are discussed in greater detail below.

i) In 1990, a particularly violent conflict between supporters of SC Farense and FC Porto received extensive media coverage and gave rise to an official inquiry. Tension between clubs from the North and the South of the country provided the background to the conflict. When the referee showed a yellow card to a Farense player, the club's supporters reacted by throwing a bottle which hit and injured the referee. The game continued in an atmosphere of great tension, with missiles being thrown onto the pitch, especially at members of the FC Porto coaching staff. The tension reached a climax at the end of the game when, outside the ground, the Farense

supporters were preparing to attack the referee and the players of FC
Porto. The police dispersed the crowd by using CS gas and firing at them.
They shot two supporters and a child, who needed to be hospitalised,
though their lives were never in danger. The police had to take action
again when a dozen Farense supporters, angered by the coverage of the
event by the RTP television channel, stoned the TV Station. The confrontation between the police and the supporters came to a halt only with the
intervention of the Mayor of Faro.

Among the preventive measures proposed by the official inquiry into
the event was the reinforcement of policing at matches considered to be of
high risk and the promotion of a violence prevention campaign in sport by
the 'National Commission for Co-ordination and Control of Violence in
Sports' (CNCF). This campaign, which was launched the following year,
was called '1991: The Year of Sports Ethics' and sub-titled 'Fair-play in
Sports' and 'No Doping'(Marivoet, 1992a).[5]

ii) In 1995, in the match between Sporting and FC Porto, a group of Sporting
fans were heading towards the players' entrance used by the away team
with the intention of shouting abuse at them when a metal fence on the
outer part of the stadium gave way. The fans fell down a five metre drop
and two young fans were killed.

iii) In the same year, in the match between V Guimarães and FC Porto, two
fan groups – the 'Insane Guys' of V Guimarães and the Super Dragões
('Super Dragons') and Dragões Azuis ('Blue Dragons') of FC Porto – were
involved in a confrontation with each other and with the police as a result
of which one police officer was killed and forty other people were injured,
three critically. Following the incident, the club managers held a press
conference in which they stressed that it was not fans in general, but only
a minority, who engaged in such acts of violence. They also strongly
criticised the media for defaming the 'people' of the North and for fanning
the traditional rivalry between the North and South, which is very strong
in Portuguese football.

iv) In the 1996 Portuguese Cup Final between Benfica and Sporting, a Sporting
supporter was killed by a distress rocket which had been launched from
the sector where the Benfica fan groups, the 'No-Name Boys' and the
Diabos Vermelho (Red Devils), were sitting. The rocket, which had been
launched to celebrate Benfica's first goal, flew across the stadium and hit a
Sporting supporter sitting in the opposite sector. The person who launched
the rocket was arrested but, following an investigation, it was concluded
that the death had been accidental. Attention was focused upon the lack
of security at the stadium, especially the fact that fans had not been searched
for dangerous or offensive objects before entering. As a result, the Portuguese
government reinforced the security measures at stadia, particularly by
tightening controls at entrances.[6]

The claques movement

Since 1976, some young members of the four big football clubs in Portugal have started watching matches in specifically created members-only areas of the stadium.[7] This development started with the supporters of Sporting Lisbon. A group of youngsters from São Jõao de Brito College came up with the idea, and started sitting together at matches. According to some of those involved in the claques, a major influence on this movement came from some college students who had returned from Brazil after having spent some time there because of the socio-political events of 1974. This point was emphasised by the Vice-President of the Fan Group Federation, whom we interviewed as part of our research into fan groups in 1989–90 (all quotations in this section are taken from this research, which is reported in full in Marivoet, 1992b). He said:

> I guarantee that the Sporting claques are based on the ideas of the Brazilian claques. That was the idea . . . the smoke we used, face powder, talcum powder and flour, the bamboo flags . . .

In the same study, other people who were involved in the claques recalled their reasons for forming or joining the claques. A young member of the management of the Juve-Leo (Sporting) claque recalled:

> What made us join . . . First of all we liked Sporting a lot, we were members of Sporting, we started going to football matches. I saw the Juve Leo members all together . . . I used to go either with my father or my uncle and I'd say 'I don't like being here'. My father was always quiet and over there were people of my own age. Over there it was 'cool' . . . the show was good. Like young people every-where, they needed to release their energy.

A young member of the Dragões Azuis fan group recalled how the claque had been formed:

> We were a group of individuals who always came to the matches . . . One brought a flag, the other a scarf . . . as we were always at the matches we got talking . . .until we reached a point of discussing the possibility of a fan group . . . of getting together and forming a claque.

Similarly a young member of Furia Azul recalled how he had helped to establish that fan club:

> We knew each other from school, the neighbourhood and . . . from going to matches every Sunday. I was one of the founders. My aim was to make the claque

official and to get more than fifty members, to make it an official thing so everybody knew of our existence.

In the early 1980s, in a second phase in the development of the movement, fan groups campaigned for official recognition by the clubs. Some of the young people in the fan groups had family ties with club managers and this facilitated the recognition of the fan groups and also helped to develop a greater awareness of their existence. During 1982, fan groups from the four major Portuguese clubs – Juventude Leonina (Sporting), Diabos Vermelhos (Benfica), Dragões Azuis (FC Porto) and Panteras Negras (Boavista) – gained official recognition from the clubs. The strong bond between fan groups and the management of the respective clubs led to the active participation of fan groups in political decision making within the clubs. Candidates running for office within the football clubs sometimes promised that, in the event of their being elected, they would give their support to the fan groups. However, these promises were not always kept, leaving some members of fan groups feeling disappointed and cheated, as the following young member of a fan group explained:

> In the elections and during the campaign period, we were given support, vans, even tickets. We didn't have to pay for anything . . . Afterwards, after winning the elections, they'd stop delivering support. I think they used us quite a bit.

These fan groups continued to grow in the 1980s. Groups already in existence increased their membership while new groups emerged and groups multiplied within individual clubs. The appearance of splinter groups baffled the management of the clubs, and also forced them into choosing which of these groups they should continue to support. This scenario became even more complicated as conflicts developed between these groups and the members in the surrounding stands who had different ways of relating to the club and of watching football. This led the fan groups to demand from the club manage-ment that they be allocated their own space in the grounds, away from the other fans. As a member of a fan group expressed it during our fieldwork in 1990:

> They have to find a way of separating the claque members from other fans. They [other fans] want to be comfortably seated but the claque has to make a noise . . . they don't like us cheering . . . they are seated next to us, then we get up and they don't like it . . . They start moaning and the claque members defend each other.

Faced with these events but not always understanding the processes at work behind them, the managements of the clubs tried to control their fan groups more rigorously. This process gave rise to the third phase of the

Portuguese fan group movement, a phase which was not unrelated to the impact in Portugal of the Heysel Stadium disaster in Brussels in 1985.

This provides the context for understanding the actions taken by the management of clubs in relation to their fan groups. Some managed to tighten their control of their groups by changing the leadership or by reducing their autonomy; this was the case with Juventude Bracarense of Clube Sporting de Braga during the 1986–87 season and with the Dragões Azuis of FC Porto and the Panteras Negras of Boavista FC in the following season. In some cases, the fan groups refused to accept this demand for increased control by the clubs, resulting in disagreement with the club, and a consequent loss of support and official recognition from it. Examples include the VIII Exército and Juventude Vitoriana of Vitória de Setúbal, two claques which were founded in 1986 and which continued without the support and official recognition of the club. In two other cases – those of the Diablos Vermelhos of SL Benfica and the Fúria Azul of Belenenses FC – relationships between the fan clubs and the management of the football clubs were ruptured following violent incidents

In the case of the Diablos Vermelhos, the breakdown in relationships with the club followed violence during a Cup semi-final. One of the young claque members we interviewed in 1990 explained the context of this breakdown in relationships:

> The elections [for positions in the football club] came and a candidate promised to support us. We campaigned for him. For a month everything was fine. We got in free. They promised us free tickets for the Cup semi-final but they kept us waiting three hours . . . and then told us they didn't have any tickets. We all saved money to buy the tickets and as revenge . . . we threw fire torches onto the pitch. We threw these because we were angry and then some violence occurred. We were angry with all that. They decided not to withdraw their support, so they gave us their support again, but only for a little while.

The difficulties in the relationship between Fúria Azul and Belenenses FC started in the 1988–89 season, when the club's management board tried to prevent the circulation of a claque sticker with a skull symbol and then tried to impose new rules and change the name of the claque. In our research into claques at this time, one young member of Fúria Azul explained the claque's intended use of the skull symbol which sparked off the controversy:

> What happened between the management and us was that, after the elections, we adopted as a symbol not only the cross of Christ but also the skull. We know that it's a bit hostile and it shows a certain aggressiveness which we don't have . . . We had the stickers made for an important match . . . which draws big crowds. The day before the match I went to pick up the stickers. I was told they'd been seized

because they wouldn't let us use the skull symbol. We were suspicious because the fan group's Board of Management had approved it . . . We saw the symbols of other claques, even foreign ones we corresponded with, which were far worse than ours. I don't understand the reaction of the Board [of the club] . . . I'm not sure if the stickers had anything to do with it or not but the Board wanted us to change the name Fúria Azul ('Blue Fury' to Alegria Azul ('Blue Joy') but I think it's completely different.

Sporting CP is the only Premier League club which continues to give support to its autonomously organised fan groups, Juventude Leonina-Juve Leo, Torcida Verde, Onda Verde and Consórcio de Claques Força, Onda e Império Verde.

One indication of the close association between fan groups and the clubs is that the former have often adopted the organisational model of the latter. The formation of a 'National Fan Group Federation', elected in a general assembly in Coimbra in 1989, also indicates the strong links with institutionalised models of the sports system.

Fan groups generally give the impression of being 'tough' and they are sometimes involved in disturbances and acts of aggression and vandalism. However, such violence tends not to be premeditated. Fan group members are aware of what is happening in other countries and may imitate the behaviour of fans in other countries, for example through the symbols or the British names they use. Violence is rarely used or engaged in for its own sake.

In 1990, the sports paper *A BOLA* published an article based on interviews with some young members of fan groups. The article was headed: 'Hooliganism File . . . the Portuguese way'. The published interviews illustrate the spirit of most Portuguese fan groups. They dismiss the gratuitous violence that occurs in other countries, notably England, and claim that the opponents are always the same ones: the 'enemy fan group, the other team and the referee. And, of course, the "coppers"!' The author of the article highlighted the 'tough' image they wanted to project:

the funniest thing was some years ago when these guys from LIVERPOOL came . . . we threw the English down the stands. With the French of 'BERNADETTE' TAPIE it was no fun. 'It was the police who did them over . . .' . . . Alcohol and drugs are ingredients that make up the menu of claques: 'having fun' at a football match, smoking 'joints' and having some drinks. It's so cool, 'that's the way to get a kick out of football' (*A BOLA*, 30 June 1990).

The capacity of group leaders to regulate conflict inside grounds, even with members who are more disposed to violent acts, and their capacity to hold a dialogue with the police about their preparations for the matches, has meant collaboration by, and acceptance of, the fan groups, which consist mainly of young students.

Since 1998, another phase has emerged in the fan group movement. A new law allows clubs to support only those claques that are properly constituted as associations and that register themselves with the Football Federation or the Football League.[8] This law requires information to be kept on members of claques and prohibits the use of symbols or expressions that incite violence, racism or xenophobia. By the 2000–01 season, two claques – Torcida Verde (Sporting) and Mancha Negra (Académica de Coimbra) – had been legally constituted and two others were in the registration phase: Diabos Vermelhos and No-Name Boys (Benfica).

The above measures constitute one aspect of the specificity of the phenomenon in Portuguese society and have contributed to making the claques more responsible for their members' actions. These measures have also facilitated a greater degree of control of fans' behaviour and have helped to prevent confrontations both among members of a single fan group, and between supporters of opposing teams.

In the 1990s, fan groups have developed outside the big city clubs. These new fan groups have come from many different parts of the country. In northern Portugal, recently formed claques include the 'Insane Boys' and the 'White Angels' at Vitória de Guimarães, the Alma Salgueirista at Sport Comércio e Salgueiros and the Mancha Negra at Academia de Coimbra, currently a second division club. In the south, recently formed claques include the 'South Side Boys' at Sporting Clube Farense and, on Madeira, the Templários at Clube Sport Marítimo. In the last decade, many claques have also modelled themselves on the Italian ultra groups and have adopted the festive participative style of supporting characteristic of the Italian groups.

The growing unity of the fan group movement in the last decade is also reflected in the appearance of its own publication, currently called the *Ultras Magazine*, which provides information about 'events' organised by the various national and international fan groups, with its own e-mail address for fans to communicate among themselves. The news items which are most striking are those relating to the choreography used during matches, while there are also many advertisements offering to exchange iconographic material, photographs and videos. The dynamic character of the current situation is also reflected in the development of the fan groups' own publications – the 'Fanzines' – which focus on the activities and affairs relating to their own clubs.

One can thus see the continuation of a process of institutionalisation of the fan group movement in Portugal, a process which is characterised by the fans' assertiveness and their ability to write about themselves, by their consciousness of collective group membership and of themselves as bearers of a tradition of supporting. This is also visible in the way in which they build their choreography in matches, where there has also been a growing tendency to display placards and scarves bearing the date of the foundation of their respective groups.

This movement has now been in existence for some two decades and there is thus among current football spectators a group of adults who acquired their youthful football experiences in a new football culture. This is evident in the way in which fan groups now interact with other supporters in the stadium. There is now a culture of what might be described as 'active participation' in the grounds, with the fan groups acting as catalysts and taking legitimate control of the action, whether this involves choreographed crowd movements, chanting or 'Mexican waves'.

The fan groups for young people now constitute organisations which have a proper constitution and formal recognition from the clubs. In addition, the clubs' managers function as go-betweens in linking the fan groups with the police in preparation for big games where extra security may be required. There is, of course, still a 'tough' image in some fan groups, which is reflected in the ritual use of violent language and in some of their physical actions in the places reserved for them during matches. There is, moreover, still a small number of violent incidents, often aimed at damaging the stands at the end of a match, especially if their own team has lost. In this situation, the police remain vigilant.

Conclusion

When reflecting on the nature of football-related violence in Portugal, there are a number of important points to bear in mind. These include: the characteristics of the reported incidents of violence; the social profile of those involved in these incidents; the specificity of the organisation of the Portuguese claques and their integration with the clubs; and the absence of a predisposition towards premeditated violence as a leitmotif for their experiences and involvement in football. All these points suggest that it may not be entirely appropriate to label those involved in these incidents as 'hooligans'. Nevertheless, incidents of violence in a football context are a reality in Portuguese society, although the level of violence has fluctuated over the years.

We can identify four important characteristics as being specific to football-related violence in Portugal. These are:

i)   the involvement of several different groups in violence. While spectators represent the bulk of those involved in the reported incidents, club managers, players and referees have also been involved.

ii) The institutionalisation of young fan groups associated with major clubs, especially in the Premier League, and the social distance between these fans and older spectators, some of whom may also be involved in incidents of violence

iii) The organisational characteristics of the young fan groups which are associated with major clubs; specifically, the occupation by these young fans of places in the stadia which are reserved for group members and the absence of premeditated violent confrontations with opposing groups of fans.

iv) The predominance of incidents of violence targeted at referees.

It may be argued that the specificity of football-related violence in Portugal suggests: (*a*) that there is a strong emotional involvement of the supporters with their teams; and (*b*) in some cases there is regional rivalry based on the assertion of the distinct cultural identities that exist within Portuguese society. The ways in which these tensions are expressed within the context of football in Portugal may be regarded as an illustration of what Dunning calls 'faction fighting'.

Using Dunning's framework, the pattern of violence in Portuguese football may be seen to be spontaneous and affective. That is to say it is related to the excitement and tension associated with football. This spontaneous and affective violence interconnects with club or territorial rivalries which are strongly experienced by male spectators who are predisposed to the use of physical force to defend their teams, and who have a code of honour which involves the idea of 'taking justice into their own hands'.

The quest for excitement on the part of claque members may involve a variety of activities, from active forms of spectating at the match to confrontation with other fans; as such, it may vary from a 'carnival parody' to explicit aggression or acts of vandalism. Thus, although there are ways in which the leaders are able to some degree to regulate the behaviour of claque members, their behaviour remains in many respects variable and not always predictable.

Chapter 13

The 'black cat' of South African soccer and the Chiefs–Pirates conflict

Cora Burnett

There was a commotion before yesterday's Kaizer Chiefs-Orlando Pirates soccer derby when a black cat was kicked to death on the field at the FNB stadium. A Chiefs' supporter grabbed the luckless cat as it ran along the grandstand and threw it towards the Pirates bench. Boikie Raphela, a security guard, then picked up the animal and kicked and hit it with a stick. Before he was led away, Raphela said the cat was bad muti

The Sunday Times, 11 May 1997.[1]

The incident

When I witnessed the notorious 'black cat incident', I was probably the only white woman in a noisy, excited crowd of 60,000 black, predominantly male supporters. Cheers and shouts of encouragement went up as the cat was propelled to and fro between Chiefs' and Pirates' supporters in the 'grandstand', before landing in front of the 'luckless' security guard who kicked it to death. This incident and the public outcry against the violence it involved as well as the guard's 'uncivilised' behaviour illustrate the existing contrast of values, ranging from approval (by soccer supporters at the game) to condemnation (by the authorities and the media). Some critics condemned the cruelty as reflecting 'the callous, disgusting disregard for life that is fast eradicating the nation's self-respect' (*Metro*, 18 May 1997: 20).

The significance of the 'black cat' incident should also be viewed in terms of its symbolic link to ideas about the supernatural and to the belief system of black soccer supporters. In this regard, it should be noted that ritual, magic and 'muti' are widely believed to play an important role in manipulating 'powers' to bring about a victory.

Although this incident serves as a metaphor for the discussion of soccer-related violence, some other and more tragic incidents will also be discussed to illustrate the seriousness of the phenomenon in Africa and particularly in South Africa. Between 11 April 2001 and 11 May 2001, 194 people were killed at soccer matches in Africa, including 121 people killed at the Accra Stadium in Ghana, one in the Ivory Coast and 29 at Lubumbnashi in the Congo, while at Ellis Park Stadium in Johannesburg, 43 people were killed at a match between two professional teams, Kaizer Chiefs and Orlando Pirates.

To make sense of such incidents, they need to be understood within their broader socio-cultural context. More specifically in South Africa, such violent incidents cannot be understood in isolation but have to be approached in relation to the social, cultural and sports contexts of the rival, predominantly black soccer supporters in South Africa.

South African soccer as a 'black sport'

Soccer in South Africa is known as the 'sport of the people', referring mainly to the black people of that country. The core market of soccer consists of black adults, who account for approximately 86 per cent of the 8.5 million following, which currently shows a rate of increase of four per cent per annum (*Premier Soccer League*, 1997). Soccer is sometimes referred to as their 'second religion'. It is a symbol of unification represented in the collective consciousness of black people who experience empowerment through their identification with powerful soccer clubs, leagues and leaders.

Following the introduction of football to black South Africans by British soldiers during the Anglo-Boer War, separate Bantu, Coloured and Indian Football Associations were established in different provinces early in the twentieth century. The aim of the 'white' ('European') government was to have football organised separately for 'non-Europeans' in order to establish control and 'to eliminate gambling and other objectionable practices' (Thabe, 1983: 5). When the Federation of South African Football Associations was formed in March 1951, the South African Bantu Association (established in 1933) did not join the other three ('White', 'Coloured' and 'Indian') associations and only later accepted a subordinate membership of the white-controlled Football Association of South Africa (FASA). Internal struggles continued after the formation of the National Professional Soccer League in 1964, which functioned against the backdrop of the lack of sponsorship and many social injustices (Thabe, 1983). Breaking away from direct government control, the South African Soccer Federation Professional League (FPL) charted a non-racial course for professional soccer and brought together the disenfranchised groups and in many ways united the marginalised communities (*The Post*, 22

February 1980: 8). Thousands of black people 'took up the armed struggle' in all spheres, negotiating for political power in the broader society through boycotting and opposing so-called 'normal' (interracial and multinational) sport in an 'abnormal' (racially segregated) society' (Bose, 1994).

The polarisation of sport along racial lines created dissent among black supporters who were segregated at soccer matches during the seventies and early eighties. The fact that whites enjoyed exclusive seating away from Indians, Coloureds and Africans who were 'lumped together' caused racial tension and conflict (*The Post*, 22 February 1997: 18). For the multinational soccer tournament of the South African Games held in 1973, when 'white' and 'non-white' teams played officially against each other for the first time, spectators were segregated 'in the normal way' (*The Star*, 16 February 1973: 1). 'Black-on-white' violence became prominent when predominantly 'white' soccer teams, such as Highlands Park, Arcadia Pepsi and Wits University played against their 'black' counterparts (Orlando Pirates, Kaizer Chiefs or Moroka Swallows).

Soccer, race and politics

The conservative 'white press' labelled the occurrence of 'black violence' during the seventies and eighties as proof that multinational sport and 'social integration' were doomed to fail because of the 'permissive' and 'violent nature' of hostile blacks. The police became, for blacks, the symbol of oppression and severe opposition was launched against their 'brutal' methods of crowd control. The use of physical force, guard dogs and a 'sneezer machine' (a police vehicle from which tear gas canisters were fired) aggravated racial tension and black-white violence (*The World*, 27 June 1977: 14). Their presence often triggered racial violence, while *The Sunday Times* (11 November 1979: 21) argued at the time that the police 'serve merely as bottle-throwing targets for the crowd whenever the spectators don't like what the referee does'.

Complaints from whites related mainly to the hooligan element ('tsotsism'), the malicious damage to property and the molestation of whites. Soccer riots were reported vividly, such as the incident where 'knife-wielding soccer fans . . . went on an orgy of window smashing and looting in Umgeni road [near Kings Park Stadium in Durban] after the match' (*The Citizen*, 24 February 1981: 1). The 'soccer riots' were met with strong opposition from whites living in the vicinity of the stadia in Johannesburg (Rand Stadium), Pretoria (Caledonian Stadium) and Durban (Kingsmead Stadium) whose property and security were threatened. They called on local councils to enforce 'discipline' and to 'honour' the Group Areas Act in keeping 'blacks in their own townships'. This coincided with politicians warning against the 'black threat' ('swart gevaar') which, it was claimed, threatened the country's 'internal stability'. White-dominated city councils saw rioting black spectators as a political threat and professional soccer was banned from government-owned stadia in the white suburbs (*Die Afrikaner*, 10 November 1980: 11). Prominent soccer leaders criticised these measures as 'racial discrimination', whereas right-wing leaders interpreted such criticism as propaganda by left-wing black organisations to lobby for international support by isolating South African sport (*The Citizen*, 24 February 1981: 1). This culminated in a 'racial' war between local city councils and black soccer leaders and supporters. *The Post* (22 February 1980: 8) criticised the banning of professional soccer as racist, stating that the dignity of black people had been 'assaulted'. The reporter stated that: 'They [white city councils] knew that any self-respecting black would not go to the stadium until he is sure that he is looked at as a person, a dignified human being, and treated as such at the stadium'.

Black opposition was unanimous, especially from the supporters of professional clubs and communities threatening to boycott the sales of major soccer sponsors and boycotting international ('rebel') soccer tours. The refusal of prominent black professional clubs (Kaizer Chiefs, Orlando Pirates and Moroka Swallows) to play against the 'international mercenaries' was met with widespread black support and 'smug satisfaction' (*The Sunday Times*, 25 July 1982: 30). They sabotaged the government's attempts to demonstrate the success of 'multiracial' soccer and to be accepted again as a member of the international soccer body (FIFA), which expelled them first in 1960, then in 1964 and again in 1976 (*The Star*, 23 July 1982: 17). 'Political football' became the order of the day and soccer became an effective tool and symbol of the struggle against apartheid. After the abolition of apartheid in the nineties and the building of stadia such as 'Soccer City' (First National Bank Stadium) on the periphery of Johannesburg in the eighties, violence shifted 'into' the stadia and changed from being mainly a form of 'resistance' or 'ethnic-related' violence to 'soccer violence' *tout court*.

The multi-faceted face of violence in the context of poverty

The core market of the Premier Soccer League consists of approximately four million black male adults scattered all over the country, most of whom have a working-class background. About 71 per cent of the supporters have a relatively low income or are unemployed according to the Living Standard Monitor Index (*Premier Soccer League*, 1997). This is consistent with earlier research, published in a report entitled *Poverty and Inequality in South Africa* in May 1998, which found that the majority of black South Africans are living below the poverty line with a monthly expenditure of R353 (£32) per adult per month (Sidiropoulos et al., 1997–98: 441). Most black people live in stressful and 'dehumanising' conditions of chronic poverty which are associated with a low educational profile as well as the absence of resources, opportunities for work and socio-political power.[2] Mechanisms to cope with poverty include the formation of social networks and the interdependent functioning of house-holds and social groups, such as same-age peer groups in the form of gangs. These youths are often turned 'out on the street' because of their inability to contribute to household income. Their economic vulnerability causes them to be dependent on their peer group for acceptance, recognition and social belonging (Winfree et al., 1994). The social and psychological security and acceptance experienced in the gang help to compensate both for the rejection they experience in other spheres of their lives and for the extreme physical violence used against them by adults (in the household and school) to coerce them into conforming to societal norms. This socialisation into a 'culture of violence' leads them in turn to use physical violence and intimidation to obtain economic resources and earn prestige among their peers and in the community (Burnett, 1998).

The stratified socio-structural position based on gender (man versus woman) and age groupings (adult versus child), correlates with the degree to which men dominate women and children as well as with the perpetuation of patriarchal ideology. Black men are themselves relatively powerless and subjected to 'structural' violence, for it is the macro-structures of society that have 'caused' their position of relative powerlessness. Their hegemonic position of relative power and domination within their communities is often maintained by the use of force as one of the few 'power sources' left to them. Violence is inclusive, all pervasive and is reflected at all levels, spiralling from macro-structures (such as oppression by the state) to communities, households and individuals. The psychological results of poverty include the erosion of compassion, a sense of marginality and inferiority, vulnerability, insecurity, anxiety, powerlessness and a 'live for the moment' mentality.[3]

Soccer matches present a public stage where men 'fight' for their prestige and that of their team, finding temporary relief from anxiety through physical violence and alcohol abuse without considering the consequences in their quest for excitement and temporary 'empowerment'. Violence expressed by men in the public sphere is status-conferring and invariably linked to their proneness to use violence in circumstances of heightened excitement and intense identification. The interrelatedness and uniqueness of soccer-related violence in the South African context, which has been referred to metaphori-cally as 'the black cat', will be explored further by analysing violent events as well as the behaviour and experiences of soccer supporters.

A research agenda

Violence is manifested in different forms and may be placed on a continuum. Its intensity has to be judged according to the norms of the society in which it occurs. For the purposes of this study, violent acts which occur at soccer events and which are judged by the media, governing bodies and supporters to be 'soccer violence' have been selected for analysis. This includes mainly acts of physical violence which are visible and in a sense measurable, as well as acts of physical injury to people and/or property (vandalism).

In an effort to establish the scope and nature of soccer violence in the South African context, relevant newspaper articles in all the major Afrikaans and English newspapers were studied. These articles covered the period from April 1977 to May 2001 as only a few incidents prior to 1977 could be traced. It is impossible to compile a complete index of soccer-related violence because of under-reporting, the political agendas of editors and the priority given to violence with political implications threatening the stability of communities. For the period specified above, 343 newspaper articles referring to incidents of physical violence that occurred at soccer matches were traced, reporting 180 incidents of soccer violence, 88 per cent of which occurred at professional or first league matches. Soccer violence was reported increasingly in the early eighties (political riots) though there was a significant decrease after 1984; in the period from 1977 to 1984, 77 violent incidents were reported compared with 34 between 1985 and 1992. There was another increase in levels of soccer-related violence after the election in 1994 with a sharp decline in 1999–2001 (see figure 1).

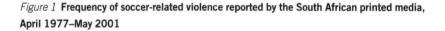

Figure 1 **Frequency of soccer-related violence reported by the South African printed media, April 1977–May 2001**

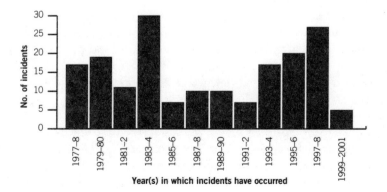

Of the 180 violent incidents reported in the print media from 1977 to 2001, 53 involved the supporters of Kaizer Chiefs and 49 those of Orlando Pirates. However, with the exceptions of three tragic incidents in which soccer supporters were killed (in April 1991, July 2000 and April 2001), there have been very few incidents of soccer-related violence reported by the South African press since October 1998 (*The Sowetan*, 11 July 2000: 2; *The Star*, 12 April 2001: 1–2). This situation may be in part a consequence of the widespread public support for 'clean soccer' in South Africa, especially as hooliganism was condemned by politicians and was perceived to have negatively influenced England's bid for the Soccer World Cup of 2006 (Jansen, 2000: 3). A spirit of fair play was successfully conveyed and argued in the appeal to FIFA when South Africa's bid failed. It is particularly significant that no violent incidents were reported in this period between supporters of arch rivals Kaizer Chiefs and Orlando Pirates. Other influences that contributed to the peace between these two professional football clubs relate to the fact that all matches between them were drawn in the 1999–2000 season, they have never met in a major knockout match or final, and they share sponsorship from the same company, Vodacom. This shared sponsorship has promoted 'fair play' initiatives and joint support as supporters are issued with jerseys with the emblems of both clubs on the front. On the surface, it seems that supporters have united to challenge Sundowns, the league winners for the past three years. However, this is a volatile situation and, as the euphoria of the 2006 World Cup bid wears off, league positions may change and major rifts may remain unresolved at managerial and grass roots level. The Ellis Park disaster, in which 43 people lost their lives, illustrates the volatility of this situation.

The 'black cat' of South African soccer

An analysis of the incidents of physical violence that were reported in the South African media over a period of approximately 24 years indicates that most incidents occurred at high profile professional (80 per cent) or first league games (eight per cent). Violent incidents included attacks on referees by supporters, acts of criminal violence such as looting and vandalism, gang warfare, riots and the 'retaliation' of fans attacking officials or players who 'prevented' their team from winning.

In one incident, a primary school boy was stabbed and killed by youths at the end of a match because of his 'brilliant' goalkeeping (*The World*, 24 April 1977: 1). Only two incidents were reported where gang 'warfare' took place at soccer events. In one incident, the wardens at Modderbee Prison on the East Rand initiated the fighting between the Big Five and Twenty-Five's during a soccer game, causing the death of three inmates (*The Sowetan*, 24 February

1997: 1). 'Retaliation' against 'supernatural powers' is illustrated vividly in an incident where the supporters of AmaZulu and Moroka Swallows attacked one another with knives and umbrellas over the yellow bag of the AmaZulu goalkeeper, which was believed to have contained 'muti' (a magic potion) (*The Sowetan*, 24 October 1983: 20). In another instance, a substitute referee stabbed two players when they argued with him, 'opening gashes above their eyes' (*The Sowetan*, 7 August 1984: 16). Violence is thus widespread. In the majority of cases, the attacks were mainly focused on the referee and linesmen who were blamed for being 'biased' by allowing or disallowing goals and/or red-carding players; angry supporters would then invade the pitch, bombard the officials with missiles or assault them physically. 'Rough' play and a variety of violent incidents on the field often triggered violence in the stands, but there were more deep-rooted causes for the eruption of violence at soccer matches, which resulted in 105 reported deaths in the period under investigation.

Trends in soccer violence

Several incidents demonstrated interracial tension between predominantly black, white (Wits University and Arcadia Pepsi), Indian (Dynamos), Portuguese (Lusitano), Jewish (Highlands Park) and Greek (Hellenic) teams. The congestion of tens of thousands of psyched-up black soccer supporters in stadia in 'white' neighbourhoods with inadequate space and 'violent' police control inevitably caused potentially explosive situations in the seventies and eighties. The collective and violent resistance to racial oppression became the main thrust of racial tension, involving rioting in predominantly white suburbs (Pretoria, Johannesburg, Durban and Cape Town) and violent clashes between black supporters and 'white' police. A leading black newspaper, *The Post* (7 December 1979: 15), reported that winning a high profile soccer match was for black supporters 'a black triumph' rather than a mere 'football victory'. Inter-racial tension and soccer violence peaked between 1977 and 1987 when 39 incidents were reported, compared to seven that occurred between 1988 and 2001. Proactive and reactive violence became the symbol of the social divide and political power.

Managerial and administrative problems often added to the frustration and indirectly triggered violent 'retaliation'. This was the case in an incident in which 15,000 frustrated black supporters attacked white officials when Orlando Pirates did not turn up for a match (*Die Transvaler*, 9 June 1980: 2). Soccer violence related to social inequality and based on the social and racial 'hierarchy' of South Africa does not, however, explain the occurrence of all the incidents at South African soccer matches. A more in-depth analysis of incidents of soccer violence occurring at matches between Kaizer Chiefs and

Orlando Pirates illustrates other factors contributing to the perpetuation of soccer violence among black supporters.

A case study of soccer violence: Kaizer Chiefs versus Orlando Pirates

Very many incidents of football-related violence have involved the fans of the Kaizer Chiefs and Orlando Pirates. Matches between these two clubs have been particular flashpoints: in the period between 1978 and 2001, there have been violent clashes between Chiefs and Pirates fans on 23 occasions, including the 'massacre' of 40 people in 1991, the further deaths of 43 people at a match in 2001 and fairly severe outbreaks of violence in 1994, 1997 and 1998 (see table 1). In order to study the conditions associated with such violence, several interviews and focus group sessions were conducted among their supporters from Soweto and Alexandra, two major 'black' townships adjacent to the city of Johannesburg. I attended several games to obtain data for in-depth analysis and the contextualisation of soccer violence. Knowledge of black soccer fans and of the experiences of people living in poverty in rural and urban areas was obtained through lengthy periods of extensive fieldwork carried out between 1978 and 1996.

Kaizer Motaung, a former Orlando Pirates player, founded Kaizer Chiefs in 1970 after he returned from a successful season playing for Atlanta Chiefs in the North American soccer league. Several former players and administrators of Orlando Pirates joined him and enjoyed a meteoric rise in the Professional Soccer League. The Kaizer Chiefs have several million supporters and approximately 100,000 card carrying members who are affiliated to 102 supporters clubs country-wide (*The Star*, 31 August 1994: 13). They are also known as the 'Amakhosi' (Zulu for Chiefs), the 'Phefeni Boys' (an area in West Orlando) and the 'cocky glamour boys'. Based in Johannesburg, they may draw 30,000 or more spectators if they play at the Johannesburg Stadium, their home ground. Supporters will come from all over the country and thousands may travel long distances to 'unite with other supporters' (*Management*, December 1985: 9–11).

The Chiefs' arch rivals, Orlando Pirates (established in 1937 in Orlando East), also enjoy nationwide popularity, with approximately 80,000 paid cardholders. Their home ground is the First National Bank (FNB) Stadium in Johannesburg, also known as 'Soccer City'. They were first known as the Sea Rovers, the Ghosts or the Buccaneers, and they now promote the slogan 'once a pirate, always a pirate'. After the split initiated by Kaizer Motaung, they regrouped despite several disputes and internal conflicts. Their supporters have often been accused of being fanatical, 'tsotsi' (hooligans) or belonging to a 'dog club'. The rivalry is ascribed to the distinction in 'class' and 'lack of humility' – the son (Kaizer Chiefs) should not be greater than the father (Orlando Pirates) (*The Star,* 7 May 1997: 22). The intense rivalry marks the stormy relationship between these two clubs as they have always been at loggerheads, competing for the top position in the National Professional League (1971–85) and the National Soccer League (1985–2000).

Several preventable 'causes' have been identified in the aftermath of the violence at matches between the Chiefs and the Pirates, especially those involving loss of life. At the Orkney disaster in January 1991, 40 people were either trampled or stabbed to death in the pandemonium and fighting that broke out at the 'friendly' match in the Oppenheimer Stadium. Armed spectators were allowed into the grounds and rival supporters were allowed to congregate on the same grandstand with no adequate barriers separating them. There were only 35 security guards to control a crowd of 20,000 and no police were on standby. When fighting broke out among hundreds of the spectators after the Chiefs scored a disputed goal, thousands of people stampeded towards the gates. A locked gate and blocked passages contributed to the deaths as the stadium was overcrowded and medical help was unavailable. Several commissions of inquiry identified inadequate infrastructure, management and security as the main reasons for the disaster and suggested that alcohol, missiles and weapons should be prohibited at games. They also recommended that the supporters should be educated about violence, and not provoked into using violence by inflammatory statements and media reporting (see table 1 for sources).

Similar explanations were offered after fighting and rioting broke out at the FNB Stadium in May 1994 when Orlando Pirates fans went on the rampage after the Chiefs were awarded a penalty in the second half of their Castle League soccer match. Hostile fans invaded the pitch and then set fire to seats causing damage estimated at R200,000 (*The Sowetan,* 2 June 1994: 1).

The most serious incident in South African football, measured in terms of the number of deaths, took place in April 2001, when 43 spectators died in a stampede as excited fans tried to get into the Ellis Park Stadium in Johannesburg in order to see a match between the Chiefs and the Pirates. The stadium was filled to capacity with 65,000 fans when another 60,000 people stampeded their way into the stadium after the gates had been closed (Ratao, 2001: 1). A journalist (Maseko, 2001: 2) who witnessed the violence at Ellis Park described the behaviour of the soccer crowd as follows:

> Tempers were running high as a stand-off developed between the masses of fans, most of whom did not have tickets, and the security men on the south side of the brimful stadium . . . 'Break down the gates', screamed an angry fan among the crowd. But the security men manning the gates would not budge. They scrummed down with the fans trying to force their way to the other side of the

Table 1 **Soccer violence between Kaizer Chiefs and Orlando Pirates
June 1978–September 2001**

Date	Place/Stadium	Type of incident	Source
June 1978	Soweto	Referee attacked by knife wielding fans.	*The Sunday Times* (11/11/79: 15)
May 1979	Rand Stadium	Referee attacked by mob.	*Die Vaderland* (22/5/79: 26)
31 January 1983	Orlando Stadium (Soweto)	Overflowing stadium – 'flare-up' between a player and his 'bench'.	*The Sowetan* (31/1/83: 1)
11 May 1983	Ellis Park Stadium (Johannesburg)	Bucks followers threw missiles on the pitch and disputed decision by referee.	*The Sowetan* (11/05/83: 20)
20 July 1983	Ellis Park Stadium	Angry Pirates fans invaded the pitch in protest against referee.	*The Sowetan* (20/7/83: 16)
21 June 1984	Ellis Park Stadium	The excited crowd rushed onto the field after goal by Chiefs.	*The Sowetan* (21/6/84: 28)
16 July 1984	Ellis Park Stadium	Angry Orlando Pirates fans invaded the pitch and interfered with linesmen.	*The Sowetan* (16/07/84:1)
26 November 1988	Ellis Park Stadium	Two supporters were killed and a security guard injured.	*Die Transvaler* (9/6/88: 8)
November 1988	Ellis Park Stadium	Pirates supporters blamed referee for disallowing goal. Supporters and security guards were injured.	The Pretoria News (18/6/88: 9)
13 January 1991	Harry Oppenheimer Stadium (Orkney)	Pandemonium and fighting broke out between armed spectators. Overcrowding and fighting – 40 deaths.	*New Nation* (24/1/91: 32) *Die Beeld* (16/2/91: 1) *The Star* (14/1/91: 1; 5/2/91: 3)
27 August 1993	Ellis Park Stadium	A riot broke out among angry fans when the gates did not open at 17.00.	*The Sowetan* (27/8/93: 45)
15 November 1993	FNB Stadium (Johannesburg)	Fans attacked each other outside the stadium. Many people were injured.	*The Sowetan* (15/11/93: 23; 16/11/93: 25)

Date	Place/Stadium	Type of incident	Source
1993	FNB Stadium	A free-for-all fight between rival fans – 76 injured and one shot dead.	*The Sowetan* (25/11/93: 23)
January 1994	FNB Stadium	Pirates fans started fighting. A number of spectators were injured.	*City Press* (22/5/94: 1)
24 January 1994	FNB Stadium	100,000 people crammed in stadium with capacity of 80,000. There were 90 casualties taken to hospital.	*The Star* (24/1/94: 3)
22 March 1994	FNB Stadium	Supporters attacked referee, linesmen and 'own' Nigerian goalkeeper. Set fire to seats in stadium.	*City Press* (22/5/94: 1)
21 May 1994	FNB Stadium	Violence erupted among Pirates supporters. They stormed the pitch and vandalised the stadium. R200,000 damage was reported.	*The Citizen* (25/5/94: 4) *The Sowetan* (2/6/94: 1) *Die Afrikaner* (27/5/94: 5)
21 May 1995	FNB Stadium	Fans set fire to seats. Inadequate security arrangements.	*Die Beeld* (31/5/95)
19 January 1997	Ellis Park Stadium	80,000 tickets sold – stadium has only a 65,000 capacity. Two men stabbed and policeman injured.	*City Press* (19/1/97: 2) *Die Beeld* (20/1/97: 5)
11 May 1997	FNB Stadium	Black cat was kicked to death.	*The Sunday Times* (11/5/97: 1)
30 March 1998	FNB Stadium	Chiefs fans threw missiles.	*The Sowetan* (30/3/98)
10 October 1998	Ellis Park Stadium	Violent clashes with police when thousands of supporters could not gain entry to the already full stadium.	*City Press* (11/10/98: 1)
11 April 2001	Ellis Park Stadium	43 spectators died in a stampede as excited fans tried to gain entry to a full stadium.	*The Star* (12/04/2001: 1–2) *The Sowetan* (12/04/2001: 1)

gate. The scene resembled a tug-of-war as the heaving mass of fans pushed and pushed and pushed . . . Ultimately the gates buckled under the force of the frenzied, marauding fans and the hapless security guards were forced to back off . . . The entire atmosphere was charged with a peculiar air of excitement and tension . . . some fans were swept away by the heaving mass of bodies surging forward. Then came the news of the tragedy.

It is clear that the occurrence of violence at soccer matches is related not only to the inadequate infrastructure identified by several earlier commissions of inquiry, but also to a 'culture of violence that spread through the townships' (*The Citizen*, 23 May 1994: 6). Although stemming from the same root, soccer violence differs from township violence in terms of its unique public stage, the level of excitement generated and the fairly large numbers involved.

Attending a top-level match in South Africa is like experiencing a carnival where thousands of black supporters, most of whom are relatively young men, create a festive mood by chanting and 'bragging' noisily about their teams and by displaying a colourful assortment of paraphernalia. Before they enter the grounds, many people coming from work might buy food and liquor from the vendors outside the stadium. A female supporter of Chiefs said that she would start preparing for a game at four o'clock in the morning. First she would cook, 'offer snuff' to her forefathers to 'ask for a victory' and then 'dress to kill for the Chiefs' in her black and yellow outfit, before taking a taxi to the game. Entering the stadium, she would team up with other Chiefs supporters on the north or western pavilion where thousands would enthusiastically chant and praise their team. A chant such as '*Helele Ma! U yeze Umkhoto!*' (Watch out! Umkhoto is coming!) is based on a freedom song and 'warns' Pirates that Umkhoto (the name of a player) is coming. A sangoma or medicine man dressed in the club's colours may wave his medicine stick, an action which is believed to chase away the 'bad spirits'. Throughout the game people shout instructions to the coaches, players and particularly to the referee. In anticipation of violence, supporters often leave the stadium towards the end of the game. One male Kaizer Chiefs supporter said that one should hurry as 'Pirates like to fight for nothing'.

During an interview, a Pirates fan agreed that he feels provoked to fight when his team has lost. He feels ridiculed and belittled when 'the glamour boys' defeat his team. He explained:

It makes me angry if they [Chiefs] laugh at us. I am so fucked up when my team loses. Chiefs get trophies with penalties and the ref's on their side. They have more sponsors and supporters – they are crowd-pullers. If your team loses and you come home after the game, they even mock you at the taxi rank. You feel that you have been robbed. I want to fight when they laugh at me. At the shebeen we watch the game to prove a mistake at the replay. Then we start fighting and people can even kill each other. Some have been drinking the whole day and smoked ganja [marijuana].

A young male supporter of the Chiefs said that he was punched at a Pirate-Sundowns semi-final game just because his Chiefs membership card fell out of his pocket. Supporters are fanatical about their team affiliation and on one occasion a young man killed his brother because they supported opposing clubs (Chiefs and Pirates).

The above incidents, perceptions and experiences indicate clearly that there are many factors contributing to soccer violence in South Africa and that the multi-faceted phenomenon should be viewed in the complex context in which it occurs. Structural fault lines create enduring dispositions that may serve as strong motivators for people to engage in violence at soccer matches. However, personal characteristics and a high level of trait anxiety – beyond the scope of this analysis – cannot be ignored as psychological factors that may lead to violent responses under certain circumstances. Supporters identify themselves with a particular soccer club of high prestige, and the extent to which they perceive themselves as fans and view the team as a 'representation' of themselves may contribute to obsessive and violent behaviour. The team becomes part of their own social identity and they cannot accept defeat as this also implies a loss of pride, self-esteem and 'bragging rights', while giving the opponents the 'right' to humiliate them (Brindley, 1982).

For supporters from an impoverished social and economic background, soccer is a symbol of their self-worth; it is a symbol of identity where the supporter gets his self-image from what happens on the field. They allow nothing to obstruct their quest for recognition and success, so frustration may lead to violence when supporters cannot gain entrance to the game or 'significant others' (players, officials and the referee) obstruct their objective (*The Citizen*, 19 February 1997: 52). This probably explains why violence often erupts at the end of the game or when it becomes obvious that a team will inevitably lose. Violence involving attacks on officials, throwing missiles or invading the pitch, is directed at the source of frustration. Poor refereeing, biased decisions and the rigging of games are indirectly 'adding fuel to the fire' (*Pace*, April 1997: 30–2). With high profile soccer teams as foci of identification, traditional rivalry and established 'worthy' opponents become the object of long-lasting feuds.

The social divide between the supporters of these teams may also reflect the hierarchy of social positions in society at large. Despite the similarity of socio-economic positions, Chiefs supporters perceive themselves to be socially superior and are concurrently identified by Pirates supporters as social 'snobs'. In the majority of cases, Pirates supporters have been accused and 'punished' as the aggressors, and it seems to be the young men who have been socialised into a life of 'aggressive masculinity' who commit acts of violence. In this sense, violence is both a manifestation of poverty and one of the few resources available for males to 'prove' themselves and to earn recognition among their peers, as in the case of 'gang fights'. In addition to these structural 'fault lines', situational factors may also contribute to the occurrence of violence at high profile soccer matches.

The violent nature and the demonstration of aggression by the players, which is part and parcel of the game plan, may create an environment where 'aggro' is appreciated and demonstrated (*Campus Sport*, September 1985: 4–5). The excitement, chanting and increased noise contribute to a festive atmosphere and heightened tension that are increased by inflammatory statements and sensationalistic media reporting. Headlines that glorify players and teams, identify 'problems' and accentuate the importance of a 'do or die clash', may influence the perception and experience of supporters. So, too, does the 'arch-rivalry' between Kaizer Chiefs and Orlando Pirates, which is highlighted by the media and which creates 'villains' and 'heroes', 'winners' and 'losers' and a culture of 'shame' and 'blame' (*The Sowetan*, 7 August 1984: 16).

Additional factors to add to the psychological and sociological 'profile' outlined above include the perception that some teams may have access to 'strong muti' or 'supernatural' powers that may favour them and create an unfair advantage. It is widely believed that most top clubs employ a 'muti man' or 'sangoma' and, to make them acceptable, hide them behind user-friendly titles such as 'technical advisers'. Practising 'magic' aimed at influencing the outcome of a game is illustrated by the following incident:

> The night before a vital match between soccer giants Kaizer Chiefs and Orlando Pirates, Chiefs officials crept into Soweto's Orlando Stadium and began to bury a slaughtered sheep behind the goal. Alerted to this unusual activity security men switched on the floodlights to reveal Pirates officials also furiously burying a sheep behind the other goal (*The Sunday Times*, 3 September 1995: 17).

Another factor widely proclaimed as contributing to the violent behaviour of supporters is the effect of alcohol. The effect of alcohol on the state of consciousness, leaving the user with an altered state and feelings of 'empowerment', may trigger the loss of self-control and cloud the individual's judgement in certain situations. Individuals gambling away their hard-earned money may have serious consequences for them and their dependants. If they (their team) lose, or appear about to lose, scapegoats or circumstances that are perceived to be contributing to the loss may 'infuriate them to the point of violence' (*Premier Soccer League*, 1997). Self-blame is relatively absent as people often remark that 'we wuz robbed' or 'cheated' out of a victory, so they feel justified in 'retaliating'. In such cases they revert to the one option available to them:

violence. They have been socialised into an acceptance of the use of violence and have probably experienced that physical violence can be a powerful instrument to obtain a sense of control and 'empowerment'. This perception, combined with a 'live-for-the-moment' mentality and a negative self-concept, is a potent motivator for violent behaviour.

Layers of understanding

The first layer relates to those manifest 'causes', identified by the media, governing bodies and soccer leaders, which are associated with mechanisms of external control. The physical structure of grounds and the immediate environment, the security measures adopted, as well as the organisation and management of big soccer events, have received priority in the media when debating 'causes' of soccer violence. Such factors clearly play a part because security fences and the partitioning of fans might safeguard people's safety and prevent disasters, such as that which occurred in Orkney in January 1991, in which 40 people were killed. However, the soccer authorities have not been able to eradicate violence at soccer matches using measures of this kind. This has led to calls for a further tightening of controls, further improvements to the infrastructure, education of fans, the fining of clubs, or a denial that soccer violence constitutes a serious problem (*Premier Soccer League*, 1997). Not all the violence occurs at the event itself. Nor can soccer-related violence be controlled by short-term measures. That is because it is embedded in the social world of the supporters who have much at stake and little to lose.

The second layer of explanation refers mainly to 'latent' causes of a more 'internal' and less directly observable nature. The norms, values and behaviour ('machismo') into which males of the working class and poverty-stricken communities are socialised are produced and reproduced by everyday experiences, in which survival and self-esteem are negotiated and enforced through physical violence (Hobbs and Robins, 1991). Even the racial violence at soccer events in the seventies and eighties can be viewed, from a Marxist perspective, as a form of resistance against the experience of powerlessness induced by the (white) state and police (Taylor, 1982a). This 'insiders' versus 'outsiders' affiliation finds violent expression in the socially stratified divisions or 'fault lines' that are established over time and offer foci for identification and prestige for the relatively powerless. The South African 'soccer hooligans' are not an import of any kind, but are products of a society scarred by chronic poverty, in which some groups are marginalised in the social, political and economic spheres. Violence is embedded in South African society and forms part and parcel of the everyday experiences of the people living in poverty-stricken communities.

Chapter 14

Soccer spectators and fans in Japan

Yoshio Takahashi

Introduction: Japan's modernisation and the dawn of soccer

In 1854, Japan abandoned its policy of isolation, resulting in the influx into the country of soldiers, mariners and teachers from the West. Until that time, Japan's external trade had been carried on through a specific controlled area. The opening of the country greatly accelerated the spread of Western civilisation, one important aspect of which was sport. According to some records, soccer was introduced to Japan in September 1873 by Lieutenant Commander Douglas of the British navy. He arrived in Japan that year as an instructor at the naval school in Tokyo, and taught the game to his students as a form of recreation.

A physical training text for schools, published in 1885 (Tsuboi and Tanaka), for the first time mentioned 'football' in the Japanese language, following which the game spread among students. After the conclusion of an alliance with Great Britain in 1902, many British teachers arrived in Japan, some of whom taught soccer at various locations throughout the country. Soccer spread, via the education system, from the major cities to the regional areas, and from higher educational organisations to elementary and junior high schools.

Soccer spectating developed through intramural and inter-school matches. In 1907, the first international match was held in Tokyo. It was between the Tokyo Higher Normal School and a Tsukiji foreign team and drew a crowd of 2,000. Five years later, Japan participated for the first time in the Olympics – they were held in Stockholm that year – following which Western sports became more popular. In 1917, Japan entered a national soccer team, consisting mostly of players from the Tokyo Higher Normal School team, in a Far Eastern tournament; this was the first time that Japan entered a national team in an international soccer event. They lost to China 5–0 in the first match and suffered a very heavy 15–2 defeat by the Philippines in the second. The criticism voiced by the spectators at such a crushing defeat was described in a book commemorating the Japan Football Association's 75th anniversary. That tournament was the impetus for the formation of the Tokyo Football Club. A football tournament sponsored by the Osaka Mainichi Press was held in 1918, followed by tournaments in Osaka, Nagoya and Tokyo. In those days, an integrated national football organisation did not exist in Japan, but the English Football Association, mistakenly thinking that Japan had held a national championship, donated a silver cup in 1919.

The gift of this silver cup from the English Football Association prompted Uchino, a Tokyo Higher Normal School Professor, to form the Japan Football Association. William Hague, representing the British Embassy, lent support to the establishment of that association by explaining how England's association was managed and how to establish tournament rules. Finally, in 1921, the All Japan Football Association was established and, beginning in that year, national championships were held annually until they were suspended during the Second World War. After the war, the championships were resumed and these tournaments have become the basis for today's Emperor's Cup. In addition, a football league for vocational school student teams was inaugurated in 1922.

Japanese soccer spectatorship

In Japan, soccer was originally played primarily in schools and amateur clubs, and spectators consisted primarily of people affiliated to these schools and clubs. An early development towards the monetarisation of sport – in this case baseball – occurred in 1907 when, at a baseball game between teams from Hawaii and Keio University, a charge for admission was made for the first time. Charging a fee to watch baseball, it should be noted, represented the monetarisation of the game, not its commercialisation. The proceeds from the fees collected were used to invite foreign teams to Japan, to send home teams abroad, or for baseball-related facilities, and not for personal profit.

The behaviour patterns of sports spectators in Japan are greatly influenced by the media. Radio broadcasting was inaugurated in 1925 and the ability to convey information to a mass audience helped to diffuse baseball to a much larger public, thus impacting greatly upon the growth of spectatorship. Kiku (1993) has noted that a national study of radio listening habits carried out in 1937 found that 63.6 per cent of those who owned a radio listened to baseball, while only 8.6 per cent listened to soccer. It is clear that at that time soccer was much less popular than baseball.

Following the Second World War, soccer – which had been interrupted by the war – was quickly revived, and Japan was permitted to return to the international stage in 1950, thus opening the way for international matches. During the 1964 Tokyo Olympics, crowds of close to full capacity watched the soccer matches. However, soccer was still not very widely known to the public, one indication of which was that the spectators were relatively quiet even when Japan defeated Argentina. On the other hand, a book commemorating the Japan Football Association's 75th anniversary described some of the fans as having been frenzied. Prior to the 1964 Tokyo Olympics, some of these more passionate soccer fans formed the Japan Soccer Association, a private fan club (this association was appropriately named, for the Japanese characters for 'association' in the title are a visible pun, containing the alternative meaning of 'crazy group'). The association publishes a journal for its members, who originally numbered more than 100, growing to 250 by the end of the 1980s. This association provides information on overseas soccer that has not been covered by the mass media, and also has some foreign articles translated. In the 1970s, it organised its own tour to support the Japanese national team on a foreign tour. That might be described as a forerunner of the Japanese sports tourism which we see today.

The Japanese Soccer League (JSL) was established in 1965 by corporate teams in order to improve Japan's soccer competitiveness. These clubs, whose parent bodies were companies, helped to enhance both corporate loyalty and corporate identity. The ease of domestic travel resulting from the building of the Tokaido 'bullet train' contributed greatly to the holding of league games throughout Japan. The Japan Soccer League received widespread coverage in newspapers and magazines and on television, resulting in a considerable expansion of the number of soccer fans. The Scottish team, Stirling Albion, which came to play in Japan in 1966, attracted 45,000 spectators to their first game and 20,000 for their second (the stadium capacity for this latter game was 20,000). In 1968, JSL matches attracted an average of 7,491 people per game. However, by 1973, by which time the number of teams had increased from eight to ten, the average attendance had decreased to 3,000. By 1981, there had been a further decrease to 1,800, with many empty seats in the stadia. Nakatsuka (1986) cited as one reason for these falling attendances the fact that Japan's national team had not been able to participate in either the World Cup or the Olympics.

In 1985, after failing to qualify for the 1986 World Cup in Mexico, Japan looked into the possibility of establishing professional teams. In 1986, two players registered themselves as professionals with the Japan Football Association. In the mid-1980s, soccer again became more popular, with an increase in the number of spectators. This increase in popularity appears to have been associated with an increase in economic prosperity, which began in the latter part of 1986, together with the promotion of professionalism. One other factor was that comic magazines using soccer as a theme became increasingly popular with children. At that time, Japanese people spent a great deal on leisure-related activities, went on trips throughout the world and shopped for expensive brand-name items. The inception of satellite broadcasting also made it possible for Japanese people to obtain real-time sports information from around the globe. A plan to turn the JSL into a professional league was initiated around 1988 and, with the economic boom in Japan, the plan received substantial funding from supportive corporations. During 1988, the decision was taken that Japan would seek to host the 2002 World Cup. The then FIFA Chairman, Joao Havelange, expressed the hope that the 2002 World Cup could be held in Asia.

In Beijing in August 1992, the Japanese national team for the first time won the Dynasty Cup, which had been started in 1990 and which involved Japan, South Korea, China and Hong Kong.[1] Also in 1992, the Yamazaki Nabisco Cup was established; this took place between September and November and involved matches between league clubs in Japan. A group called 'Supporters', which had not previously existed, came to the stadia and, by singing and playing horns, supported the teams. The games in the Nabisco Cup attracted an average of 11,111 paying spectators. Later in the autumn, the Japanese national team also won the Asia Cup which was held in Japan. Favourable conditions, such as professionalisation of the game, an excellent economic climate and victories by the home team provided an environment in which soccer's popularity was set to explode. Finally, the J-League, which was the professional league formed out of the JSL, began in May 1993. The opening match attracted a large television audience, with 32.4 per cent of those who owned a television watching the match. The average match attendance for J-League matches during 1993 was 17,976, rising to 19,598 in 1994, but falling to 16,922 in 1995. After 1995, the J-League boom to some extent subsided but during 2001 the average attendances again increased, partly because of the impact of the forthcoming 2002 World Cup and partly because of the influence of the soccer lottery, which was initiated in 2001. Trends in match attendances for the period from 1993 to 2001 are shown in table 1.

Table 1 **Trends in the number of participants in the J-League**

Year	Total spectators	Average spectators	Number of teams
1993	3,235,750	17,976	10
1994	5,173,817	19,598	12
1995	6,159,691	16,922	14
1996	3,204,807	13,353	16
1997	2,755,698	10,131	17
1998	3,666,496	11,982	18
1999	2,798,005	11,658	16
2000	2,655,553	11,065	16
2001	2,199,521	17,319	16

As of 11 August 2001

Football-related research in Japan

Members of the Scientific Research Department and the Medical Committee of the Japan Football Association participated in the first International Congress on Sports Medicine Applied to Football, which was held in Rome in 1979. In the following year, a meeting on Soccer Medicine and Science Research was held in Japan in order to publicise scientific knowledge concerning soccer.

Research on soccer in Japan is described in depth in the *Scientific Research Review Series on Sports*, by Asami et al. (1981). However, there was no mention of any studies concerning Japanese spectators and it is only recently that studies of football spectators have been made at soccer stadia.

Nakazawa (1998; 1999) and Nakazawa et al. (2000) have conducted such studies on a chronological basis, beginning in the year prior to the inauguration of the J-League. Nakazawa analysed the characteristics of spectator behaviour through profiling the spectators from a marketing standpoint. Harada and Fujimoto (1999) conducted research concerning the degree of sponsor-recognition on the part of the spectators. The research of Kisanuki and Esashi (1996) and Nakazawa et al. (2000) focused on gender differences. Takahashi et al. (1994), similarly to Desmond Morris (1983), reported on how J-League spectators dressed and what they brought with them at the time the J-League was launched. Uemuki et al. (1996) and Takahashi (1996) reported on the factors that motivate spectators to attend matches, while Shimizu (2001) reviewed research about British hooligans and studied the culture of J-League supporters. In addition, a few foreign researchers such as Horne (1996) and Birchall (2001) began to develop an interest in Japanese football.

J-League supporters

The present culture of soccer spectators at stadia has been greatly influenced by the inauguration of the J-League. Viewing soccer at stadia created a new lifestyle for some. According to research conducted by Takahashi (1993) in the first year of the J-League at Kashima Stadium, 68 per cent of male and 90 per cent of female spectators were 'novices' who had started going to stadia to watch football matches only in the last three years. According to a study by Nakazawa et al. (2000), 82.9 per cent of soccer spectators have attended stadia only since the inception of the J-League.

The sexual composition of crowds is 60 per cent male and 40 per cent female (Nakazawa 1998, 1999; Takahashi, 1993). Football crowds in Japanese stadia are filled with large numbers of women and children and there is a significant difference in this respect from what one sees in European stadia. In terms of the age structure of Japanese football crowds, 50 per cent of spectators are in their teens and twenties, less than 30 per cent are in their thirties and under 20 per cent are over forty.

The cheering style of the Japanese has developed since the inception of the J-League. Initially, the cheering style, with the use of horns, resembled that of many European countries, and that of Brazil, using samba rhythms. Cheering by those behind the goal demonstrated their love for their club. The spectators displayed their club's colours by wearing items sold by the club, such as uniforms, scarves, flags and bandanas. Writing from the perspective of an Englishman, Birchall (2001: 6) commented on the differences between the cheering styles and stadium services of the J-League, and the controlled enthusiasm of the Japanese supporters, and those in Europe:

> Outside the railway station, the posts of the low, chain-link fence lining the pavement are topped with small metal footballs. The shop selling local souvenir sweet bean cakes has typical Japanese paper lanterns, also shaped like soccer balls. I had boarded the bus with a line of people wearing orange and yellow Shimizu S-Pulse shirts and carrying orange and yellow Shimizu S-Pulse banners. It wasn't a rowdy crowd. There was no pushing or shouting. There were no policemen on horses with riot helmets. At least half of the people on the bus were young women, some of them with children.

Later, Birchall (2001: 8) continues:

> The two teams had broken from the line-up; the small children, the bunches of flowers and the big, fluffy, yellow mascot had been removed, and the crowd, and the drums, were starting in earnest – 'ESS-PULSE ESS-PULSE, BOOM BOOM BOOM. ESS-PULSE ESS-PULSE, BOOM BOOM BOOM.' At the front of the crowd, standing at the head of the samba band, a single figure in orange held up both his hands and the whole stand hushed. The leader signalled and the drums began again, this time with the entire band sweeping into the full samba rhythm. Now the whole stand was moving as one, jumping from side to side, the fans throwing their arms forward at the end of the chant, like a massive coordinated aerobic lesson.

Finally, Birchall (9–10) adds:

> At the half-time whistle, I went in search of snacks as the aisles filled up with people obeying the rules against smoking while watching the game. This being Japan, the snack scene is particularly well developed. Throughout the first half, polite young women had wandered up and down the stands, dispensing Asahi beer in plastic cups. At half-time, people were queuing for corn-on-the cob,

barbecued on an open flame in a corner of the stadium, while more polite young women shouted 'irrashaimasse', 'at your service', with all the enthusiasm of waiters at the finest sushi restaurant. Such are the rewards of social order.

Unable to find a soggy hamburger or sinister hot-dog, I bought a neat, plastic bento box with rice, fish and some other more uncertain pickled things, complete with disposable wooden chopsticks. In Europe, disposable wooden chopsticks would be considered potentially dangerous weapons.

At Nihondaira Stadium, fans can wash and brush up at a sink with an unbroken mirror. That wouldn't happen in Europe. The fifty-foot drop from the parapet of the walkway to the ground wouldn't happen in Europe. And what of the garbage bins, neatly divided for burnable and non-burnable rubbish? Where else in the world can you watch football, and sort your trash?

As the second half got under way, I munched the remains of my rice and fish, sipped my beer and watched the drama.

There have been some fieldwork studies of Japanese soccer spectators. Takahashi (1993) studied a group of supporters of the Kashima Antlers, called 'Infight', who sit behind the goal. Shimizu (2000) analysed the Urawa Reds 'Crazy Calls', reporting on their rowdy, masculine behaviour. The central figures in both groups have changed since the groups were originally formed. Prior to a game, a supporter group will decide such matters as how to conduct their cheering. Supporter groups also follow the Japanese national team in order to cheer it on. These groups are very much aware of the existence of the media, to the extent that they transmit images of themselves through the media, thereby celebrating and demonstrating their own existence as groups. There are significant differences between supporter groups in terms of their behaviour. For example, the difference between the rowdy behaviour of some groups and the behaviour of the supporters who followed the national team in the World Cup in France in 1998 was demonstrated by the admirable conduct of the latter in cleaning the stands following the French World Cup.

Violence and incidents at stadia

Though they are normally polite, Japanese soccer spectators do occasionally engage in violence. The J-League initially did not seek to regulate the behaviour of the supporters' groups. However, there have been incidents when some supporters have protested against the referee's decisions and on occasions supporters have created a ruckus when their team played badly and lost. During the Yamazaki Nabisco Cup (Urawa Reds *v* Nagoya Grampus, held 7 October 1992), supporters left their seats and entered the field, interrupting the game and, during the same match, a drunken spectator threw an object onto the field, hitting a coach. These incidents were reported in the Japanese newspapers as an indication of hooliganism, though Ohsumi (1998), in referring to those articles, has argued that some journalists lacked a precise understanding of the meaning of the term 'hooligan'. However, rowdiness on the part of supporters has not gone away.

In October 1997, at a qualifying match for the 1998 World Cup, about a thousand supporters surrounded the stadium and threw eggs and plastic bottles at the World Cup personnel. In an incident in the Kashiwa no Ha Stadium in 1999 (see table 2), supporters protested when their home stadium was to be moved to a location further away. Although altercations among supporters and destructive behaviour towards stadium facilities have not been reported, a considerable number of such actions are believed to have taken place.

Ohsumi (1998) has argued that the reason why large numbers of media reporters attend matches has less to do with the level of play in the J-League and rather more to do with the 'show' created by the supporters. Ohsumi also argued that the mass media influence the behaviour of supporters. Shimizu (2000) has similarly argued that the public image of supporters has been shaped by media reporting.

Clubs and associations have taken measures to try to ensure the safety and comfort of spectators. Following an incident in which a young man leaped onto the field during a high school tournament and fractured a bone, the front three rows of seats in the national stadium in Tokyo were roped off in order to prevent spectators from getting onto the field. The J-League has introduced rules common to all clubs at all games and, in the event of a violation of these rules, the J-League debriefs the club which hosted the match and issues a stern warning to the club. However, they have not taken measures to separate the entry gates for 'home' and 'away' supporters, as is common in many European stadia. A list of major incidents involving supporters in the period from 1992–2000 is given in table 2.

Proposed measures to counter violence and disturbances at the Korea/Japan World Cup 2002

Approximately 4,700,000 foreigners visit Japan each year. For the 2002 World Cup finals, the Japanese government estimates that approximately 425,000 people will come to Japan. Travel agencies estimate that 129,000 people will go back and forth between Japan and Korea. During the World Cup finals, many spectators will move from one location to another, and special preparations will be required to counter violence and ensure the safety of spectators.

Table 2 **Major supporter incidents**

7 October 1992	Urawa Stadium	Fans invaded the pitch (interrupting the game), throwing objects which hit a coach.
December 1993	Utsunomiya Green Stadium	Trouble between security guards and supporters.
19 November 1993	Toyama	About 30 fans invaded the pitch, creating problems among security guards, cameramen and supporters.
26 April 1995	Ohmiya Soccer Stadium	Fans invaded the pitch and tried to attack the goalkeeper.
23 September 1995	Restaurant in Urawa City	A player became violent towards a supporter.
7 May 1997	Urawa Stadium	About 500 supporters surrounded a team's bus, throwing coins and eggs.
10 May 1997	Mizuho Stadium	Violence broke out among the supporters.
26 October 1997	National Stadium	About 1000 supporters surrounded a stadium, throwing eggs and plastic bottles
24 April 1999	Kashiwa no Ha Stadium	Smoke flares were ignited, and a huge piece of cloth was used to protest.
April–July 2000	Urawa Reds supporters at away games	Objects were thrown onto the field, smoke flares and firecrackers were ignited.
29 July 2000	Sapporo	Smoke flares were ignited, plastic bottles were thrown, supporters invaded the pitch and tried to attack a cameraman.

Sources: Reports by Shimizu (2000) and Ohsumi (1998)

In Japan, the term 'hooligan' is not widely known. The violent behaviour of hooligans became a topic of conversation largely because of the incidents that occurred at the 1998 World Cup Finals in France. However, since Japan has not really experienced such behaviour, the Japanese do not fully comprehend the meaning of 'hooliganism'. Nevertheless, images transmitted during the World Cup in France helped to convey the meaning of the word to the general public. British and German hooligans, in particular, became notorious in Japan. The Japan World Cup Organising Committee for 2002 (JAWOC) identified security as a key item involved in planning for the Cup and they advocated the building of cooperative relationships between security experts and municipal police organisations.

Staff members of the JAWOC and the KOWOC (Korea World Cup Organising Committee for 2002) participated in the European Union's special soccer security meetings held in Blackburn, England, in February 1998. In October of that year, personnel from Japan's National Police Agency visited the Korean National Police Agency to affirm total cooperation between them. In August 1999, the Tokyo Metropolitan Police Agency and the Seoul Metropolitan Police Agency exchanged signatures on a friendship document, thereby strengthening their cooperative relationship. The JAWOC formed a security department, the chief of which was seconded from the National Police Agency. In the following year, the personnel of the security department attended an international conference relating to security at the European Championships (Euro 2000), and learned first-hand how European countries deal with such matters. Japan's policy on security is to emphasise the importance of international co-operation and to seek 'soft security', through which the Cup event can be fully enjoyed by the public. The security guidelines for the Cup were established in January 2000 and made public on the Internet. In March 2001, those working for the JAWOC attended a British soccer security symposium sponsored by the British Council, to which personnel of the British National Criminal Intelligence Service (NCIS) and journalists were invited as guest speakers. One hundred and fifty people, including representatives of the police, municipal government organisations and journalists, attended that symposium and discussed a variety of topics, including safety manuals, the use of 'stewards', examples of how European governments and police agencies deal with these matters, and the importance of control rooms.

Korea also has a division in charge of security. Conferences attended by those responsible for security arrangements have been held in both Japan and Korea, thereby confirming the commitment in both countries to the importance of security. These also highlight the commonalities but also the differences in their respective security systems, for in each country the organisations primarily responsible for security have their own particular structures. In Japan, in cooperation with other governmental organisations, the police, private security companies and volunteers all enjoy a degree of autonomy, whereas in Korea, responsibility lies mainly with the police and the military. NHK, Japan's public broadcasting station, describes the JAWOC's security system as being unique.

As the above section makes clear, security preparations for the 2002 World Cup have been under way for some time. However, following the terrorist attacks on New York and Washington on 11 September 2001, security arrangements for the World Cup will be further tightened and will take into account the national teams which qualify for the finals.

The 2002 World Cup and the Japanese

Developments in information technology and the globalisation of the economy and information have brought about significant changes in the awareness and the lifestyle of the Japanese people. The 2002 World Cup, which inherently contains the possibility of promoting social change, is expected to influence Japanese society in a variety of ways. The fact that Japan will be one of the hosts for the 2002 World Cup will focus attention on the Japanese players, probably leading to the transfer of a number of leading players from Japanese clubs to foreign clubs in return for huge amounts of money. This transfer of excellent Japanese players to overseas clubs will, in turn, help to foster global awareness among the Japanese. Players such as Nakata, Ono, Inamoto and Nishizawa, who already play for overseas clubs, have attracted the attention of the Japanese media, thereby enhancing the trend for Japanese players increasingly to be drawn to overseas clubs. As a consequence, the J-League has been constrained to introduce innovations in its management and marketing style.

The outflow of domestic 'stars' may possibly reduce the commitment to and involvement with local and community clubs but, on the other hand, the multi-faceted character of the globalisation process may possibly prompt people to identify themselves more with a local symbol. The Japanese, who tend to integrate themselves into the local community, may in future need to establish their personal identity within a more diversified society. In so doing, individuals will need to communicate with others and take greater individual responsibility for managing changing patterns of relationships on their own rather than being compelled to do so by others. In this context, it might be suggested that, in an increasingly diversified society, fans who cheer and support their team in a disciplined manner may be seen as searching for a common sentiment and a common sense of reality through the sharing of time and space with others. Finally, it should be noted that, although the sociological study of soccer in Japan is barely under way, with the 2002 World Cup as a catalyst it is beginning to attract more attention.

Chapter 15

A walk on the wild side: exposing North American sports crowd disorder

Kevin Young

In this chapter, I want to tackle the view, still held in some quarters, that there is no serious or 'patterned' fan violence in North American sport. Though the research has often been impressionistic and the theorising frail, there is copious evidence to suggest that North American sports crowds have articulated their aggressive and violent proclivities with regularity throughout the twentieth century. Whether one focuses on mêlées breaking out at 'prize fights' at the turn of the century, brawling baseball and football fans during the inter-war years, or injurious and destructive post-event outbursts throughout the last quarter of the twentieth century, it is clear that North American sports crowd disorder is neither new nor uncommon (Atyeo, 1979; Smith, 1983; Guttmann, 1986; Dunning, 1999). Indeed, those convinced that rambunctious North American sports crowds are very recent phenomena, or are restricted to any single sport, would do well to remember that one of the longest and most destructive of all North American riots followed an ice hockey game in Montreal in the mid-1950s (Katz, 1955; Duperrault, 1981; Young, 1988; Bélanger, 1999), long before the contemporary trend in post-event rioting more typically associated with grid-iron football, baseball, and basketball. The so-called 'Rocket Richard Riots' lasted two days and resulted in dozens of injuries and thousands of dollars worth of damage.[1]

Despite the level and frequency of North American sports crowd disorder, the social and official responses to soccer hooliganism in many countries around the world and to sports crowd disorder in North America have been quite dissimilar. As an expansive literature on hooliganism (see Taylor, 1982a; Williams et al., 1984; Dunning et al., 1988; Murphy et al., 1990a; Giulianotti, 1994) attests, football-related disorder has prompted solicitous reactions from politicians, police, sports authorities, and the media in numerous settings. For instance, it has precipitated, in the case of the UK, new legislation[2] and, in the case of the 'Euro 2000' games which were played in Belgium, record-setting policing manoeuvres. By contrast, North American sports crowd disorder has been the subject of relatively little serious debate and official attention. Simply put, the stigma (Goffman, 1963), stereotypes (Hall, 1978) and moral panic (Murphy et al., 1988; Young, 1986, 1988) which have long been associated with soccer and its fans in the UK and elsewhere have been avoided in North America. While this may be justified in terms of the relative scale of disorderly incidents, it can be argued that North American sport has shown a stubborn, if perhaps faultering, resilience in maintaining its 'squeaky clean', family-centred, and essentially 'safe' image despite the fact that crowd disorder is well known and has clearly changed the configuration of stadia and game-day experiences for fans and authorities in a number of sports. This suggests that North American sports crowd disorder is both constructed and requires deconstruction not only at the behavioural level but also at the political and ideological levels (Young, 1988; Young, 2002).

The view that North American sports crowd disorder is insignificant is not only inaccurate but also insidious, for realistic crowd control and security measures can only proceed on the basis of well-grounded information regarding the nature and extent of the 'problem'. However, it is emphatically not being suggested here either that soccer hooliganism in Europe and miscellaneous North American fan disorders represent social problems of the same magnitude, nor that they are one and the same thing. While there are some common sociological threads in crowd disorders on both sides of the Atlantic[3] and in the global context more generally,[4] and while the problem may reflect similar social processes in those contexts, it is also clear that many aspects of sports crowd disorder are heterogeneously articulated and culturally specific.[5]

North American sports crowd disorder: nature and extent

Because in-depth research is scarce (there is a modest psychological and sociological literature that is in need of updating, for example, Smith, 1975, 1976; Arms et al., 1979, 1980; Case and Boucher, 1981; Lewis, 1982; Smith, 1983; Goldstein, 1989; Young, 1988), information on the demographics of North American sports crowd disorder is limited to police, sports team and media reports, which are not always credible or accurate. Though the following characteristics repeatedly surface in crowd disorder scenes and are familiar to the authorities, they provide us with no more than an elementary outline of who is involved in the phenomenon.[6]

Predictably, though there are occasional cases of females involved in North American fan violence, most offenders tend to be young males. This suggests that, as with other forms of physical violence, North American sports crowd disorder is both gendered and, usually, an activity of youth. Both casual atten-ders and season-ticket holders have been involved in a variety of disorderly actions. Apart from Listiak's (1981) case-specific study of class-related bar behaviour during the Canadian Football League's 'Grey Cup' (which is outdated and unlikely to be generalisable) and also from preliminary thumbnail sketches offered by Lewis (1982) and Smith (1983), very little is known about the social class background of offenders. However, since some of the rowdiest crowds are US college football crowds,[7] a positive correlation between poor education and involvement in disorders should not be assumed, while a high level of education should not automatically be seen as preventing involvement in crowd disorder.

Questionnaire responses from teams in four professional leagues (National Basketball Association, National Football League, Canadian Football League, Major League Baseball) in the 1980s strongly indicated that the majority of offenders who were ejected from stadia for disorderly behaviour or who were involved in other stadium-based disturbances were white (Young, 1988). However, there is also evidence that race and youth factors have coalesced in disorderly crowd behaviour in both Canada and the US, especially with respect to street-gang involvement in post-event conflicts (Johnson, 1993; Nelson, 1994).

The nature of the problem

As with most classification schemes, the following scheme is by no means exhaustive, though it does chronicle some key components of North American sports crowd violence. These components, far from being mutually exclusive, often occur simultaneously.

Missile throwing

There is substantial evidence that North American fans have participated in missile throwing – the projection of objects onto the playing surface and/or at participants/fans – for many decades; as far back as the 1930s and 1940s, players have complained of being struck by cans, bottles, batteries, coins and other missiles launched from the 'bleachers' (the uncovered stands) (Greenberg, 1977: 26–7; Green, 1984: 111). On the basis of a longitudinal content analysis of the North American press, Young (1988) found that, prior to the 1960s, such incidents were given minimal coverage in the media and may have been of low frequency. It is difficult to ascertain whether the incidence of missile throwing has changed, but certainly media reports of fans throwing objects onto the field of play and at players have increased since that time.

Such was the extent of the problem in the 1970s that professional baseball in the US became almost synonymous with missile throwing, as Runfola described in 1976:

In the 1973 Championship Series between the New York Mets and the Cincinnati Reds, for example, after Pete Rose punched the Mets' Bud Harrelson, fans in Shea Stadium pelted Rose with bottles, beer cans and garbage. During the 1974 baseball season, Bob Watson, the Houston outfielder, hit the wall and lay semi-conscious, bleeding from facial wounds, prompting a group of fans to pour beer on him. Violence became such a way of life at Madison Square Gardens' Felt Forum in 1974 that there were three riots where bottles were thrown, property damaged and people injured (Runfola, 1976: 304).

The tradition continues. The numerous missiles thrown from the stands onto the playing surface during the projectile-riddled 1996 World Series included batteries, cans, bottles and food (*Sports Illustrated*, 4 November 1996: 20).[8] Several further incidents took place in 1999: at a college football game in Colorado in September, student fans threw bottles at police and sprayed them with mace when their attempts to destroy the goalposts were thwarted (*National Post*, 6 September 1999: B2); in October, a Denver Bronco player almost lost an eye after being hit by what has been described as a 'battery-powered snowball'; and in December, fans of the Vancouver Grizzlies pelted Houston Rockets' rookie Steve Francis (who had previously declined an opportunity to play for the Grizzlies) with tennis balls and coins (*Sports Illustrated*, 13 December 1999: 27).

Numerous sports have been affected by missile throwing, but the evidence suggests that field sports like baseball and football have been particularly targeted. In addition to the aforementioned missiles, flagrantly dangerous objects such as golf balls and marshmallows weighted down with coins and metal are also thrown with some regularity by the often huge American college football crowds (Herbert, 1994; Riseling, 1994). Worryingly, the use of such objects in crowd disorder hints at the preconceived rather than the spontaneous nature of the practice, for one hardly arrives at a football game carrying such objects 'accidentally'. Perhaps partly because the spatial context of ice hockey is different – the game being played indoors with smaller, more conspicuous crowds – this popular team sport has been less susceptible to missile throwing, although throughout the 1970s and 1980s Canadian hockey fans showed their penchant for the bizarre by 'releasing' live and dead animals and fish onto the ice.[9] Throughout the 1990s, this author observed university students throwing such objects as fish and pigs' trotters from the stands during varsity ice hockey games. While it has become a recognised aspect of hockey culture in many North American cities (it is not uncommon for fans to throw programmes, cups and the like onto the ice to stop play – especially when the home team is 'shorthanded' or in need of a 'time-out') – this behaviour is far more disruptive than it is threatening or injurious.

Although the throwing of missiles has been a fairly common form of fan disorder in both North America and the UK in certain sports, a significant difference may lie in their intended targets. In the UK, the use of ammunition and missiles aimed by soccer hooligans at rival fan groups, players of the opposing team and the police inside and outside the ground has been a recognisable aspect of hooligan behaviour since the 1970s (Marsh et al., 1978; Dunning et al., 1988). In contrast, in North America, missiles have been more commonly thrown at players – sometimes one's own – or simply with the intention of disrupting play. There have been incidents in which a group of fans has attacked a rival group with missiles (for example, fans of the New York Yankees and the Detroit Tigers have been known to 'rain' beer and missiles on sections of opposing fans; see *Toronto Star*, 15 September 1985: A16), but they are infrequent. Also noteworthy, however, are missile assaults upon police by unruly fans in several post-event incidents, such as in Vancouver in 1994 (British Columbia Police Commission, 1994; City of Vancouver, 1994; Vancouver Police Department, 1995) and Los Angeles in 2000 (*Daily Mail*, 21 June 2000: 27).

Use of weapons and firearms

Couched in terms of the wider concern about the place of weapons and firearms in North American – and particularly American – society and especially among young people, there has been much conjecture about the presence and use of weapons at North American sports events. However, no systematic research has been carried out on this issue. This is not to say that weapons are not smuggled into sports stadia and confiscations show that, in fact, they are. The following examples provide a sense of the forms that weapon use assumes:

i)   Guns, knives and other weapons have featured prominently in the numerous post-event riots across the continent (Nelson, 1994; Tolliver, 1994).
ii) Crowd violence at Toronto high school basketball games in the 1990s became so persistent that security measures, including the hiring of armed guards, were significantly increased before, during and after games. One guard claimed that 'searches now routinely turn up small knives, scissors, and [other] makeshift weapons' (*Toronto Star*, 22 January 1995: A6).
iii) Gunfire erupted at a 1996 high school football game in Monrovia, California, wounding two people and sending terrified fans rushing from the bleachers (*Boston Globe*, 5 October 1996: 72).
iv) A belligerent fan following golf star Tiger Woods was ejected at a 1999 PGA event. When searched by security officers, a loaded semi-automatic handgun was found in his waist-pack (*Calgary Herald*, 2 February 1999: C1).

The fact that weapons have been used criminally in post-event misconduct raises troubling questions both for scholars and the authorities. Firstly, how many fans arrive armed at sports events? Secondly, since armed rioters in post-event incidents have been known to join the fray without actually attending the game, it seems inaccurate to attribute all of the damage and injury incurred in those contexts to sport spectators. In general, where the use of weapons is concerned, we can say that observational reports, such as that offered by Chicago attorney Scott Nelson (1994), suggest that weapon use is an ongoing concern in some sports-related disorders. Many of the aforementioned missiles obviously qualify as 'weapons' in terms of the way in which they are used, as do the mace and tear gas deployed by college football fans at the Colorado–Colorado State game in September 1999 (*National Post*, 6 September 1999: B2). However, the only valid way of summarising the extant information on this topic is to acknowledge that we actually know very little and that no consistent patterns have been identified. Clearly, more data are needed before generalisations about the dimensions of the presence and use of weapons and firearms in North American sports crowd disorder can be made.

Field invasion
While field invasions are statistically uncommon in all North American sports, there have nevertheless been many cases during the latter half of the twentieth century. Incidents have generally been associated with victory celebrations on and around the playing area. When the New York Mets won the World Series in 1969, for example, jubilant fans burst onto the Shea Stadium field and proceeded to rip up the sod and home plate. Numerous championship victories in baseball and football since then have been followed by similar incidents.

However, not all field invasion cases have been related to victory celebrations, as the following examples illustrate:

i)   In the summer of 1974, the Cleveland Indians promoted a 'Nickel Beer Night' at a game due to be played against the Texas Rangers. The plan backfired when fans, many of whom were intoxicated, bombarded players and officials with bricks, cans, and bottles. A riot ensued in which dozens of players and officials were injured, and the game was forfeited to Texas (*New York Times*, 6 June 1999: 35).

ii) In the summer of 1977, a promotional 'Disco Demolition Night' was hosted by the Chicago White Sox. In order to gain entry into the Cominskey Park 'doubleheader', fans were required to bring a disco record and to pay just 98 cents. The idea, which was to destroy the widely ridiculed disco records on the field of play between games, backfired when up to 7,000 fans used them as missiles and started a riot in which bases, turf and the batting cage were destroyed. The second game was abandoned (Snyder and Spreitzer, 1983: 202).

iii) At the Toronto Blue Jays' home opener in 1986, I observed hundreds of marauding spectators clash with police on horses behind the home-run fence for no fewer than six innings of the game:

> Three Metro policemen were injured and 125 people were ejected yesterday during the Blue Jays' rowdy home opener against Baltimore Orioles . . . Metro Police said 45 charges were laid, most of them alcohol-related . . . Stadium announcers twice urged fans to stay off the field and 'let the outcome of the game be determined by the players' . . . But even as that announcement was being made, fans in the bleachers were massing behind the right field wall for an assault on mounted policemen and Blue Jays security guards who defended the grounds near the playing field . . . About 200 fans kicked over steel barriers and sprinted across the park towards unoccupied field level seats on the other side, 50 yards away (*Toronto Sun*, 15 April 1986: 15).

The anomalous nature of this field invasion, however, is indicated by the fact that this was the only incident of its kind during the 1986 season and there has been no similar incident in Toronto since then.

Although exclusively game-centred explanations for fan violence have justifiably received criticism for ignoring the broader social context giving rise to sports crowd disorder, the Chicago and Cleveland cases clearly show that the particulars of game contexts should not be overlooked. In the Chicago case, the club was heavily criticised for not having the foresight to expect problems at a mid-summer's 'double-header' involving cheap beer, cheap tickets and a potentially dangerous hand missile. Of course, the capacity for such events to backfire so embarrassingly also emphasises the need for careful security preparations in hosting sports events.

Property destruction and vandalism

Destruction and vandalism at North American stadia have, like other forms of disorder, most commonly been associated with team victory revelry in play-offs and other important games. For example, fans of both collegiate and professional football have been associated with the destruction and even the theft of goalposts for several decades. Goalposts have been dismantled or removed at dozens of college venues including McMaster University in Canada (*McMaster University Silhouette*, 28 October 1982: 5), Yale University (where an 18-year-old Harvard student was critically injured when a metal section of the posts fell on her head), Northwestern University and the University of Illinois. At Penn State University in the 1980s, the goalposts were dismantled so frequently that the Athletics Department 'offered $4500, the cost of new ones, to the Student Activities Fund if fans refrained from tearing down any more' (*Sports Illustrated*, 28 November 1983: 27). Dozens of other colleges and universities across the continent have experienced similar problems (*National Post*, 6 September 1999: B2).

As a result of these and other unruly fan practices, it is not uncommon for stadia personnel to smear goalposts with grease and for playing areas to receive a significant police presence, with 'attack' dogs and horses, at the conclusion of games. One of the ugliest and most injurious field invasions in recent memory occurred at the University of Wisconsin-Madison in 1993. In a scene eerily reminiscent of the television pictures of the Heysel Stadium tragedy of 1985, organisers watched helplessly, making numerous announcements, as thousands of fans poured onto the playing area. Dozens of fans dismantled the goalposts as injured fans receiving medical attention lay sprawled about them. Over seventy people were injured, six critically. Mounted police horses were brought in to enable ambulances to reach the injured (*Sports Illustrated*, 8 November 1993, 60–5; Beecher, 1994: 24).[10]

Though property destruction and vandalism have usually been linked to post-event revelry and rioting, isolated incidents have occurred which demonstrate that this type of disorder can also be a response to team defeat and/or action involving the players. At the end of the 1986 baseball season, for example, following the New York Mets' failure to clinch the National League East title in Philadelphia, approximately a thousand fans rioted. In a scene again reminiscent of some British hooligan scenarios[11] – and this suggests that such events can potentially happen in North America if the conditions are right – dozens of seats were ripped from their moorings by Mets fans and used as ammunition against players, officials and police. More recently, two people were arrested and a boxing official injured when a chair-throwing mêlée broke out after a heavyweight boxing bout in Atlantic City. Over 50 people were reportedly involved in the fight, which occurred after one boxer was knocked out and out of the ring by his opponent (*Calgary Herald*, 8 November 1999: C8).

Fan fighting

There is compelling evidence that sports crowd disorder such as fan fighting has social origins (see Smith, 1983; Dunning et al., 1988) and that parallel causes can be traced across various sports and geographic settings. However, this is not to suggest that aspects of the phenomenon such as fighting are monocausal, or to deny the significance of 'situational' factors. For instance, perhaps partly due to the unique social and structural context of North American sport (travel on a huge continent is geographically and financially prohibitive; fan support between numerous sports and levels of sport is widely distributed; team franchises are extremely mobile; high season ticket sales are normal), fan fighting at North American sports has not taken the form of the routinised rival gang episodes of British and European soccer, and certainly organised 'super crews' or 'firms' of fighters in the European sense have not appeared to date.

The majority of incidents of fan-to-fan aggression occurring at North American games involve individuals or small groups of supporters participating in activities such as common assault, drunken and disorderly behaviour and confrontations with police. Less frequently, episodes of fighting involving larger numbers of fans have occurred. The *Los Angeles Times* reported a Rams play-off game in 1986 as follows:

> According to the Anaheim Police Department, there were 14 fights in the stands, 2 arrests, 8 citations issued, and 19 fans ejected. Now, 14 fights among 60,000 people isn't alarming, until you consider that most of the fights involved many participants. Entire sections, in some cases (25 November 1986: 3).

On an even larger scale were two riots that broke out during Monday Night NFL games at Schaefer Stadium in Foxboro, Massachusetts. *Sports Illustrated* (13 October 1980: 29) described the first, in 1976, as:

> a frightening evening during which a fan was stabbed, a police officer assaulted and his gun stolen, and drunkenness and brawling resulted in the arrest of more than 60 people. 35 others were treated at hospitals.

The second riot, in 1980, was described as 'another night of sheer horror', when a man was killed in a car accident outside the stadium, traffic jams led to fans not reaching their seats until half-time, and 50 arrests and 100 evictions were made. The report continued:

> youths rampaged through the parking lot, snapping off auto antennas, kicking in car doors and urinating on tires . . . bonfires were built, and fighting continued 'till the wee hours of Tuesday morning.

In 1985, over the course of three days of baseball between Toronto and Detroit, more than 200 fans were ejected for fighting and drunkenness and at a 1996 heavyweight boxing match at Madison Square Gardens, a post-contest riot involving dozens of fighting fans lasted 30 minutes and injured 22 people (*Sports Illustrated*, 19 August 1996: 58–63).

It should be reiterated that these types of cases remain exceptions to the normal pattern of sports crowd disorder, although on the basis of the frequency of press reports they apparently became more common in the 1970s and 1980s. It is difficult to estimate the exact frequency of fighting because, unlike the larger and more dramatic incidents, cases of interpersonal fan violence at North American sports go largely unreported in the mainstream media. However, interview and questionnaire data from club officials suggest that the vast majority of games involve cases of interpersonal dispute or aggression (Young, 1988).

Generally speaking, collective episodes of fan fighting, especially involving rival groups, are far more rare in North American sports than in, for instance, British soccer, although teams such as the New York Yankees, the Detroit Tigers and the New York Rangers have become infamous for the consistently bellicose behaviour of some of their fans. This has led, in the cases of several teams, to efforts to 'retake' stadium sections from chronically violent fans by closing them. Similar attempts by British soccer clubs throughout the 1970s and 1980s to make grounds safer by closing sections of the 'ends' (areas of the stadium known for territorial fan behaviour and symbolism) have been widely reported (Murphy et al., 1990a: 90–1).

Time and location of disorder
Unlike British soccer where, in the 1970s and 1980s, increases in stadium security had the unintended effect of displacing hooligan encounters to outside the ground and enhanced the possibility of violent exchanges taking place long before or after the game (Stuttard, 1985), North American crowd disorder has primarily taken place during games and inside stadia. Whereas a trip to a British soccer match, particularly for fans predisposed to hooligan encounters, commonly lasts much longer than the duration of the game itself – it often includes, for example, collective drinking sessions before and after games (Williams et al., 1984; Coakley, 1998: 204) – the history and culture of North American sports events have traditionally resulted in a far more 'privatised' and comfortable form of spectatorship.[12] For instance, parking facilities allow fans to arrive at and leave many events alone without requiring public transport. There is generally a far less intense and intimidating police presence at North American events and all-seater stadia mean that fans do not experience the same physical closeness with fellow spectators as the British fan (though this situation has changed at most top-level British clubs over the last decade).[13] In many respects, the cultural circumstances and experiences of the British and North American game day are quite dissimilar. Under such conditions and despite occasional concern over 'tailgate parties',[14] North American sports crowd disorder usually takes place within the boundaries of the game itself. Post-event riots which do not, of course, occur on a weekly basis, provide a notable exception to the rule.

Post-event riots
The most predictable and widely publicised form of North American fan disorder, the post-event riot,[15] involves forms of Saturnalia that may become

violent and destructive. Behaviours such as mass inebriation, fighting, looting, vandalism, vehicle destruction and physical and sexual assault are not uncommon during these episodes (Johnson, 1993; *Daily Mail*, 2 June 2000: 27).

Cases of post-event rioting can be found across the twentieth century, but no period matches the last three decades either for frequency or for damage to persons and property. During this period, post-event conduct has left a long trail of arrests, damage and injury across the continent. Even in what one Canadian newspaper called the 'friendliest of all celebration riots' – a celebration that took place following the Blue Jays' second consecutive World Series victory in 1993 – there was damage running into thousands of dollars, there were several arrests, and a young, pregnant woman lost an eye (*Calgary Herald*, 28 October 1993: A13).

The locations of post-event riots include, but are not limited to, New York (1969), Pittsburgh (1971), Philadelphia (1980), Toronto (1983), Detroit (1984, 1990), San Francisco (1985), Montreal (1986), Hamilton, Ontario (1986), Chicago (1991, 1992, 1993, 1994, 1996, 1997), Dallas (1993, 1994), Montreal (1993), Vancouver (1994), Denver (1998, 1999) and Los Angeles (2000). Probably the most catastrophic injury toll in a post-event riot is the eight deaths in Detroit in 1990; on that occasion, in addition to dozens of arrests and injuries related directly to the behaviour of 'celebrating' fans, four people were killed by an errant driver (Johnson, 1993). After three consecutive Chicago Bulls NBA (National Basketball Association) Championships between 1991 and 1993, the cumulative damage reported by Chicago police included 1700 arrests, over 100 police cars burned or destroyed, two people shot dead and approximately $8 million worth of damage to property. These events led directly to major changes in policy with respect to policing post-event gatherings in Cook County, Illinois (Nelson, 1994). After the Vancouver Canucks were beaten by the New York Rangers in the 1994 Stanley Cup Final (following a game played in New York), up to 70,000 people poured into the Vancouver downtown core. Police deployed tear gas to disperse the crowd and fired a rubber bullet. Over 200 people were injured, 50 people were arrested, and dozens of shops and properties were damaged (*Macleans*, 27 June 1994). Most recently, following the L. A. Lakers' 2000 NBA World Championship victory against the Indiana Pacers, police battled with rioting fans outside the Los Angeles Staples Centre, trapping inside other fans, players and celebrities for several hours. Twelve people were injured and a further dozen arrested (*The Guardian*, 21 June 2000: 12–13).

Post-event rioting is not confined to professional teams. Though they receive less media attention, there have been numerous cases involving college and high school teams. For example, stemming from post-game celebrations following Arkansas's victory over Duke in the National Collegiate Athletic Association (NCAA) basketball title game in 1994, 119 fans were arrested and several others were injured (*Sports Illustrated*, 25 April 1994: 10). Again, similar cases have occurred in North American amateur sport.

The policing – and indeed the sociological understanding – of such episodes are not made easier by the fact that many participants are known not to have attended the sports event in question or even to be game attenders at all. For example, according to police (Johnson, 1993; Nelson, 1994), several post-event troubles in Chicago and Detroit in the early 1990s displayed evidence of street gang involvement which led to concerns with so-called 'band-wagoning'. Such a possibility serves to underscore the need for socio-logical assessments of the phenomena which address not only the sport-specific cultures and conventions but also wider questions relating to, for example, gender, race, age and poverty and to what Elias and Dunning (1986) called the 'quest for excitement' in modern societies.

The extent of the problem

In seeking to estimate the extent of sport-related disorder, we are immediately confronted with familiar criminological problems of measurement (Hagan, 1991: 32–80). For example, what exactly is being measured and what is being left out? Are we measuring actual incidence levels or public sensitivities to a perceived problem about which people are increasingly curious or concerned? This dilemma is exacerbated by the fact that there is no single statutory legal category called 'crowd violence' which would facilitate the easy collection of data. It is further exacerbated by the fact that sports clubs (which operate as commercial businesses and hence fear negative marketing) have been loath to share their experiences and records with researchers (Young, 1988). There are also problems associated with the political economy of sport which prevent us from knowing the dimensions of the phenomenon more reliably. For example, sports crowd disorder is often defined and reported quite differently by clubs and security personnel. In my own research, I discovered that, perhaps because they work with it 'hands on', security personnel are far more likely to acknowledge the existence of a fan violence 'problem'; professional sports administrations (teams, leagues, governing bodies) often seem less willing to do so.[16] A possible partial explanation for this is offered below with respect to ownership, alcohol, and reputational issues.

In the absence of any systematically collected and empirically replicated regional or national surveys, the limited evidence as it stands restricts us to analyses at the level of particular localities – for instance: how many fights or ejections occur at National Football League (NFL) games at a particular stadium? How predictable are post-event riots in particular areas? Which games pose the biggest problems for police?

Useful preliminary profiles of, in Smith's words, 'who riots', can be found in Lewis (1982) and in Smith (1983: 172–7), but both sources are nearly two decades old. My earlier research with professional sports teams suggested that incidence levels for weekly sports events were quite low and that the majority of games take place largely without incident. For example, information from CFL (Canadian Football League), NFL, and Major League Baseball clubs indicated that during games there are often between three and thirty ejections or arrests per game, with alcohol being a major factor (Young, 1988). Disorder at college and university games can pose a far greater problem for the police (according to its Chief of Police, the University of Wisconsin regularly ejected over 100 football fans per game from Camp Randall Stadium in the 1980s; see Riseling, 1994), as can behaviour at and in response to end-of-season, play-offs, or other special games at the professional or amateur level.

The response of North American authorities to fan violence

It is clear that, in the last thirty years, North American sports and legal authorities have perceived a need to improve security and violence control at sports events. Having treated sports crowds more or less with 'kid gloves' until the mid-1970s, sports and security groups have begun to introduce much more severe measures both in anticipation of, and in response to, crowd disorder. These changes have generally taken the form of revisions to security procedures and efforts to anticipate and decrease abusive, profane, threatening, or violent behaviour. Concrete changes include, but are not limited to, the following organisational and security trends at North American sports stadia:

i) Changes in ticketing procedures and the introduction of educational programmes aimed at improving spectator orderliness (Riseling, 1994).
ii) Increases in fines for trespassing on the field of play and the introduction of local by-laws against field encroachment; a heightened police presence at the end of play.
iii) Improved security arrangements including the use of 'hi-tech' surveillance systems, screening procedures at entrances, use of police dogs and horses and significant increases in the number of security personnel at games.
iv) Modifications in alcohol concessions, including the sale of low alcohol beer, the banning of hard liquor and the earlier termination of sales; co-ordinated efforts between 'stakeholders' to reduce alcohol-related behaviour at sports events.
v) Remodelling of stadia including the construction of protective tunnels for players and officials to enter/exit the field safely and the construction of designated 'family' enclosures.

vi) Temporary closure of entire bleacher sections known to house chronically rambunctious fans. This occurred at professional baseball stadia in Detroit and Chicago in the 1980s.

vii) Judicious security planning in anticipation of post-event revelry and the assignment of special investigation units. For example, the City of Chicago spent $3.2 million preparing for a post-event 'celebration' following the Bulls' NBA World Championship in 1993 (*Calgary Herald*, 16 June 1997: D4).

viii) Improvements in criminal intelligence preparations in advance of national and international sports tournaments and festivals. This has included the international exchange of information on football hooligans in advance of the 1994 World Cup (Van Zunderd, 1994) and on possible 'terrorist' activity prior to the 1996 Summer Olympic Games in Atlanta (Kelley, 1994).

ix) Punitive legal responses to those involved in anti-social fan behaviour. For example, a man controversially charged with instigating the 1994 National Hockey League (NHL) Stanley Cup riots in Vancouver was sentenced to a year in jail (*Calgary Herald*, 15 June 1996: A8), and a drunken hockey fan who poured beer over a player's head at a 1997 NHL game was sentenced to 30 days in jail and fined $1,000 (*Calgary Herald*, 4 February 1997: A1).

While these examples focus on fan behaviour and responsibility at sports events, critical questions of accountability have also been directed at athletes themselves and at the police and other authorities. For example, fines and other sanctions have been imposed on players for making what could be perceived by fans as provocative gestures. The NFL's attempt in the 1990s to prohibit the infamous 'sack dance' and 'excessive' celebration in the end zone are cases in point. Also, concern that police had reacted with unwarranted force in the 1994 Vancouver ice hockey incident, and conjecture that the death of a fan shot by a policeman could have been prevented, led to widespread criticism and to the preparation of three official reports, all of which 'determined' different causes for the riot (British Columbia Police Commission, 1994; City of Vancouver, 1994; Vancouver Police Department, 1995).

Notwithstanding these examples of the increasingly thorough and strict policing of sports crowds and intermittent questions raised about how best to control them, North American authorities have reacted to crowd disorder on essentially local levels. Other than occasional attempts to have the US Congress address the issue of violent sports fans – most of which seem to have been ineffective or stymied – no wide-ranging legislation has been introduced to curb the problem and state legislators do not seem to have given the problem of sports crowd disorder much thought. At a hearing of the Congressional Subcommittee dealing with the Sports Violence Act of 1980, it was argued that 'one of the greatest threats to the future of sports of every kind, here and abroad, is mayhem on the field and crowd violence' (Mottl, 1980: 3), but although the problem of crowd violence in the US shows no sign of diminishing, legislative debates at this level have subsided and no concrete action has been taken with respect to federal policy.

Since it is thought to be a major precipitant of fan violence (many of the manifestations of North American sports crowd disorder described above are routinely attributed to it), the perceived role of alcohol and official reactions to that role are particularly worthy of note. On the one hand, concern that alcohol consumption might precipitate violence has prompted not only restrictions on sales of alcohol and increased frisking and confiscation procedures at many stadia, but also extensive, continent-wide efforts to reduce alcohol-related misconduct linked to sports events. For example, TEAM (Techniques for Effective Alcohol Management), the largest programme of its type, represents co-ordinated efforts with many professional sports teams/leagues, especially baseball. Similar, but local, programmes also exist in particular cities, such as the 'Game Plan: Safe Ride Home' programme at Toronto's SkyDome (City of Vancouver, 1994: 6). On the other hand, it remains the case that the vast majority of North American stadia continue to sell beer and/or hard liquor and that sport, sports spectatorship and sports business are enmeshed in what can only be called a 'culture of alcohol'. For example, the accounting firm, Ernst and Young, reported that beer/alcohol are by far the most popular products advertised at American sports stadia. In 1994, for instance, the New York Islanders' Nassau Colisseum displayed no fewer than 130 alcohol signs (*Sports Industry News*, 21 January 1994: 28; 22 January 1994: 38).

Although many stadia have reduced the strength and volume of alcohol they sell and frequently terminate sales prior to the conclusion of games, at least one interpretation of these practices is that they are public relations strategies used by clubs to mollify frustrated orderly fans and other concerned parties. Earlier data showed that clubs experiencing problems with inebriated fans have at times underplayed the extent and seriousness of the offences taking place (Young, 1988). This may be explained by the fact that many North American clubs are either sponsored or owned by breweries, or that stadia and their concessions are controlled not by the teams themselves but by external organisations. In these ways, then, the official reactions to the role of alcohol in sports-related disorder seem at least contradictory and possibly hypocritical. Despite the perceived primary role of alcohol in North American fan violence, it seems premature to anticipate any facsimile of Britain's 1985 'Control of Alcohol Bill' (Williams, 1985) in the near future.

The germane point here is that alcohol continues to feature prominently in the varied articulations of sport-related violence. As is demonstrated by the existing evidence on, for instance, sport-related hazing (abusive initiation practices) (Bryshun and Young, 1999), the excessive behaviour of current or retired 'superstar' athletes, as well as the myriad of alcohol-related scandals across the continent involving – usually male – athletes (Benedict and Klein, 1997), what might be called a 'sport-alcohol-masculinity-aggression complex' is obviously a matter of concern for authorities and sports officials alike. In brief, the various well-intended efforts to deal reasonably and responsibly with the negative impact of alcohol are positioned paradoxically against the culture of modern sport whose corporate and gender alliances (with alcohol) seem firmly rooted.[17]

Summary

It has been several decades since *Newsweek* proclaimed that 'the spectacle of the ugly American sports fan has been assuming increasingly frightful proportions' (17 June 1974: 93) and Yeager (1977: 93) similarly referred to 'increasingly brutal spectator outbursts and injuries to participants' and insisted that crowd disorder was 'the new violence in [North American] sports'. In fact, neither claim was entirely accurate. Fan violence was certainly not new. And although there is evidence that particular articulations of the phenomenon were becoming more widely reported in the popular media and that they were being freshly constructed as 'new' social problems (Young, 1988), there was, at that time, little firm evidence to suggest that they were becoming 'increasingly brutal'.

Since the 1970s, the research on and thus our knowledge of North American sports crowd disorder have expanded, but what we know about the phenomenon remains unsatisfactory on a number of levels, particularly with regard to extent/frequency issues and theoretically informed interpretation. It should be said that a number of barriers to understanding the problem more accurately continue to face researchers: the view that there is no serious or patterned fan violence in North America remains popular; police detection is difficult; no specific legal classifications of sports crowd disorder offences exist that could facilitate the ready use of 'official' data; and clubs are reluctant to open up their records. A further complicating factor is that sports crowd disorder in North America is extremely diffuse and not confined to any particular sport or level of play. There are, in this sense, easier phenomena to study.

There seems little doubt that in the 1970s and 1980s, sports crowd and player violence in North America were the focus of considerable attention both in the media and in academe and that a sizeable literature developed. This literature included, as Melnick (1989: 170) noted, 'some solid theoretically grounded work, [though] empirical investigations [were] far more numerous'. It is also true that during the last decade of the twentieth century sociologists of sport continued to probe the varied manifestations of North American sports-related violence. Though in my view less expansive and encapsulating than it could be (Young, 2000, 2001), the ensuing body of work has nevertheless been impressive. It includes, for example, investigations into: abusive initiation practices (Bryshun and Young, 1999); violent rituals in ice hockey (Weinstein et al., 1995; Collings and Condon, 1996); physicality and aggression among both male and female athletes (Rail, 1990, 1992; Messner, 1992; de Garis, 1997; Young, 1997); athletes involved in crimes away from the arena (Melnick, 1992; Crosset et al., 1995; Benedict and Klein, 1997); aspects of sports-violence litigation (Barnes, 1991; Young, 1993; Young and Wamsley, 1996); media coverage styles and their interface with corporate alliances (Gillett et al., 1996; Wenner, 1997); the intersection of youth, sport and violence (West, 1996); and a burgeoning literature on sports-related pain and injury (Curry and Strauss, 1994; Nixon, 1994a, 1994b; Young et al., 1994; Pike, 1997; Young and White, 1999).

Remarkably, however, this body of work is almost entirely restricted to violence both by and to athletes themselves. In other words, the recent sports violence research in North America has neglected the very real problem of crowd disorder, save for the occasional summary in edited anthologies (McPherson et al., 1989), introductory texts (Leonard, 1993; Bryant and McElroy, 1997; Coakley, 1998), or updates of the present kind. To my knowledge, the last in-depth empirically based examination of North American sports crowd disorder was conducted in the mid-1980s (Young, 1988) and can no longer be considered representative of current circumstances. Moreover, perhaps the most considered theoretical explanation of North American sports crowd disorder in the last decade has come not from someone currently empirically engaged in the topic in the US, Canada, or Mexico,[18] but from a Briton who acknowledges not being involved in primary research on the North American question at all (Dunning, 1999: 165). The fact that Dunning has probably written more on the topic of sports-related violence than any other living sociologist, and has arguably theorised it more rigorously than any other, does little to obscure the minimal attention given to the phenomenon by North American sociologists of late.[19, 20]

North American sports crowd disorder may not have posed as ominous or as consistent a problem as football hooliganism in Britain, Europe or other parts of the world. Nevertheless, the purpose of this chapter has been to challenge the clearly flawed view that there is no serious or patterned sports crowd disorder in North America. This view is at odds both with a constellation of evidence to the contrary, as well as with the varied interventionist efforts of the authorities which are themselves based on the perception of a need to address a real social problem in responsible ways.

Chapter 16

Towards a global programme of research into fighting and disorder at football

Eric Dunning
Patrick Murphy
Ivan Waddington

Writing on the Internet in 1996 about European studies of football hooliganism, Peter Marsh and a group of colleagues had this to say:

> Research on football violence has been a growth industry since the late 1960s in Britain, and academics in other European countries have been steadily catching up since the mid-1980s. To many observers, ourselves included, the subject is now probably over-researched and little in the way of new, original insights have been forthcoming in the past decade (Marsh et al., 1996: 1).

We disagree with this diagnosis. There are at least four reasons for disputing the idea that football hooliganism has been over-researched. These are that:

i) explanation of the phenomenon remains a hotly disputed issue;
ii) understanding of the social and psychological roots and parameters of football hooliganism, among policy makers as well as academics, journalists and members of the general public, remains generally low;
iii) the problem has not yet yielded – at least in most countries[1] – to public efforts to contain or eradicate it; and
iv) as many of the contributions to this volume show, it has been possible simply by widening the base to include countries outside Europe to break new ground and provide fresh insights.

The studies included in this volume represent a foundation which could be used to construct an international programme of collaborative research into football hooliganism and related issues. In the second half of the twentieth century, football hooliganism came to pose a near-global threat to the existence of the game, and solid, research-based knowledge represents the best hope there is of effectively countering this threat. Let us begin a preliminary exploration of some of the problems that will have to be addressed in an international programme of comparative research into the persistent and seriously troublesome issue of fighting and disorder at football.

The first tricky issue in any such future programme of cross-cultural research is that of identifying the degree to which the claims of scholars relating to differences between groups, regions, countries and historical periods are apparent rather than real. Many of the disagreements between scholars who study football hooliganism appear to us to be principally a question of ideological and related perspectival differences. Writers of a left-wing persuasion, for example, tend to stress the alienation of subordinates and exploitation by powerful groups as causes of football hooliganism, whereas people who lean towards the right are more likely to demonise football hooligans and to stress the elements of individual responsibility and choice that are involved. Writers on the left are also more likely to point to the causal role of a country's agents of social control – its police and politicians – in creating such problems. Scholars further to the right will be more likely to stress the role of these agents in controlling and/or solving the problem. In our view, however, such approaches and explanations are not necessarily mutually exclusive. What is needed is some means of getting beyond ideologically influenced understandings to the core balance of similarities and differences in the 'real world' of football hooliganism. Let us look at what we take to be some of the main 'real world' sources of similarity and difference. We shall start with similarities. The discussion is intended to be illustrative rather than exhaustive.

The first common element in the background of football hooliganism internationally is the fact that top-level football everywhere, whilst it is work for professional players and those otherwise occupationally involved in the game, is, for the spectators, a leisure pursuit one of the principal *raisons d'être* of which is emotional arousal, the generation of excitement (Elias and Dunning, 1986; Dunning, 1999). Authors such as Armstrong (1998: 296–8) and Giulianotti (1999: 53–4) are, we think, pointing broadly to the same phenomenon when they invoke Bakhtin's (1968) concept of carnival, Turner's (1977; 1982) concept of liminality and Csikzentmihalyi's (1975) concept of flow in this connection. Whenever a large crowd turns up to watch an exciting leisure event, it is highly probable that some of its members will abandon their self-controls and behave in disorderly and sometimes violent ways. Others will seek deliberately to heighten the excitement. Again, spectators will sometimes be provoked into violent behaviour if a football match fails to live up to expectations and the anticipated level of excitement is not generated. Under such circumstances, the violence may take the form either of direct protest or of acting in disorderly ways to counter the boredom and disappointment of an unexciting match. We hasten to add, of course, that violence is by no means the only response at matches of this kind. Fans also respond humorously and in ways intended to encourage their team. And violence can also, under certain conditions, take a ritual, metonymic form (Marsh, 1978; Marsh et al., 1978).

Ignoring for present purposes the question of the specific situational 'triggers' which 'spark' violence at sports events, it can be suggested that the probability of such violence as does take place, and its probable seriousness, is likely to vary between countries, classes and other subgroups according to their levels and trajectories of civilisation (and de-civilisation) – according to where they stand at a specific point in time in a civilising (or de-civilising) process. The probability of spectator violence at football and other sports is also likely to be increased by the degree to which spectators identify with the contending teams and the strength of their emotional investments in and commitments to the victory of the teams that they support. In its turn, this will vary to the extent that the spectators have been socialised into and adhere to the values of the 'fair play' ethos, i.e. the idea that taking part in sport for fun and sticking to the rules are more important than winning.

In Britain and many other countries, commitment to the fair play sports ethos atrophied in the course of the twentieth century, largely in conjunction with processes of monetarisation, commercialisation and professionalisation. Many English fans for example – and we speak of them because we know them best – have come to claim that they are 'passionate' about the teams they support, and they certainly seem to be heavily emotionally committed to victory. In short, their egos and identities are deeply involved with the fortunes of their teams. This means that, besides the strength and firmness of their socialisation into fair play values, the strength of spectators' emotional investment in and commitment to the victory of their sides is liable to be a consequence of the centrality and significance of football in their lives; that is, whether it is one among a number of sources of meaning and satisfaction for them or just the only one. Spectators for whom identification and emotional involvement with a soccer team are *the* central source of meaning in their lives seem likely, *ceteris paribus*, to be among those most liable to behave in disorderly and perhaps violent ways in soccer and related contexts if their self-controls slacken and they lose their inhibitions. Further to this, the centrality of soccer in people's lives is likely to differ, *inter alia*, in terms of such variables as: the location of the game in their country's prestige hierarchy of sports; its positioning in their country's class, ethnic and gender structures; people's degrees of sexual satisfaction; whether they have a regular partner or are married and, if so, how happily; the numbers and degrees of closeness of their friends; their levels of education; the degree to which they are able to obtain satisfaction from their occupational work; what their hobbies are; and, indeed, whether they are able to find employment at all. However, in Britain, what one might call the 'core football hooligans' tend not to be people who simply lose their self-controls. They are groups which are organised to varying degrees, whose members have a predisposition to fight, and whose fighting usually involves a degree of premeditation. The same holds true for some of the Italian and French 'ultras' (see chapters 10 and 5) and for some of the Argentinian and Peruvian 'barras bravas' (see chapters 2 and 11).

The second common element in football hooliganism which we believe is probably internationally shared relates more directly to fighting. *All* societies in the world today remain characterised by general forms of male dominance, especially in the public sphere, and hence are permeated by patriarchal values and institutions. It is true that there are differences between countries in the degree of male dominance, and there are variations within countries – for example between social classes, regional and ethnic groups . Changes in gender relations are also continuing to occur. Furthermore, there are stylistic differences between, for example, Hispanic ideals of machismo (see chapters 2 and 11) and North European, North American and Antipodean masculine ideals (see chapters 15 and 3). Yet in spite of all these variations, a general characteristic of patriarchy is the expectation that males will be aggressive and fight, that a willingness and ability to fight in specific situations – for example for one's country in a war or for one's wife and children if they are attacked – constitute a key mark of what it means to be a 'man'. Football is a context which is conducive to patriarchal fighting behaviour, because the game itself involves a 'play-' or 'mock-fight' component, and because, despite the successes of women's football around the world in recent years, the game originated as a male preserve and continues to this day to be permeated by masculine and patriarchal values (Dunning, 1999). (Of course, this is true not just of soccer but of sport in general. Indeed, it is more true of sports such as boxing, a sport which has its share of fighting fans but who have not received anything like the degree of adverse publicity accorded to their football counterparts (Sheard, 1997, 1998; Sugden, 1996).) What our general argument so far means is that, whenever large numbers of males – especially males divided by passionate support for rival teams – assemble in the context of an exciting leisure event such as a football match, fighting among some of them is not an improbable outcome. Our discussion so far, however, deals mainly with fighting which is *ad hoc* and situationally generated. We must next pay attention to those fans who go to football matches with the *intention* of fighting.

Some forms of fighting at football are generated through the way in which the game is embedded in wider social contexts. In consequence, more or less organised groups of fans – 'firms', 'crews', 'ultras', 'barras bravas', 'torcidas organizadas' – sometimes attend matches with the intention of fighting their counterparts who support the opposing side. It has even been suggested that, in some countries, Portugal (chapter 12) and Greece (chapter 7) for example, club owners sometimes incite and even pay their fans to fight opposing fans. In all these cases, the violence involves a substantial degree of premeditation, planning and organisation. The Leicester research (Dunning et al., 1988; Murphy et al., 1990a) suggests that, in England, fans who go to matches intending to fight – those who are not satisfied simply with vicariously experiencing 'battle excitement' by watching the 'mock fight' on the field of play – first began to be drawn to the game in substantial numbers in the 1960s. The Leicester research also suggests that the unintentional 'advertising' of the game by the mass media as an occasion where exciting and, above all, violent action regularly takes place, played an important part in attracting fans of this kind to soccer. This implies that the forms and extent of media coverage of soccer in particular countries will be one of the influences on their patterns of soccer hooliganism, contributing to its escalation under certain circumstances and its de-escalation under others (Dunning, 1999 and see chapter 1 above). Highly publicised fighting in soccer contexts also means that the game can become attractive to extremist political groups as a place for recruiting street fighters and engaging in kinds of terrorist activity in order to gain publicity for their cause (chapter 6). Evidence points to a group called 'Combat 18' – combat on behalf of Adolf Hitler ('A' and 'H' being the first and eighth letters of the alphabet) – as being regularly involved in English football hooliganism, both at home and abroad. There is also evidence of right-wing involvement in football hooliganism in Belgium and Spain, and in contributions to this volume such evidence is presented for Argentina (chapter 2), France (chapter 5), Germany (chapter 6) and Italy (chapter 10). And in some countries, for example England, Germany (chapter 6) and Greece (chapter 7), left-wing groups have sometimes fought and otherwise campaigned against fascists or racists in football-related contexts.

Similar patterns of football hooliganism and fan behaviour also occur in conjunction with the shared characteristics of particular linguistic/cultural areas. Examples are the barras bravas patterns of Spanish America (chapters 2 and 10), and the similarities that arose in Eastern Europe as a consequence of Soviet domination and its downfall (chapters 4 and 8). Similarities can also arise from processes of diffusion within and between countries. Such processes usually involve the members of some groups adopting aspects of the behaviour of other groups, nearly always groups which are, or which they perceive to be, more powerful, prestigious or successful in some respects than they are themselves. Such behaviour tends to be seen and felt by members of the adopting groups – these processes involve emotional as well as rational/ cognitive components – as meeting specific needs in ways which they perceive to be better than their own equivalent forms. For example, starting in the late 1960s, young football fans in continental European countries started to adopt some of the forms of behaviour – patterns of chanting, singing and fighting – developed by English fans and English hooligans. They did so, it seems reasonable to surmise, because compared with their own forms of behaviour, they saw them as:

i) conducive to the generation of greater excitement;
ii) expressive of greater commitment to one's team; and
iii) as constituting more of a challenge to the football and state authorities.

Such processes involved modelling based on direct observation of the behaviour of English (and sometimes Scottish) hooligans or fans whose clubs were playing abroad, as well as modelling based on watching English football fan behaviour on television. This whole pattern is probably best seen as having been connected with the predominance of English 'youth culture' and 'pop culture' models in that period. Two things need to be added. The first is that processes of diffusion occurred in the reverse direction as well. For example, it is likely that the fashion of wearing 'casual' clothes to football was introduced into Britain by the fans of English and Scottish teams which were successful in European competitions in the late 1970s and early 1980s, and who had seen and admired the clothing styles of Italian fans. The now wide-spread use of face-paints seems to have originated in the Netherlands and spread from there. And more localised processes of diffusion involved the spread of the 'ultra' style from Italy to France and Portugal (chapters 5 and 12). The second thing worthy of note is that these processes of diffusion rarely involve slavish adoption. Rather, they almost invariably entail modification and adaptation by the receiving group or groups as they merge the adopted patterns with their own distinctive cultural forms. This brings us to the question of differences.

We have already discussed differences in patterns of football hooliganism and fan behaviour within and between countries which occur in conjunction with processes of 'civilisation' and 'de-civilisation'. Related differences are likely to arise in relation to the particular trajectories of economic, political and cultural development of different countries and regions. Ethnic and racial patterns are likely to be important in this connection (chapters 3, 9 and 13). So, too, are political histories: whether countries have had a Nazi/fascist past (chapters 6, 10 and 12); a Communist past (chapters 4 and 8); a democratic one (chapters 1, 3, 5 and 15); or whether they have experienced military dictatorship (chapters 2 and 7).[2] Different political histories of these kinds are likely to be a significant influence on patterns of policing and these, in their turn, are likely to have significant effects on the behaviour of fans.

To the extent that they involve breaking the law, football hooliganism and its equivalents are probably best defined as forms of 'expressive criminality'. It is worth remembering, however, that both hooliganism and sports crowd violence generally can also involve or be a pretext for criminality of an instrumental kind (chapter 15). A final point is that there is often an element of intergenerational rivalry and tension involved in football hooliganism. This can take the form, or involve elements, of an adolescent *rite de passage.* It sometimes involves older people as well, however, and when it does, it tends to be more politicised and more seriously violent.

Notes

Chapter One

1 'Soccer', the term by which Association Football is known especially in the United States, Canada and Australia, is used to distinguish it from their own forms of the game. It is an abbreviation of the word 'association'.

2 The term 'hooligan' apparently entered common English usage in the late nineteenth century as a term for describing 'gangs of rowdy youths'. It is possibly a corruption of 'Houlihan', the name of an Irish family who lived in London at that time and who were renowned for their love of fighting (Pearson, 1983: 40).

3 'Fan' is an abbreviation of the term 'fanatic'.

4 When discussing how to tackle the problem of football hooliganism in the wake of the Heysel tragedy, the Prime Minister, Margaret Thatcher, apparently asked leading figures in the Football Association whether spectators were an essential ingredient at matches.

5 Together with our former research assistant, John Williams, we wrote three books on the subject: *Hooligans Abroad* (1984, 1989); *The Roots of Football Hooliganism* (1988); and *Football on Trial* (1990).

6 Reported in *The Guardian*, 7 October 1999.

7 Skirmishes between Liverpool and Juventus fans took place in several parts of Brussels, especially in and near the city centre, in the hours before the match. Whilst the Juventus 'ultras', the closest to Italian equivalents of the English football hooligans, were mainly housed at the match on segregated terracing, the Liverpool hooligans shared a terrace with non-hooligan Italians, many of whom had been sold tickets on the day of the match in violation of UEFA's regulations. It was the latter fans who were attacked in a terrace charge and it was from their ranks that the 39 victims came.

8 Continental fans in the 1970s and 1980s also began to imitate English/British fans' behaviour more generally, for example in their songs and chants. The adoption by British fans of the 'casual' style was, of course, an example of diffusion in the opposite direction, from Italy to England, Scotland and Wales, and also to France and Portugal.

9 Standing terraces were made illegal at grounds staging top-level English matches as a result of the implementation of Lord Justice Taylor's recommendations in his enquiry into the Hillsborough tragedy of 1989.

10 The implication here is that their arguments are reminiscent of the convolutions of Ptolemy of Alexandria and subsequent pre-Copernican astronomers as they struggled to fit empirical observations into their 'geocentric' or earth-centred view of the solar system.

11 'Figurational' or 'process sociology' is the synthesising approach to the subject pioneered by Norbert Elias. See, for example, his *What is Sociology?* (1978).

12 The occupations of two Germans were provided in these newspapers, a tattoo shop manager and an apprentice mechanic.

13 Upper and middle class people, of course, often play comparatively violent sports like rugby. They can also behave violently in private and cause the state's monopoly of physical violence to be used. Further to this, research shows that, since the 1960s, a small but relatively stable percentage of English football hooligans has come from the higher reaches of the social scale.

14 In patriarchal societies, that is in most societies up to now, males are generally expected to fight in defence of their families, tribes or nations. Careers in the military and the police also involve a direct training in the use of violence. The hypothesis developed here is an attempt to explain a way in which a form of aggressive male habitus can develop and persist as a result of structural arrangements, relatively independently of specific and deliberate planning.

15 Patterns of aggressive masculinity of this sort will be liable to spread beyond the families and communities where their original sociogenesis takes place so that their bearers pick on less aggressive males at school, on the streets, at work, in pubs, clubs and at football grounds, constraining those of the latter who choose 'fight' rather than 'flight' to become more aggressive themselves.

16 In militaristic societies, of course, females and older males often exert pressure on young men which increases the violence of the latter's behaviour.

17 German students of football hooliganism seem agreed that the problem in their country is not class related or connected to patterns of social stratification in any way (see chapter 6). To our knowledge, however, German scholars rarely if ever provide occupational, income, educational and other relevant data which would allow outside observers to assess the validity of this conclusion.

Chapter Two

1 Data from the newspaper *Clarín* of Buenos Aires, 28 May 1998, Sports, p. 5.

2 Extra police officers are assigned to manage security at football matches. However, the number of additional officers is decided in a Committee of Security in which the clubs are not represented; the assignment of police officers is therefore almost exclusively a police decision. The extra funds allocated to the police are distributed between the police force and individual policemen, for whom the work generates extra income. There have been cases in which the police have neglected security problems at the end of a match (when violence is most likely to take place) in order to collect their extra payments for attending the match. Given the low wages of the police in Argentina, these sums are relatively important in their monthly income.

3 Several important aspects of violence (time of occurrence, the number of victims, those responsible for the violence, repercussions of the violence) were examined in reports covering thirty years and published in three newspapers from Buenos Aires, each with its own distinct readership.

4 This was a campaign organised jointly by the AFA and the monopoly owner of TV transmissions, TyC. It used several different means of communication (press, radio and television, and leaflets at stadiums). For an analysis, see Calvo (1998).

5 De Ipola alleges that biological metaphors have their origin in the discourse of the French reactionary nationalism of the second half of the nineteenth century, and from there they have become an habitual topic of right-wing discourses.

6   A more detailed analysis can be found in Coelho et al. (1998).

7   By using the plural I want to point out the group characteristic of our work. The statements contained in this chapter could not have been made without the joint work of the whole team. All are young graduates of the University of Buenos Aires.

8   Between 1996 and 1998, more than 300 interviews were carried out with militant fans of Argentine football teams, mostly from Buenos Aires, although fans of teams from the interior of the country were also interviewed.

9   The clearest sign of this expansion is the 'footballisation' of television: the hundreds of hours of sport programmes, and the fact that the ten most widely watched programmes on Argentine television in 1998 were sport transmissions.

10   Players also become part of the mass media show: they are new members of the local jet set, they flood the screens, the advertising announcements; they become erotic symbols, the subjects of sexual desire. Thus, their relationship with the fans becomes increasingly distant.

11   I have developed elsewhere the idea that the national team had lost this capacity for summoning national commitment. See Alabarces (1999).

12   In the case of Racing Club, one of the tribes is called 'Racing Stones', from their predilection for the rock band, the 'Rolling Stones'. Another tribe is called 'The 95' simply because, coming from the North of Buenos Aires, they go to the stadium on bus number 95.

13   Dal Lago and Moscati (1992) suggest this stigmatisation is focused on youth. However, we believe it to be focused on the intersection of youth and class, that is, on the youth of the popular classes. See Alabarces and Rodríguez (1996: 61–74).

14   These remarks are drawn from our previously cited work which was based on interviews. A first analysis in terms of the perception of violence on the part of the fans can be found in Guindi (1998).

15   A good description can be found in a journalistic British reference: see McCaughn, 1999.

16   But comparison of the violence used by different classes is impossible. In spite of the possibility of micro-sociologically analysing what we can recognise as violent characteristics in the daily life of the popular classes, the presence of institutional violence by dominant classes is prior and omnipresent. Recognition of this is necessary for moving from the realm of comparison to the realm of causation.

17   Hector Souto was a 17-year-old fan of Racing Club who was killed by 'barras bravas' of Huracan during a match. Police inquiries showed that the 'barras' were protected and financed by club leaders.

18   The case of 'Door 12' happened in 1968, after a match between Boca and River. Seventy-one people died in a crush against a door, presumably closed by police. The case was never investigated, nor were those responsible identified. One of our informers offered a political explanation: the hinchada of Boca would have sung the 'Peronist March' during the match, a song that identified them as then outlawed Peronistas. Police then caused the disaster as a reprisal. Argentine history suggests the plausibility of this type of explanation, despite its conspiratorial character.

19   In 1985, Adrian Scaserra, a 14 year old who was with his father attending his first football match at a stadium, was killed by a police bullet during massive police repression at Independiente's stadium. Those responsible for his death were never found.

Chapter Five

1   For a description in English of the social history of French football, see Mignon (1994a: 273–98; 1999: 79–97).

2   The analysis in term of a hierarchy of values is based on Dumont (1966).

3   I shall not go further into this issue in this context. However, it should be noted first, that football culture in France has to be understood not only as an expression of the people but as a collective production involving different kinds of social actors; and second that there is a special link between disorderly Parisian supporters and the club.

4   I have used here the case of Paris Saint-Germain. However, surveys in Metz, Saint-Etienne and Marseille show, with some variations, the same general picture. All these surveys were carried out between 1994 and 1999 (Mignon, 1994b; 1997; 2000).

5   I am using here a very broad definition of hooligans. The common definition used by the police and the media refers to those who make trouble and have been arrested for this reason or who are known for their activism.

6   One of the 'Kop de Boulogne's' leaders came from an educated and affluent background.

7   In the sixties, schoolchildren were taught that there were ten cities of more than 100,000 inhabitants in France.

8   For a description of these processes see for example Dubet and Lapeyronnie (1992).

9   The following analysis is founded on ethnographic and quantitative studies conducted between 1994 and 1999. The research included interviews with ordinary and ultras supporters and convicted hooligans.

10 As developed in interactionist sociology.

Chapter Six

1   'Regularisation', in the sense of a practice or institution becoming more regular, especially through the formulation and following of rules.

Chapter Seven

1   The research was carried out under the auspices of the Greek Centre of Criminology, Department of Sociology, Panteion University. The programme was directed by A. E. Astrinakis and M. G. Stylianoudis. The research staff consisted of four doctoral candidates as research coordinators, five special researchers and nine postgraduate students as research assistants.

2   For purposes of our research, we classified the matches we observed as *interlocal*, *local* and *neighbourhood*, that is, on the basis of the areas from which the teams draw their main spectatorship and fans. This classification only partly coincides with the threefold alignment of the 1st National Division, the 2nd National Division and the 3rd Amateur Division.

3   Aigaleo is a working-class city adjacent to, and traditionally a rival of, Peristeri. For many years, the fans of the two cities have engaged in aggressive rivalry with each group considering the other as their greatest enemy.

4   In the course of our research with 'the Genuines', participant observation mainly consisted in developing a very close, almost intimate contact over a period of one and a half years with two of their local members, and looser and sporadic contacts with four other local members.

5   A PhD in social anthropology which was based on a study of the soccer fan and hard-core fan cultures and groupings of Olympiakos, carried out at the same time as our own project,

reached similar conclusions to us in relation to social demarcations, social organisation and subcultural patterns of Olympiakos fans. See Papageorgiou (1995).

6   See Siamou and Playanakou (1998); Siamou et al. (1999); Haralambopoulos (in progress); Hadjantoniou (2001).

7   See also Siamou (in progress).

Chapter Ten

1   In Italy, as a rule, the most popular parts of the stadium are the ends that abut onto the terraces. The 'distinti' area – the name already points to a difference of status as compared to the popular stadium end – runs along the length of the pitch and is located opposite the stand.

2   Data gathered from a scan of the following dailies: *Il Resto del Carlino, La Repubblica, L'Unita* and *La Gazzetta dello Sport.*

3   Out of 59 incidents recorded in the period of study, 33 involved southern Italian teams and 25 took place in minor divisions (Serie C and Amateur Championship).

4   The Archive-Observatory is part of a project called 'Progetto Ultras'. The latter has two essential aims: to uphold the values connected with football fan culture and to limit the intolerant behaviour present in the world of football support through social/community-type work conducted together with the fans themselves.

5   In Italy, for some years now, the Police Study Centre in Brescia has been processing and publishing data relating to incidents, season by season. These data, however, are not reliable since they make no distinction between football hooliganism and mere wild behaviour by fans.

6   For example, West Ham, founded by a group of steel workers; Sheffield United, created by artisan cutlers; Manchester United, set up by workers engaged in building the railway network. On this topic see Taylor (1969: 204–6).

7   See, for example, Dunning et al. (1986c). Recent studies have, however, given different results, which suggest that the hooligans have a broader social base. See Kerr (1994) and Armstrong (1998).

8   On this topic see, among others, Balestri and Podaliri (1998).

9   According to Dunning, this mechanism is based on the principle of ordered segmentation, i.e. on the fact that youth groups belonging to the same community, but independent of each other, have the tendency to unite according to a fixed sequence when faced with the possibility of a conflict with youth groups of other communities. See Dunning et al. (1988: 201 et seq.). Note that in Italy this mechanism does not operate in the cities where there are two rival fan groups. In this case, the two fan groups do not ally to face away fans.

10   For an analysis of the social disintegration among young people, see, for example, Berzano (1998). From the enquiry carried out in Turin it emerges that the district groups and gangs that had characterised the urban area up to the 1980s have been almost totally disappearing.

11   We describe the world of the ultras as a 'movement' because that is how they define themselves, and also because this world does not greatly diverge from the definition given by Melucci of the concept of movement: 'a collective phenomenon that manifests with a certain unity, but that within contains highly differentiated significances, forms of action and modes of organisation'. See Melucci (1982: 15).

12   In 1998, thanks also to the activity of the Progetto Ultras, the strategy of confrontation and dialogue centred on ultras' themes has become a common practice. The topics dealt with at

meetings concern the original mentality of the ultras, the rights of fans, and the defence of football fan culture in the face of the onslaught of the soccer industry.

Chapter Eleven

1   According to the popular tradition Alianza Lima was founded in 1901 by a group of black workers. From this point of view, Alianza has been identified with the poor, especially with the Afro-Peruvian culture.

2   Taking as a poverty indicator the index of unsatisfied basic needs prepared by the National Statistics and Data Institute in 1998.

3   Survey conducted by the National Statistics and Data Institute. Source: Piqueras, 1998.

Chapter Twelve

1   Among the existing studies of violence and values in Portuguese society, the works by Braga da Cruz and Reis (1983), Pais (1998), França (1993) and Barreto (1996) are of particular significance.

2   The Portuguese Football Federation penalised Benfica for this disturbance with a suspension of eight matches at their stadium, and a pecuniary fine.

3   In 1977, the government formed an interministerial working group with the participation of one representative of the Portuguese Football Federation and one from the Central Football Referees Commission, with equal representation from other sports, to study aspects related to violence in sports grounds and the security measures to be taken. In 1979, the obligatory presence of police at sports events was withdrawn, unless there was a full capacity crowd, or when considered necessary by the Federated bodies. Since 1980, the Government has issued a number of decrees about the closure of stadia and the obligation to take security measures, such as those relating to fences and access tunnels when violent incidents occur. At the core of this vacillation regarding policy towards violent incidents at matches is the controversy it caused among club managers when their clubs were penalised for the supporters' behaviour. The measures which have been enacted sought, on the one hand, to try to prevent acts of violence by penalising supporters (these penalties may adversely affect their own clubs) and, on the other hand, highlighted the lack of security in stadia, especially on and around the pitch.

4   Eight per cent of the reported incidents occurred, in descending order, in handball, roller hockey, basketball, and volleyball.

5   This campaign was directed at clubs, schools and the general public. It owed its political–institutional existence not only to the existing violence in sports but also to the fact that the Under-20 Football World Cup took place in Portugal and the Hockey World Cup in Paris, as well as Portugal's eventually unsuccessful bid to host the 1998 Football World Cup.

6   As a consequence of this incident, the Government passed a law forbidding the taking of explosive devices to any civic event (Law 8/97 of 12/4–DR I–A 86). The National Stadium where the incident occurred was rebuilt in accordance with the safety standards of sports grounds, the reconstruction being concluded in 1999.

7   In the 1989–90 football season, we conducted research on the national pattern of violence in sport and as part of this project we studied the fan groups – claques – of the seven major Premier League clubs. This study was included in the 'Comparative Multinational Investigation

by the European Council on Football Hooliganism'. Twelve claques were studied through participant observation and interviewing the group leaders: Panteras Negras (Boavista-Porto); Fúria Azul (Belenenses-Lisboa); Dragões Azuis and Super Dragões (FC Porto); Diabos Vermelhos and Força Benfiquista (Benfica-Lisboa); Juventude Bracarense (SC Braga); Juventude Leonina-Juve Leo, Torcida Verde, Onda Verde and Consórcio de Claques Força, Onda e Império Verde (Sporting-Lisboa); VIII Exército/Juventude Vitoriana (VF Setúbal). Some results from this study have been included in this chapter; the full results of the study are published in Marivoet (1992b).
8   Law 38/98 of 4/08 (DR I–A 178).

Chapter Thirteen

1   Details of references from the popular media appear in the text and are not referenced separately in the list of references. Some page numbers are not indicated as they do not appear in the sources obtained from the Johannesburg City Library and the Sowetan Library.
2   The effects of poverty were qualified and quantified in the second and third Carnegie Reports on Poverty in South Africa. The first report was Wilson and Ramphele (1989). The second was conducted by SALDRU (South Africa Labour and Development Research Unit) for the World Bank (1995).
3   These conclusions are drawn from my PhD thesis (Anthropology), entitled 'Violence in the Context of Poverty in Davidsonville' and completed in 1996 at the Rand Afrikaans University, and from research by J. C. Kotzé published in 1993 by Juta (Kenwyn).

Chapter Fourteen

1   The Dynasty Cup was discontinued from 1998.

Chapter Fifteen

I would like to express my gratitude to Michael Atkinson, Eric Dunning and David Stead for their help with earlier drafts of this paper.

1   In March 1955, Francophone sports icon, Maurice Richard of the Montreal Canadiens, was suspended by Anglophone NHL President, Clarence Campbell, for a stick-swinging incident and was thus prevented from reaching what looked like a certain single-season goal-scoring record. When Campbell attended the Canadiens' next home game, he was subjected to verbal and physical abuse and a smoke bomb was set off in the stadium. A two-day riot ensued on the streets of Montreal (Mark et al., 1983: 84).
2   For example, the Football Offences Act was enacted in April 1991. A response to a prolonged period of fan-related violence connected to English soccer and in the immediate post-Hillsborough context, the Act introduced restriction and exclusion orders designed to prevent fans convicted of football-related offences from attending football matches. The powers of magistrates to impose domestic and international banning orders on those convicted of soccer-related offences were strengthened by subsequent legislation following disorders involving English fans at the Euro 2000 Championships.

3   Since sports crowd disorder on both sides of the Atlantic is overwhelmingly a 'male preserve' (Dunning, 1986), the most obvious of these sociological 'threads' is perhaps gender.

4   See chapter 1 for an innovative interpretation of soccer hooliganism as a 'world social problem'.

5   The issue of cultural specificity in the expression of violence is important. For instance, the manner in which spectators from European countries differentially articulate their allegiance to the game of soccer has been discussed by Williams and Goldberg (1989).

6   These demographic characteristics of those involved in sports crowd disorder represent a compilation of data derived from several sociological studies and from my own 1988 study which used questionnaire, interview and archival procedures with sports clubs, sports administrators, legal officials, fans and the media. Though this profile summary is admittedly outdated, I know of no systematic sociological update since it was first produced.

7   At the conclusion of the Colorado–Colorado State (American) football game held in Denver in September 1999, student fans used mace and tear gas and rushed onto the field to steal the goalposts. One officer commented that 'the crowd was the most unruly he had ever seen, and he had done Broncos games since 1967' (*National Post*, 6 September 1999: B2).

8   Of the newspaper and magazine sources cited in this paper, *Sports Illustrated*, the *Boston Globe*, *New York Times*, *Los Angeles Times*, *Newsweek* and *Sports Industry News* are all published in the United States. The *National Post*, *Toronto Star*, *Calgary Herald*, *Toronto Sun*, *McMaster University Silhouette* and *Macleans* are all published in Canada. The *Daily Mail* and *Guardian* are national daily British newspapers.

9   One example of this behaviour which continues to take place at the professional level is that in Detroit, where fans throw octopuses onto the ice when the NHL's Red Wings score a goal in the play-offs. The practice began in 1952 when the Red Wings needed an unusual eight play-off games to win the Stanley Cup.

10 Although caused by different sets of crowd dynamics and cultural circumstances, the two incidents nevertheless shared seriously injurious outcomes. As with the Heysel tragedy, many of those affected by the Wisconsin incident had no unlawful intentions but were simply caught up in the crowd surge and eventual crush.

11 There are numerous examples from British soccer that could be used to illustrate this argument; one of the most cited is the nationally televised English cup tie between Luton Town and Millwall in March 1985, when dozens of fans tore seats from their anchors and used them in a missile attack upon a surprised and unprepared police contingent (Stuttard, 1985).

12 For a structural comparison of sports crowd disorder in the UK, USA and Canada, see Young (1988: 148–95). Coakley (1998: 204) also details stark differences in appearance and style between some North American stadia and some British soccer grounds.

13 Although they have not been entirely removed from all stadia, many of the traditional 'all standing' areas of British soccer grounds were changed to seating sections in the post-Hillsborough period as a safety precaution.

14 Essentially collective celebrations held in stadia parking lots prior to and/or following sports events, 'tailgate parties' are normally law-abiding affairs but occasionally involve unruly behaviour. Alcohol tends to feature prominently.

15 Since episodes of this kind have been associated both with team victory and team loss, the term 'post-event riot' is preferred here to the widely used but misleading classification 'celebration riot'.

16 For example, on several occasions during my doctoral research (Young, 1988), I became aware of clubs minimising violence and/or security problems that their own security personnel emphatically acknowledged. In fact, the only way I became aware of fan disorder at certain clubs was through security personnel violating club policy and making their records available to me, orally or in hard copy. Simply stated, while many professional clubs continue to deny a crowd disorder problem, I have never, then or more recently, spoken to anyone who works in sports crowd security who has argued that North American sports fans are becoming less rowdy.

17 The relationship between alcohol and sports-related violence (Young, 2001) clearly requires more in-depth consideration. This relationship has been brought into sharp relief on both sides of the Atlantic by the drunken exploits of European, and particularly English, soccer fans at Euro 2000 and of US rioters at the Los Angeles Staples Centre incident. In addition to the ambiguous position taken on the alcohol-violence question by clubs owned or sponsored by breweries, other paradoxes on this matter can be found at the elite level. Perhaps none is more bizarre than Manchester United's marketing of its own brand of whisky, Manchester United Premier Blend (*Sports Illustrated*, 6 May 1996: 24). Manchester United is among the most successful soccer clubs in the world; their fans are also known for incidents of hooligan violence, much of which has been drink-related.

18 Strictly speaking, any assessment of North American sports crowd disorder should also consider Mexico. Again, despite known cases of Mexican crowd violence, the literature, or at least that portion of it written in or translated into English, is severely limited.

19 Of course, it is possible that I may unwittingly have misrepresented North American work on sports crowd disorder and that more primary research and theoretical assessment than I have acknowledged has been done or is being developed.

20 Indisputably a pioneer in the sociological study of sports violence, particularly as it pertains to football hooliganism, Eric Dunning's substantive and interpretive work has been widely influential both among his own and subsequent generations of sport scholars. Similarly, in North America, it is unlikely that anyone has contributed as much to the sociological understanding of sports-related violence, in all its different dimensions, on and off the field, as Michael Smith. Though clearly in need of updating, Smith's landmark text, *Violence and Sport* (1983), remains one of the most panoramic sociological explorations of the North American scene. Anyone interested in probing the 'standard deviations' of North American sports crowds should regard Smith's book and his many other contributions (1975, 1976, 1978) as essential reading.

An internationally respected scholar, Smith died in June 1994. He is greatly missed by his colleagues and friends.

Chapter Sixteen

1 Denmark in the 1970s may be an exception. The media and the authorities there defined football rowdies as 'roligans' (friendly hooligans).

2 We realise, of course, that the categories of fascism and military dictatorship overlap in many ways.

Bibliography

Abraham, T. (1999) 'Juego salvaje', *Clarín*, Buenos Aires: 9 March 1999: 16.

Alabarces, P. (1999) 'Postmodern times: Identities, violence and mass media in Argentine football', pp. 77–85 in G. Armstrong and R. Giulianotti (eds), *Football in the Making*. London: Macmillan.

Alabarces, P. and M. G. Rodríguez (1996) *Cuestión de pelotas. Fútbol, deporte, sociedad, cultura*. Buenos Aires: Atuel, 61–74.

Allan, J. (1989) *Bloody Casuals*. Glasgow: Famedram

Althusser, L. (1969) *For Marx*. Harmondsworth: Penguin.

Aly, G. and S. Heim (1993) *Vordenker der Vernichtung. Auschwitz und die deutschen Pläne für eine neue europäische Ordnung*. Frankfurt/M.: Fischer.

Andorka, R. (1997) 'Bevezetés a szociológiába', *Osiris* (Budapest): 91–4.

APOYO (1996) 'Informe de las razones de la inasistencia a los estadios de fútbol en el Perú'. Lima: ADPF.

Archetti, E. (1985) *Fútbol y ethos*. Buenos Aires: FLACSO, Serie Investigaciones.

Archetti, E. (1992) 'Calcio: un rituale di violenza?', pp. 241–69 in P. Lanfranchi (ed), *Il calcio e il suo pubblico*. Naples: Edizione Scientifiche Italiane.

Archetti, E. and A. Romero (1994) 'Death and violence in Argentinian football', pp. 37–72 in R. Giulianotti, N. Bonney and M. Hepworth (eds), *Football, Violence and Social Identity*. London: Routledge.

Arms, R. L., G. W. Russell and M. L. Sandilands (1979) 'Effects on the hostility of spectators of viewing aggressive sports', *Review of Sport and Leisure*, 4: 115–27.

Arms, R. L., G. W. Russell and M. L. Sandilands (1980) 'Effects of viewing aggressive sports on the hostility of spectators', pp. 133–42 in R. M. Suinn (ed.), *Psychology in Sports: Methods and Applications*. Minneapolis, MN: Burgess.

Armstrong, G. (1998) *Football Hooligans: Knowing the Score*. Oxford: Berg.

Armstrong, G. and R. Harris (1991) 'Football hooliganism: theory and evidence', *Sociological Review*, 39 (3): 427–58.

Armstrong, G. and D. Hobbs (1994) 'Tackled from behind', pp. 196–228 in R. Giulianotti, N. Bonney and M. Hepworth (eds), *Football Violence and Social Identity*. London and New York: Routledge, 196–228.

Asami, T., M. Isokawa, E. Iwamura, J. Ohashi, N. Ohata, S. Sugiyama, H. Togari, N. Fumoto and M. Matsumoto (1981) *Soccer Scientific Review on Sports*. Tokyo: Shintaiikusha.

Astrinakis, A. E. (1991) *Subcultures of the Working-class Youth: The British Subcultural Theorization and the Greek Experience*. Athens: Papazesis [In Greek].

Astrinakis, A. E. (1996) 'Subcultures of hard-core fans in West Attica: Central research findings, and discussion of theoretical issues', pp. 469–542 in A. E. Astrinakis and L. Stylianoudis (eds), *Heavy Metal, Rockabilly, and Hard-core Fans. Youth Cultures and Subcultures in Athens' Working-class Districts (West Attica)*. Athens: Greek Letters [In Greek].

Astrinakis, A. E. and L. Stylianoudis (eds) (1996) *Heavy Metal, Rockabilly, and Hard-core Fans. Youth Cultures and Subcultures in Athens' Working-class Districts (West Attica)*. Athens: Greek Letters [In Greek].

Atyeo, D. (1979) *Violence in Sports*. Toronto: Van Nostrand Reinhold.

Bairner, A. (1997), '"Up to their knees"? Football, sectarianism, masculinity and Protestant working-class identity', pp. 95–113 in P. Shirlow and M. McGovern (eds), *Who Are 'The People'? Unionism, Protestantism and Loyalism in Northern Ireland*. London: Pluto.

Bairner, A. (1999a) 'Soccer, masculinity and violence in Northern Ireland: Between hooliganism and terrorism', *Men and Masculinities*, 1 (3): 284–301.

Bairner, A. (1999b) 'Masculinity, violence and the Irish peace process', *Capital and Class*, 69: 125–44.

Bairner, A. (2001a) 'Masculinidad, musculatura y cristianismo en las representaciones corporales del unionismo en el Ulster', pp. 99–115 in Carolina Sánchez-Palencia and Juan Carlos Hidalgo (eds), *Masculino Plural: Construcciones de la Masculinidad*. Universitat de Lleida.

Bairner, A. (2001b) 'Gender, class and nation', *Peace Review*, 13 (1): 21–6.

Bairner, A. and P. Darby (1999) 'Divided sport in a divided society', pp. 51–72 in J. Sugden and A. Bairner (eds), *Sport in Divided Societies*. Aachen: Meyer & Meyer.

Bairner, A. and P. Shirlow (1998) 'Loyalism, Linfield and the territorial politics of soccer fandom in Northern Ireland', *Space and Polity*, 2 (2): 163–77.

Bairner, A. and P. Shirlow (1999) 'The territorial politics of soccer in Northern Ireland', pp.152–63 in G. Armstrong and R. Giulianotti (eds), *Football Cultures and Identities*. Basingstoke: Macmillan.

Bairner, A. and P. Shirlow (2000) 'Territory, politics and soccer fandom in Northern Ireland and Sweden', *Football Studies*, 3 (1): 5–26.

Bakhtin, M. (1968) *Rabelais and his World*. Cambridge, MA: MIT Press.

Bakhtin, M. (1987) *La cultura popular en la Edad Media y en el Renacimiento*. Madrid: Alianza.

Balestri C. and C. Podaliri C. (1998) 'The ultras, racism and football culture in Italy', in Brown A. (ed.), *Fanatics*. London: Routledge.

Barnes, J. (1991) 'Recent developments in Canadian sports law', *Ottawa Law Review*, 23: 623–706.

Barreto, A. (ed.) (1996) *A Situação Social em Portugal, 1960–1995*.

Becker, P. (1982) 'Haut'se, haut'se, haut'se in'ne Schnauze. Das Fußballstadion als Ort der Reproduktion sozialer Strukturen', pp. 72–84 in G. A. Pilz (Hrsg.), *Sport und körperliche Gewalt*. Reinbek: Rowohlt.

Beecher, C. (1994) 'Crowd control: When sports fanatics turn violent', *Illinois Quarterly*, May/June: 22–5.

Bélanger, A. (1999). 'The last game? Hockey and the experience of masculinity in Quebec', pp. 293–311 in P. White and K. Young (eds), *Sport and Gender in Canada*. Toronto: Oxford University Press.

Bell, D. (1990) *Acts of Union: Youth Culture and Sectarianism in Northern Ireland*. London: Macmillan.

Benavides, Martin (1997) 'Fútbol y Tradiciones Inventadas: el caso de Alianza Lima', Undergraduate thesis, Pontificia Universidad Católica del Perú.

Benedict, J. and A. Klein (1997) 'Arrest and conviction rates for athletes accused of sexual assault', *Sociology of Sport Journal*, 14: 86–95.

Berzano, L. (1998) *Giovani e violenza*. Turin: Ananke.

Birchall, J. (2001) *ultra NIPPON – How Japan Reinvented Football*. London: Headline (paperback edn).

Blake, A. (1996) *The Body Language: The Meaning of Modern Sport*. London: Lawrence & Wishart.

Boethius, U. (1995) 'The history of high and low culture', pp. 12–38 in J. Fornas and G. Bolin (eds), *Youth Culture in Late Modernity*. London: Sage.

Bose, M. (1994) *Sporting Colours: Sport and Politics in South Africa*. London: Robson.

Braga da Cruz, M. and M. Reis (1983) *Criminalidade e Delinquência Juvenil em Portugal*. Lisboa: Instituto de Ciências Sociais.

Brindley, J. M. (1982) 'Disruptive crowd behaviour: A psychological perspective', *Police Journal*, 55: 28.

British Columbia Police Commission (1994) *Report on the riot that occurred in Vancouver on June 14–15, 1994*. Vancouver.

Brodie, M. (1985) *Linfield 100 Years*. Belfast: Linfield Football and Athletic Club.

Bryant, J. and M. McElroy (1997) *Sociological Dynamics of Sport and Exercise*. Englewood, CO: Morton.

Bryshun, J. and K. Young (1999) 'Sport-related hazing: An inquiry into male and female involvement', pp. 269–93 in P. White and K. Young (eds), *Sport and Gender in Canada*. Toronto: Oxford University Press.

Buford, B. (1991) *Among the Thugs*. London: Secker & Warburg.

Burnett, C. (1998) 'School violence in an impoverished South African community', *Child Abuse and Neglect*, 22 (8): 789–95.

Calvo, F. (1998) 'Asesinos, Traficantes y Delincuentes. Una Campaña contra la Violencia en el Fútbol'. Buenos Aires: mimeo.

Carter, R. (1950) *Footballer's Progress*. London: Sporting Handbooks.

Case, R. W. and R. L. Boucher (1981) 'Spectator violence in sport: A selected review', *Journal of Sport and Social Issues*, 5 (2): 1–15.

Castel, Robert (1991) 'De l'indigence à l'exclusion: la désafiliation', pp. 137–68 in *Face à l'exclusion: le modèle Français*. Paris: Editions Esprit.

Castro, Raúl, (1995) 'U-Norte: de la marginalidad a la representación colectiva', pp. 27–39 in M. Benavides, R. Castro and A. Panfichi (eds), *Fútbol, Identidad, Violencia y Racionalidad*, Temas en Sociología No.1, Faculty of Social Sciences, Pontificia Universidad Católica del Perú, Lima.

České slovo, 1920–25.

České slovo večerní, 1920–37.

Chueca, L. F. (1998) 'Las Palabras de la Tribu. Aproximaciones a la producción verbal de las barras bravas de Alianza Lima', *Flecha en Azul* (6/7): 22–32. Lima: CEAPAZ.

City of Vancouver (1994) *Review of Major Events – Riots: A Background Paper*. Vancouver.

Clarke, J. (1978) 'Football and working class fans: Transition and change', pp. 37–60 in R. Ingham (ed.), *Football Hooliganism: The Wider Context*. London: Inter-Action Imprint.

Coakley, J. (1988–89) 'Media coverage of sports and violent behavior: An elusive connection', *Current Psychology: Research and Reviews*, 7: 322–30.

Coakley, J. (1998) *Sport in Society: Issues and Controversies*. New York: McGraw-Hill.

Coelho, R., A. Lobos, J. Sanguinetti and A. Szrabsteni (1998) 'Del lugar común al estigma. La cobertura de la violencia en el fútbol en la prensa argentina', paper to the IV Jornadas de Investigadores de la Cultura, Instituto Gino Germani, Facultad de Ciencias Sociales, Buenos Aires, November.

Cohen, S. (1980) [1972] *Folk Devils and Moral Panics: The Creation of Mods and Rockers*. London: MacGibbon & Kee.

Cohen, S. and J. Young (eds) (1981) *The Manufacture of News: Social Problems, Deviance and the Mass Media*. London: Constable.

Collier, R. (1998) *Masculinities, Crime and Criminology*. London, Sage.

Collings, P. and R. Condon (1996) 'Blood on ice: Status, self-esteem and ritual injury among Inuit hockey players', *Human Organizations*, 55 (3): 253–62.

Collins, R. (1990) 'Stratification, emotional energy, and the transient emotions', pp. 27–57 in T. D. Kemper (ed.), *Research Agendas in the Sociology of Emotions*. NY: SUNY Press.

Cooper, B., T. W. Sepotekele and J. Rantao (2001) 'Fury of the fans as 43 die in soccer's worst night', *The Star*, 12 April: 1.

Coyle, P. (1999) *Paradise Lost and Found. The Story of Belfast Celtic*. Edinburgh: Mainstream.

Crosset, T., J. Benedict and M. MacDonald (1995) 'Male student-athletes reported for sexual assault: Survey of campus police departments and judicial affairs', *Journal of Sport and Social Issues*, 19: 126–40.

Csikzentmihalyi, M. (1975) *Beyond Boredom and Anxiety*. San Francisco: Jossey-Bass.

Curry, T. and R. H. Strauss (1994) 'A little pain never hurt anyone: A photo-essay on the normalization of sports injuries', *Sociology of Sport Journal*, 11: 195–208.

Curtin, C., H. Donnan and T. M. Wilson (1993) 'Anthropology and Irish urban settings', pp. 1–21 in C. Curtin, H. Donnan and T. M. Wilson (eds), *Irish Urban Cultures*. Belfast: Institute of Irish Studies, Queen's University.

Dal Lago, A. and R. De Biasi (1994) 'Italian football fans: culture and organization', pp. 73–89 in R. Giulianotti, N. Bonney and M. Hepworth (eds), *Football Violence and Social Identity*. London and NY: Routledge.

de Garis, L. (1997). '"Be a buddy to your buddy:" Violence, aggression and masculinity in boxing'. Paper presented at the annual meeting of the North American Society for the Sociology of Sport, Toronto, November 5–8.

De Ipola, E. (1985) *Ideología y discurso populista*. México: Folios.

Downes, D. (1966) *The Delinquent Solution: A Study in Subcultural Theory*. London: Routledge & Kegan Paul.

Dubet, F. and M. Lapeyronnie (1992) *Les Quartiers d'Exil*. Paris: Le Seuil.

Duke, V. (1990) 'Perestroika in progress? The case of spectator sports in Czechoslovakia', *British Journal of Sociology*, 41: 145–56.

Duke, V. (1994) 'The flood from the east? Perestroika and the migration of sports talent from Eastern Europe', in J. Bale and J. Maguire (eds), *The Global Sports Arena*. London: Frank Cass.

Duke, V. and L. Crolley (1996a) 'Football spectator behaviour in Argentina: a case of separate evolution', *Sociological Review*, 44: 272–93.

Duke, V. and L. Crolley (1996b), *Football, Nationality and the State.* Harlow: Longman.

Dumont, L. (1966) *Homo Hierarchicus.* Gallimard.

Dunning, E. (n.d.) 'Zuschauerausschreitungen. Soziologische Notizen zu einem scheinbar neuen Problem', pp. 123–32 in N. Elias and E. Dunning, *Sport im Zivilisationsprozeß.* Münster: Lit Verlag.

Dunning, E. (1986) 'Sport as a male preserve: Notes on the social sources of masculine identity and its transformations', pp. 267–84 in N. Elias and E. Dunning, *Quest for Excitement: Sport and Leisure in the Civilizing Process.* Oxford: Basil Blackwell.

Dunning, E. (1994) 'The social roots of football hooliganism: A reply to the critics of the "Leicester School"', pp. 128–57 in R. Giulianotti, N. Bonney and M. Hepworth (eds), *Football Violence and Social Identity.* London and NY: Routledge.

Dunning, E. (1996) 'Fußballrowdytum im Prozeß – soziologischer Perspektive: einige theoretische und historische Bemerkungen', pp.10–16 in Europäische Akademie des Sports (Hrsg.) *Fußball und Fangewalt. Zusammenfassung einer grenzüberschreitenden Expertentagung.* Rhede.

Dunning, E. (1999) *Sport Matters: Sociological Studies of Sport, Violence and Civilisation.* London, New York: Routledge.

Dunning, E., P. Murphy and J. Williams (1986a) 'Spectator violence at football matches: towards a sociological explanation', *British Journal of Sociology,* XXXVII (2): 221–44.

Dunning, E., P. Murphy and J. Williams (1986b) '"Casuals", "terrace crews" and "fighting firms": Towards a sociological explanation of football hooligan behaviour', pp. 164–83 in D. Riches (ed.), *The Anthropology of Violence.* Oxford and New York: Basil Blackwell.

Dunning, E., P. Murphy and J. Williams (1986c) 'Spectator violence at football matches: towards a sociological explanation', pp. 245–66 in N. Elias and E. Dunning, *Quest for Excitement.* Oxford: Basil Blackwell.

Dunning E., P. Murphy and J. Williams (1988) *The Roots of Football Hooliganism: An Historical and Sociological Study.* London: Routledge.

Dunning, E., P. Murphy and I. Waddington (1991) 'Anthropological versus sociological approaches to the study of soccer hooliganism: some critical notes', *Sociological Review,* 39 (3): 459–78.

Dunning, E. and K. G. Sheard (1979) 'Der tolerierte Hooliganismus', pp. 191–2 in W. Hopf (Hrsg.), *Fussball. Soziologie und Sozialgeschichte einer populären Sportart.* Bensheim: päd. extra Verlag.

Dunning, E and K. Sheard (1979) *Barbarians, Gentlemen and Players.* Oxford: Martin Robertson.

Duperrault, J. R. (1981). 'L'affaire Richard: A situational analysis of the Montreal hockey riot', *Canadian Journal of History of Sport,* XII: 66–83.

Dwertmann, H. (1991) *Sportalltag und Dorfkultur. Eine Studie über den Konstitutionsprozeß des Sports in einem ländlichen Verein.* Oldenburg: BIS.

Dwertmann, H. (1996) 'Sport, wie ihn Hannover so hochklassig nie gesehen hat'. Hannover 96 in der städtischen Öffentlichkeit, pp. 245–71 in L. Peiffer and G. A. Pilz (Hrsg.), *Hannover 96. 100 Jahre – Macht an der Leine.* Hannover: Schlütersche Verlagsanstalt.

Dwertmann, H. (1997) 'Die Rolle Carl Diems im nationalsozialistischen Regime', in *Sozial- und Zeitgeschichte des Sports,* 11. Jg., H. 2, 7–47: Meyer & Meyer.

Dwertmann, H. (1998) 'Annäherungen an eine Theorie der Bewegungszivilisation. Soziologische Untersuchungen zur historischen Entwicklung und gesellschaftlichen Bedeutung des Sportes', Habilitationsschrift: Universität Oldenburg.

Eisen, G. (1993) *Spielen im Schatten des Todes. Kinder und Holocaust.* München, Zürich: Piper.

Eisenberg, C. (1997) 'Deutschland', pp. 94–129 in C. Eisenberg (Hrsg.), *Fußball, soccer, calcio. Ein englischer Sport auf seinem Weg um die Welt.* München: Deutscher Taschenbuch.

Ek, R. (1996) *Hooligans. Fakten – Hintergründe – Analysen.* Worms: Cicero.

Elbaum, J. (1988) 'Apuntes para el "aguante". La construcción simbólica del cuerpo popular', pp. 134–46 in P. Alabarces, R. Di Giano and J. Frydenberg (eds), *Deporte y sociedad.* Buenos Aires: Eudeba.

Elias, N. ([1939] 2000) *The Civilizing Process.* Oxford: Blackwell.

Elias, N. (1978) *What is Sociology?* London: Hutchinson.

Elias, N. (1981) *Über den Prozeß der Zivilisation,* 2. Bd. Frankfurt/M.: Suhrkamp.

Elias, N. (1986) *Was ist Soziologie?* München: Juventa.

Elias, N. (1992) *Studien über die Deutschen.* Frankfurt/M: Suhrkamp.

Elias, N. (1996) *The Germans: Studies of Power Struggles and the Development of Habitus in the Nineteenth and Twentieth Centuries.* Oxford: Polity (trans. with a preface by E. Dunning and S. Mennell).

Elias, N. and E. Dunning (1986) *Quest for Excitement: Sport and Leisure in the Civilizing Process.* Oxford and NY: Blackwell.

Elias N. and E. Dunning (1992) *A Busca da Excitação.* Lisboa: Difel.

Elias, N. and E. Dunning (n.d.) *Sport im Zivilisationsprozeß.* Münster: Lit Verlag.

Elias, N. and J. L. Scotson (1993) *Etablierte und Außenseiter.* Frankfurt/M.: Suhrkamp.

Elias, N. and J. L. Scotson (1994) *The Established and the Outsiders,* 2nd edn, with a new introduction by Norbert Elias. London: Sage (First published in 1965 by Frank Cass)

Ember, M. (2001) A kis Magyar "focista forradalom", Eso, IV. éfv. 1.sz. 2001.

Espinosa, Atilio (1999) 'Mi barrio es zona crema: territorialidad y conflicto en un grupo barrial de la Trinchera Norte', pp. 223–70 in A. Panfichi and M. Valcarcel (eds), *Juventud: Sociedad y Cultura.* Lima: Red de Ciencias Sociales.

Farin, K. and H. Hauswald (1998) *Die dritte Halbzeit. Hooligans in Berlin-Ost.* Berlin: Tilsner.

Ferreira de Almeida, J. (1990) *Valores e Representações Sociais.* 'Portugal os Proximos 20 Anos', vol. VIII, Lisboa: Fundação Calouste Gilbenkian.

Figueiredo, E. (1988) *Conflito de Gerações. Conflito de Valores.* 'Portugal os Proximos 20 Anos', vol. II, Lisboa: Fundação Calouste Gulbenkian.

Finn, G. P. T. and R. Giulianotti (1998) 'Scottish fans, not English hooligans! Scots, Scottishness and Scottish football', pp. 189–202 in A. Brown (ed.), *Fanatics: Power Identity and Fandom in Football.* London: Routledge.

Földesi, S. G. (1996) 'Racism and xenophobia in Hungarian football stadia', pp.169–86 in U. Merkel and W. Tokarski (eds), *Racism and Xenophobia in European Football.* Aachen: Meyer & Meyer.

Football Association (n.d.) *World Cup England 2006: Our Invitation to the World,* London: Football Association. (Unpaginated).

Ford, A. and F. Longo (1991) 'La exasperación del caso'. Buenos Aires: Mimeo.

França, L. (ed.) (1993) *Portugal – Valores Europeus, Identidade Cultural.* Lisboa: Instituto de Estudos para o Desenvolvimento.

Francia, F. (1994) 'I sostenitori del Pisa', in *Rassegna Italiana di Criminologia,* 3.

Free, M. (1998) '"Angels" with drunken faces? Travelling Republic of Ireland supporters and the construction of Irish migrant identity in England', pp. 219–32 in A. Brown, *Fanatics! Power, Identity and Fandom in Football.* London: Routledge.

Friedeburg, L. v. (Hrsg.) (1965a) *Jugend in der modernen Gesellschaft.* Köln, Berlin: Kiepenheuer & Witsch.

Friedeburg, L. v. (1965b) 'Zum Verhältnis von Jugend und Gesellschaft', pp. 176–90 in L. v. Friedeburg (Hrsg.), *Jugend in der modernen Gesellschaft.* Köln, Berlin: Kiepenheuer & Witsch.

Fritsch, S. and G. A. Pilz (1996) 'Vom "Schlachtenbummler" zum "Hooligan". Zur Sozialgeschichte der Fußballbegeisterung und Fußballrandale bei Hannover 96', pp. 204–26 in L. Peiffer and G. A. Pilz (Hrsg.), *Hannover 96. 100 Jahre – Macht an der Leine.* Hannover: Schlütersche Verlagsanstalt.

Galland, O. (1991) *Sociologie de la jeunesse.* Paris: Armand Colin.

Gillett, J., P. White and K. Young (1996) 'The Prime Minister of Saturday night: Don Cherry, the CBC, and the cultural production of intolerance', pp. 59–72 in H. Holmes and D. Taras (eds), *Seeing Ourselves in Canada: Media Power and Policy.* Toronto: Harcourt Brace.

Giulianotti, R. (1991) 'Scotland's tartan army in Italy: The case for the carnivalesque', *Sociological Review,* 39 (3): 503–30.

Giulianotti, R. (1994) 'Taking liberties: Hibs casuals and Scottish law', pp. 229–62 in R. Giulianotti, N. Bonney and M. Hepworth (eds), *Football, Violence and Social Identity.* London: Routledge.

Giulianotti, R. (1995) 'Football and the politics of carnival: An ethnographic study of Scottish fans in Sweden', *International Review for the Sociology of Sport,* 30 (2): 191–217.

Giulianotti, R. (1996) '"All the Olympians: A thing never known again?" Reflections on Irish football culture and the 1994 World Cup finals', *Irish Journal of Sociology,* 6: 101–26.

Giulianotti, R. (1999) *Football: A Sociology of the Global Game.* Cambridge: Polity.

Giulianotti, R. and J. Williams (eds) (1994) *Game without Frontiers.* England and USA: Arena.

Goffman, E. (1963) *Stigma.* Englewood Cliffs: Prentice Hall.

Goffman, E. (1967) *Interaction Ritual.* NY: Anchor.

Goldstein, J. H. (1989) 'Sports violence', pp. 81–8 in D. S. Eitzen (ed.), *Sport in Contemporary Society: An Anthology.* New York: St. Martin's Press.

Green, L. (1984) *Sportswit.* New York: Harper & Row.

Greenberg, P. S. (1977) 'Wild in the stands'. *New Times,* 9, 11 November: 24–63.

Guindi, B. (1998) 'El juego de las percepciones. Un análisis en recepción de la violencia en el fútbol', paper to the IV Jornadas de Investigadores de la Cultura, Instituto Gino Germani, Facultad de Ciencias Sociales: Buenos Aires.

Guttmann, A. (1986) *Sports Spectators.* New York: Columbia University Press.

Hadas, M. and V. Karády (1995) 'Futball és társadalmi identitás', *Replika* 17–18 szám: 89–119.

Hadjantoniou, T. (2001) 'A Criminological Approach to a Music Culture: The Case of Hip Hop in Athens', unpublished MA dissertation, Panteion University, Athens.

Hagan, J. (1991) *The Disreputable Pleasures: Crime and Deviance in Canada.* Toronto: McGraw-Hill Ryerson.

Hall, S. (1978) 'The treatment of football hooliganism in the press', pp. 15–37 in R. Ingham (ed.), *Football Hooliganism: The Wider Context.* London: Inter-Action Inprint.

Harada, M. and J. Fujimoto (1999) *Research Report on Tarami All Star Soccer '99*, Division of Sport Management, Osaka University of Health and Sports Sciences.

Haralambopoulos, T. (in progress) 'A Social Psychological Approach to Heavy Metal Music', PhD in progress, Panteion University, Athens.

Hargreaves, John (ed.) (1986) *Sport, Power and Culture*. Cambridge: Polity in association with Basil Blackwell, Oxford.

Harper, C. (1989–90) 'A Study of Football Crowd Behaviour'. Lothian and Borders Police: Mimeo.

Harrington, J. A. (1968) *Soccer Hooliganism*. Bristol: John Wright.

Harrison, P. (1974) 'Soccer's tribal wars', *New Society*, 29: 602.

Hay, R. (1994) 'British football, wogball or the world game? Towards a social history of Victorian soccer', *Australian Society for Sports History: Studies in Sports History*, 10: 44–79.

Heatherington, K. (1998) *Expressions of Identity: Space, Performance, Politics*. London: Sage.

Heineken, P. (1993 [1898]) *Das Fussballspiel*. Hannover: Schäfer.

Heitmeyer, W. and J. I. Peter (1992) *Jugendliche Fußballfans. Soziale und politische Orientierungen, Gesellungsformen, Gewalt*. Weinheim, München: Juventa.

Helgadottir, B. (1993) 'Return of the violent fans', *The European*, 23 September.

Herbert, T. (1994) 'Setting the tone: Sportsmanship in intercollegiate athletics'. Paper presented at conference on 'Sports Violence: Issues for Law Enforcement', University of Illinois, Chicago, 28–30 March.

Hermann, H. U. (1977) *Die Fußballfans. Untersuchungen zum Zuschauersport*. Schorndorf: Hofmann.

Hobbs, D. (1988) *Doing the Business. Entrepreneurship, the Working Class, and Detectives in the East End of London*. London: Clarendon Press.

Hobbs, D. and D. Robins (1991) 'The boy done good: football violence, changes and continuities', *Sociological Review*, 33 (3): 551–9.

Hopf, W. (Hrsg.) (1979) *Fussball. Soziologie und Sozialgeschichte einer populären Sportart*. Bensheim: päd. extra Verlag.

Horak, R. (1991) 'Things change: Trends in Austrian football hooliganism from 1977–1990', *Sociological* Review, 33 (3) 531–48.

Horne, J. (1996) 'Sakka' (soccer) in Japan', *Media Culture & Society*, 18 (4): 527–47.

http://www.iol.co.za.general/newsview (2001) 'Ghana disaster not the end of World Cup hopes'. Retrieved: 10 May at 15.25.

Hudson, P. (1999) 'Withdrawal symptoms', *When Saturday Comes*, London, April: 146.

Hughson, J. (1992) 'Australian soccer – "ethnic" or "Aussie": The search for an image', *Current Affairs Bulletin*, 68 (10): 12–16.

Hughson, J. (1996a) 'The wogs are at it again: Media reportage of Australian soccer riots', paper presented to the *No Longer Black and White* Conference, University of Melbourne.

Hughson, J. (1996b) 'A Feel for the Game: An Ethnographic Study of Soccer Support and Social Identity', Unpublished PhD thesis, University of New South Wales.

Hughson, J. (1997) 'The bad blue boys and the "magical recovery" of John Clarke', pp. 239–59 in G. Armstrong and R. Giulianotti (eds), *Entering the Field: New Perspectives in World Football*. Oxford: Berg.

Hughson, J. (1998) 'Is the carnival over? Soccer support and hooliganism in Australia', pp. 170–79 in D. Rowe and G. Lawrence (eds), *Tourism, Leisure, Sport: Critical Perspectives*. Sydney: Hodder.

Hughson, J. (2000) 'The boys are back in town: soccer support and the social reproduction of masculinity', *Journal of Sport and Social Issues*, 24 (10): 8–23.

Hutchins, B. and M. G. Phillips (1997) 'Selling permissible violence: the commodification of Australian rugby league 1970–1995', *International Review for the Sociology of Sport*, 32 (2): 161–76.

Innenministerium des Landes Nordrhein-Westfalen (Hrsg.) (1993) *Nationales Konzept 'Sport und Sicherheit'.* Düsseldorf.

Instituto do Desporto (1993) *La Violence Associee au Sport au Portugal. Investigation Multinationale Comparative du Conseil de l'Europe sur le Hooliganism dans le Football.* Lisboa: Instituto do Desporto.

Izaguirre, I. (1998) 'Presentación. Reflexiones sobre la violencia', pp. 5–13 in I. Izaguirre (ed.), *Violencia social y derechos humanos.* Buenos Aires: Eudeba.

Jansen, H. (2000) 'Mbeki the "diplomat" not provoked' (translation), *Beeld*, 19 May: 3.

Japan Football Association (1996) *Japan Football Association 75 Annals.* Tokyo: Baseball Magazine, Sha Co Ltd.

Johnson, W. O. (1993) 'The agony of victory', *Sports Illustrated*, 5 July: 30–7.

Katz, S. (1955) 'Strange forces behind the Richard hockey riot', *Macleans*, (17): 11–110.

Kelley, W. D. (1994) 'Developing security plans for the 1996 Olympics'. Paper presented at conference on 'Sports Violence: Issues for Law Enforcement', University of Illinois, Chicago, 28–30 March.

Kennedy, J. (1989) *Belfast Celtic.* Belfast: Pretani.

Kerr, J. H. (1994) *Understanding Soccer Hooliganism.* Philadelphia: Open University Press.

Kiku, K. (1993) *The Historical Sociology of 'Modern Professional Sports'.* Tokyo: Fumaido, p. 237.

King, A. (1997a) 'The postmodernity of football hooliganism', *British Journal of Sociology*, 48 (4): 576–93.

King, A. (1997b), 'The Lads: masculinity and the new consumption of football', *Sociology*, 31 (2): 329–46.

King, A. (1998) *The End of the Terraces: The Transformation of English Football in the 1990s.* London: Leicester University Press.

Kisanuki, H. and S. Esashi (1996) 'Gender differences in motives of spectators at a soccer game', *Japan Journal of Sport Sociology* (4): 106–14.

Kitchen, L. (1966) 'The contenders', *The Listener*, 27 October 1966.

Klein, M. (1989) (Hrsg.) *Sport und soziale Probleme.* Reinbek: Rowohlt.

Kleinert, C., W. Krüger and H. Willems (1998) 'Einstellungen junger Deutscher gegenüber ausländischen Mitbürgern und ihre Bedeutung hinsichtlich politischer Orientierungen', pp. 14–27 in Bundeszentrale für Politische Bildung (Hrsg.), *Aus Politik und Zeitgeschichte*, 24 (7).

Kotzé, J. C. (1993) *In their Shoes: Understanding Black South Africans through their Experiences of Life.* Kenwyn: Juta.

Kourakis, N. ([1988] 1991) 'A final report on the violence in Greek soccer terraces', pp. 299–443 in *Essays Honoring the Contributions of E. Daskalakis.* Athens: Panteion University of Social and Political Sciences. Section of Criminology [In Greek].

Krausz T. (1996) 'Soccer and racism in Hungary. Or: what's the Ajax-Fradi conflict all about?', *Eszmélet*, Spring 29: 146–73.

Lagrange, Hugues (1995) *La Civilité à l'épreuve: crime et sentiment d'insécurité.* Paris: PUF.

Lapassade, G. (1965) 'Rebellen ohne Grund', pp. 191–9 in L. v. Friedeburg (Hrsg.), *Jugend in der modernen Gesellschaft*. Köln, Berlin: Kiepenheuer & Witsch.

Leonard, W. (1993) *A Sociological Perspective of Sport*. New York: Macmillan.

Lewis, J. M. (1982) 'Fan violence: An American social problem', *Research in Social Problems and Public Policy*, (12): 175–206.

Lindner, R. (Hrsg.) (1980) *Der Fußballfan. Ansichten vom Zuschauer*. Frankfurt/M.: Syndikat.

Listiak, A. (1981) '"Legitimate deviance" and social class: Bar behavior during Grey Cup week', pp. 532–63 in M. Hart and S. Birrell (eds), *Sport in the Sociocultural Process*. Dubuque, Iowa: Wm. C. Brown.

Lourenco, N. and M. Lisboa (1988) *Dez Anos de Crime em Portugal. Análise longitudinal da criminalidade participasda às polícias (1984–1993)*. Lisboa: Centre de Estudos Judiciarios.

Maffesoli, M. (1990) *El tiempo de las tribus*. Barcelona: Icaria.

Magyar Sportévkönyv [Hungarian Sport Year Book] 1995, 1996, 1997, 1998, 1999, Ládonyi László (ed.), Aréna 2000.

Malcolm, E. (1983) 'Popular recreation in nineteenth-century Ireland', pp. 40–55 in O. MacDonagh, W. F. Mandle and P. Travers (eds), *Irish Culture and Nationalism, 1750–1950*. London, Macmillan.

Marivoet, S. (1989) *Evolution of Violence Associated to Sports in Portugal (1978–1987)*. Lisbon: Ministério da Educação/Direcção Geral dos Desportos.

Marivoet, S. (1992a) 'Une campagne national pour l'éthique sportive: bilan et perspectives. L'exemple du Portugal', *Revue Sociologie Santé*, 7: 251–7.

Marivoet, S. (1992b) 'Violência nos espectáculos de futebol', *Revista Sociologia Problemas e Práticas*, 12: 137–54.

Mark, M., F. B. Bryant and D. R. Lehman (1983) 'Perceived injustice and sports violence', pp. 83–105 in J. H. Goldstein (ed.), *Sports Violence*. New York: Springer.

Marsh, P. (1978) *Aggro: The Illusion of Violence*. London: Dent.

Marsh, P. (1980) 'Leben und "Laufbahnen"auf den Fußballrängen', pp. 117–38 in R. Lindner (Hrsg.), *Der Fußballfan. Ansichten vom Zuschauer*. Frankfurt/M.: Syndikat.

Marsh, P., K. Fox, G. Carnibella, J. McCann and J. Marsh (1996) *Football Violence in Europe*. The Amsterdam Group. Oxford: Social Issues Research Centre.

Marsh, P., E. Rosser and R. Harré (1978), *The Rules of Disorder*. London: Routledge & Kegan Paul.

Maseko, L. (2001) 'A swirling mass of humanity', *Sowetan*, 8 February: 2.

Matza, D. (1964) *Delinquency and Drift*. New York, London, Sydney: John Wiley.

McCaughn, M. (1999) 'Police on permanent death duty', *The Guardian*, 15 February 1999: 10.

McPherson, B., J. E. Curtis and J. W. Loy (eds) (1989) *The Social Significance of Sport: An Introduction to the Sociology of Sport*. Champaign, IL: Human Kinetics.

Melnick, M. (1989) 'The sports fan: A teaching guide and bibliography', *Sociology of Sport Journal*, 6: 167–75.

Melnick, M. (1992) 'Male athletes and sexual assault', *Journal of Physical Education, Recreation and Dance*, May/June, 32–5.

Melucci A. (1982) *L'invenzione del presente*. Bologna: Il Mulino.

Messner, M. (1992) *Power at Play: Sports and the Problem of Masculinity*. Boston, MA: Beacon.

Metifogo, D. and V. Martinez (1996) *Informe sobre las Barras Bravas*. Departamento de Psicologia, Universidad de Chile, Santiago.

Mignon, P. (1992) 'La società francese e il calcio', pp. 285–300 in P. Lanfranchi (ed.), *Il calcio e il suo pubblico*. Napoli: Edizione Scientifiche Italiane.

Mignon, Patrick (1994a) 'New supporter cultures and identity in France: the case of Paris Saint-Germain', pp. 273–98 in R. Giulianotti and J. Williams (eds), *Game Without Frontiers: Football, Identity and Modernity*. Aldershot: Arena.

Mignon, Patrick (1994b) *La société du samedi. Supporters, ultras et hooligans*. Institut des Hautes Etudes de la Sécurité Intérieure.

Mignon, Patrick (1997) *Les publics du football à Paris, Metz et Saint-Etienne: approche quantitative*, Ligue Nationale de Football.

Mignon, Patrick (1999) 'Fans and heroes', pp. 79–97 in H. Dauncey and G. Hare (eds), *France and the 1998 World Cup: The National Impact of a World Sporting Event*. London: Cass.

Mignon, Patrick (2000) *Les Clubs professionnels et le supportérisme: quelle politique?* Ligue Nationale de Football.

Mommsen, Hans (1976) 'Der Nationalsozialismus: Kummulative Radikalisierung und Selbstzerstörung des Regimes', pp. 785–90 in *Meyers Enzyklopädisches Lexicon*, vol. 16.

Moorhouse, H. M. (1991) 'Football hooligans: old bottle, new wines?' *Sociological Review*, 33 (3): 489–502.

Morris, D. (1983) *The Soccer Tribe* (Japanese edition). Tokyo: Shogakukan.

Mosely, P. (1994) 'Balkan politics in Australian soccer', *Australian Society for Sports History: Studies in Sports History*, 10: 33–43.

Mosely, P. (1995) *Ethnic Involvement in Australian Soccer: A History 1950–1990*. Canberra: Australian Sports Commission.

Mottl, R. (1980) Paper presented before the US Congressional Subcommittee on Crime, 30 September.

Murphy, P., E. Dunning and J. Williams (1988) 'Soccer crowd disorder and the press: processes of amplification and de-amplification in historical perspective', *Theory, Culture and Society*, 5: 645–93.

Murphy, P., J. Williams and E. Dunning (1990a) *Football on Trial: Spectator Violence and Development in the Football World*. London: Routledge.

Murphy P., J. Williams and E. Dunning (1990b) 'Soccer crowd disorder and the press: processes of amplification and deamplification in historical perspective', in P. Murphy, J. Williams and E. Dunning, *Football on Trial*. London: Routledge.

Nakatsuka, Y. (1986) 'The Sociological Background to the Professionalization of Japanese Soccer', Unpublished Master's thesis, Tsukuba University.

Nakazawa, M. (1998) 'Survey on J-League spectators', research paper, Tsukuba University, (Reported in Japanese and English).

Nakazawa, M. (1999) 'Survey on J-League spectators', Research paper, Tsukuba University.

Nakazawa, M., S. Hirakawa, D. Mahony, M. Hums, J. Tokari and Y. Nakatsuka (2000) 'Female spectators in the J-League', *Journal of Japan Society of Sports Industry*, 10 (1): 45–57.

Nelson, S. (1994) 'Celebration riots: a retrospective'. Paper presented at conference on 'Sports Violence: Issues for Law Enforcement', University of Illinois, Chicago, 28–30 March.

Nixon, H. L. (1994a) 'Coaches' views of risk, pain, and injury in sport with special reference to gender differences', *Sociology of Sport Journal*, 11: 79–87.

Nixon, H. L. (1994b) 'Social pressure, social support, and help seeking for pain and injuries in college sports networks', *Journal of Sport and Social Issues*, 13: 340–55.

Ohsumi, Y. (1998) *The Happiness of the Urawa Reds.* Tokyo: Aspect Corporation.

Ortiz, R. (1991) 'Lo actual y la modernidad', *Nueva Sociedad,* Caracas, November–December: 56–70.

Ortiz, R. (1996) *Otro territorio.* Buenos Aires: UNQ.

Pais, Elza (1998) *Homicídio Conjugal em Portugal–Rupturas Violentas da Conjugalidade.* Lisboa: Hugin.

Pais, J. M. (1996) *Culturas Juvenis.* Lisboa: Instituto Nacional Casa da Moeda.

Panayotopoulos, N. (forthcoming) *Legal State and Social State in Greece.* Athens: Patakis [In Greek].

Panfichi, A. (1995) 'Fútbol e identidad: esta urgencia de decir nosotros', pp. 16–26 in M. Benavides, R. Castro and A. Panfichi (eds), *Fútbol, Identidad, Violencia y Racionalidad,* Temas en Sociología No.1, Faculty of Social Sciences, Pontificia Universidad Católica del Perú, Lima.

Panfichi, A. and J. Thieroldt (1998) *Modelos de conducta y valores de un grupo de jovenes de las barras bravas de Alianza Lima,* informe cualitativo. Lima: UNICEF–AS Niño Intimo.

Papageorgiou, D (1995) 'Madness and Sickness: Conceptions and Practices of Sports Club Members in Greece', unpublished PhD thesis, University of Aigeon.

Pearson, G. (1983) *Hooligan: A History of Respectable Fears.* London: Macmillan.

Peiffer, L. and G. A. Pilz (Hrsg.) (1996) *Hannover 96. 100 Jahre – Macht an der Leine.* Hannover: Schlütersche Verlagsanstalt.

Pike, E. (1997) 'Self, stigma, and significant others: Some preliminary thoughts on the social construction of sport-related injury', pp. 249–60 in P. de Nardis, A. Mussino and N. Porro (eds), *Sport: Social Problems and Social Movements.* Rome: Edizioni Seam.

Pilz, G. A. (1979) 'Zuschauerausschreitungen im Fußballsport. Versuch einer Analyse', pp. 171–90 in W. Hopf (Hrsg), *Fussball. Soziologie und Sozialgeschichte einer populären Sportart.* Bensheim: päd. extra Verlag.

Pilz, G. A. (Hrsg.) (1982) *Sport und körperliche Gewalt.* Reinbek: Rowohlt.

Pilz, G. A. (1991) 'Sportjournalismus oder die Unfähigkeit zur kritischen Distanz', pp. 249–62 in R. Horak und W. Reiter (Hrsg.), *Die Kanten des runden Leders. Beiträge zur europäischen Fußballkultur.* Wien: Promedia.

Pilz, G. A. (1994) *Jugend, Gewalt und Rechtsextremismus.* Münster: Lit Verlag.

Piqueras, M. (1998) 'Buen Gobierno, Seguridad Publica y Crimen Violento', Master's thesis, Universidad Católica del Peru.

Poláček, K. (1957) *Muži v offsidu.* Praha: Československy spisovatel.

Policia Nacional del Peru, VI region Lima (1996a) 'Estudio operativo sobre la violencia juvenil y la violencia deportiva'.

Policia Nacional del Peru, VI region Lima (1996b) 'Informe sobre las pandillas juveniles en Lima y Callao'.

Portelli, A. (1993) 'The rich and the poor in the culture of football', pp. 77–88 in S. Redhead (ed.), *The Passion and the Fashion: Football Fandom in the New Europe.* Aldershot: Avebury.

Pramann, U. (1980) *Das bisschen Freiheit. Die fremde Welt der Fußballfans.* Hamburg: Gruner & Jahr.

Premier Soccer League (1997) Annual Report 1996/7 of the Premier Soccer League. South Africa. Unpublished document.

Rail, G. (1990) 'Physical contact in women's basketball: A first interpretation', *International Review for the Sociology of Sport,* 25 (4): 269–85.

Rail, G. (1992) 'Physical contact in women's basketball: A phenomenological construction and contextualization', *International Review for the Sociology of Sport*, 27 (1): 1–27.

Ratao, J. (2001) 'Death their reward for following the sport they loved', *The Star*, 12 April: 1.

Redhead, S. (1991) *Football with Attitude*. Manchester: Wordsmith.

Revista del Instituto de Defensa Legal, Ideele, special edition 1995.

Riseling, S. (1994) 'Law enforcement responds to sports violence'. Paper presented at conference on 'Sports Violence: Issues for Law Enforcement', University of Illinois, Chicago, 28–30 March.

Rizakos, S. (1996) 'Sport culture and forms of fans' organizations in Peristeri of West Attica', pp. 404–40 in A. E. Astrinakis and L. Stylianoudi (eds), *Heavy Metal, Rockabilly, and Hard-core Fans: Youth Cultures and Subcultures in Athens' Working-class Districts (West Attica)*. Athens: Greek Letters [In Greek].

Robins, D. and P. Cohen. (1978) *Knuckle Sandwich: Growing Up in a Working Class City*. Harmondsworth: Penguin.

Robson, G. (2000) *'No One Likes Us, We Don't Care': The Myth and Reality of Millwall Fandom*. London: Berg.

Rodríguez, M., A. Martínez, G. Díaz and M. Conde (1998) 'Aliens en territorio prohibido. Una aproximación al estudio de la mujer y el fútbol', paper to the IV Jornadas de Investigadores de la Cultura, Instituto Gino Germani, Facultad de Ciencias Sociales, Buenos Aires, November.

Romero, A. (1985) *Deporte, violencia y política (crónica negra 1958–1983)*. Buenos Aires: CEAL.

Romero, A. (1987) *Deporte y violencia*. Buenos Aires: CEAL.

Romero, A. (1994) *Las barras bravas y la 'contrasociedad deportiva'*. Buenos Aires: CEAL.

Roversi A. (1992) *Calcio, tifo e violenza. Il teppismo calcistico in Italia*. Bologna: Il Mulino.

Roversi, A. (1994) 'The birth of the "ultras": the rise of football hooliganism in Italy', pp. 377–8 in R. Giulianotti and J. Williams (eds), *Game Without Frontiers: Football, Identity and Modernity*. Aldershot: Arena.

Runfola, R. (1976) 'Violence in sports: reflections of the violence in American society', *New York Times*, 11 January: 304–5.

Salvini A. (1988) *Il rito aggressivo, dall'aggressivit . . . simbolica al comportamento violento: il caso dei tifosi ultras*. Florence: Giunti.

Schulz, H. J. and R. Weber (1982) 'Zuschauerausschreitungen – Das Problem der Fans', pp. 55–71 in G. A. Pilz (Hrsg.), *Sport und körperliche Gewalt*. Reinbek: Rowohlt.

Sheard, K. G. (1997) 'Aspects of boxing in the Western "civilizing process"', *International Review for the Sociology of Sport*, 32 (1): 31–57.

Sheard, K.G. (1998) '"Brutal and degrading": the medical profession and boxing, 1838–1984', *International Journal of the History of Sport*, 15 (3): 74–102.

Shimizu, S. (2000) 'Supporter – a symbol and memory', *Soubun-kikaku*, Tokyo, 3: 75–90.

Shimizu, S. (2001) 'The study of supporter cultures', *Japan Journal of Sport Sociology*, 9: 24–35.

Siamou, I. (in progress) 'A Comparative Study of Two Youth Subcultural Groups in Working-class Districts of Athens (West Attica)', PhD in progress, Panteion University.

Siamou, I. and S. Playanakou (1998) *Night Life and Recreational Drug Use in Athens*, unpublished research monograph, Mental Health University Research Institute (MHURI), University of Athens, Medical School.

Siamou, I., M. Spyropoulou and S. Playanakou (1999) 'Comparison of the psychosocial characteristics of drug-using and non-drug-using club-party goers', MHURI, University of Athens, Medical School, in *2000: New Strategies for Drug Use*, IREFREA, Lion/France, 1999.

Sidiropoulos, E., A. Jeffrey, H. Forgey, C. Chipps, T. Corrigan, T. Mophuthing, A. Helman, and T. Dimant (1997/98). *South Africa Survey*. Johannesburg: South African Institute of Race Relations.

Siklóssy L. (1928) *A magyar sport ezer éve, II. – Széchenyi-Wesselényi és még egy nemzedék (1820–1874)*. Budapest: Országos Testnevelési Tanács.

Slepička, P. (1989) 'Divácký prožitek sportovníko utkání', *Teorie a praxe*, 5: 296–300.

Slepička, P. (1991) *Spectator Reflexion of Sports Performance*. Prague: Karolinum.

Smith, M. D. (1975) 'Sport and collective violence', pp. 277–333 in D. W. Ball and J. W. Loy (eds), *Sport and Social Order: Contributions to the Sociology of Sport*. Reading, MA: Addison–Wesley.

Smith, M. D. (1976) 'Hostile outbursts in sport', pp. 203–5 in A. Yiannakis (ed.), *Sport Sociology: Contemporary Themes*. Dubuque, Iowa: Kendall/Hunt.

Smith, M. D. (1978) 'Precipitants of crowd violence', *Sociological Inquiry*, (48): 121–31.

Smith, M. D. (1983). *Violence and Sport*. Toronto: Butterworths.

Snyder, E. and E. Spreitzer (1983) *Social Aspects of Sport*. Englewood Cliffs: Prentice Hall.

Stallybrass, P. and A. White (1986) *The Politics and Poetics of Transgression*. London: Methuen.

Steavenson, W. (1997) 'Violence 1 – Football 0: football fans in Eastern Europe are following their Western neighbors' example of hooliganism', *Time Magazine*, 149 (21).

Stöss, R. (1999) *Rechtsextremismus im vereinten Deutschland*. Bonn: Friedrich Ebert Stiftung.

Stryker, S. (1994) 'Freedom and constraint in social and personal life: toward resolving the paradox of self", pp. 119–38 in G. M. Platt and C. Gordon (eds), *Self, Collective Behavior and Society: Essays Honoring the Contributions of R. Turner*. Greenwich, Connecticut & London, England: JAI Press Inc.

Stuttard, I. (producer) (1985) *Hooligan*. Thames Television, England.

Stylianoudis, L. (1996) 'Spectacle in sports: a reading of a football match', pp. 377–402 in A. E. Astrinakis and L. Stylianoudis (eds), *Heavy Metal, Rockabilly, and Hard-core Fans. Youth Cultures and Subcultures in Athens' Working-class Districts (West Attica)*. Athens: Greek Letters [in Greek].

Sugden, J. (1996) *Boxing and Society*. Manchester: Manchester University Press.

Sugden, J. and A. Bairner (1988) 'Sectarianism and soccer hooliganism in Northern Ireland', pp. 572–78 in T. Reilly, A. Lees, K. Davids and W. J. Murphy (eds), *Science and Football*. London: Spon.

Sugden, J. and A. Bairner (1993) *Sport, Sectarianism and Society in a Divided Ireland*. Leicester: Leicester University Press.

Sugden, J. and S. Harvie (1995) *Sport and Community Relations in Northern Ireland*. Coleraine: Centre for the Study of Conflict, University of Ulster.

Takahashi, H. (1996) 'A study of the factors related to the frequency of attendance at home games of Sanfrecce Hiroshima', *Journal of Japan Society of Sports Industry*, 6 (1): 7–19.

Takahashi, Y. (1993) 'The incantation is soccer. The result is to make a city "an Iron Clamp"', *Monthly Asahi*, 5 (10): 244–61. Tokyo: Asahi Shinbun.

Takahashi, Y. (1994) *Sociology of Soccer*. Tokyo: Japan Broadcast Publishing Co.

Taylor, I. (1969) 'Hooligans: Soccer's Resistance Movement', *New Society*, 7 August 1969:

204–6.

Taylor, I. (1971a), 'Football mad: a speculative sociology of football hooliganism', pp. 352–77 in E. Dunning (ed.), *The Sociology of Sport: a Selection of Readings*. London: Frank Cass.

Taylor, I. (1971b) 'Soccer consciousness and soccer hooliganism', in S. Cohen (ed.), *Images of Deviance*. Harmondsworth: Penguin.

Taylor, I. (1975) '"Vom Fußball besessen". Einige soziologische Spekulationen über Fußball-Vandalismus', pp. 245–71 in K. Hammerich and K. Heinemann (Hrsg.), *Texte zur Soziologie des Sports*. Schorndorf: Hofmann.

Taylor, I. (1982a) 'On the sports violence question: soccer hooliganism revisited', pp. 152–96 in J. Hargreaves (ed.), *Sport, Culture and Ideology*. London: Routledge & Kegan Paul.

Taylor, I. (1982b) 'Putting the boot into working class sport: British soccer after Bradford and Brussels', *Sociology of Sport Journal*, (4): 171–91.

Taylor, P., Lord Justice (1990) *Inquiry into the Hillsborough Stadium Disaster: Final Report*. London, HMSO.

Thabe, G. A. L. (1983) *It's a goal! 50 years of Sweat, Tears and Drama in Black Soccer*. Johannesburg: SANFA.

The History of Physical Education Subcommittee of the Japan Society of Physical Education, Health and Sport Sciences (1967) The Course of the Japanese Sport Century. Tokyo: Baseball Magazine Sha Co.

Tolliver, G. (1994) 'Celebration riots: A retrospective'. Paper presented at conference on 'Sports Violence: Issues for Law Enforcement', University of Illinois, Chicago, 28–30 March.

Triani G. (1990) *Mal di stadio. Storia del tifo e della passione per il calcio*. Roma: Edizioni Associate.

Trivizas, E. (1980) 'Offences and offenders in football crowd disorder', *British Journal of Criminology*, 20 (3): 281 ff.

Tsuboi, G. and S. Tanaka (1885) *Outdoor Games or Outdoor Exercises*. Tokyo: Kinko-do, Tokyo. Reprinted edn, Baseball Magazine Sha Co.

Turner, R. and L. Killian (1987) *Collective Behavior*. Englewood Cliffs, NJ: Prentice Hall.

Turner, V. (1977) *The Ritual Process*. Ithaca: Cornell University Press.

Turner, V. (1982) *From Ritual to Theatre*. New York: Performing Arts Journal Publications.

Uemukai, K., I. Takenouchi, E. Okuda and K. Katsura (1996) 'An analysis of factors affecting spectators' identification with professional football teams in Japan', *Nagoya Journal of Health, Physical Fitness and Sports*, 19 (1): 39–45.

Vamplew, V. (1994) 'Violence in Australian soccer: the ethnic contribution', *Australian Society for Sports History: Studies in Sports History*, 10: 1–15.

Van der Brug, H. H. (1986) *Voetbalvandalisme*. Haarlem: De Vrieseborch.

Van der Brug, H. H. (1994) 'Football hooliganism in the Netherlands', pp. 174–95 in R. Giulianotti, N. Bonney and M. Hepworth (eds), *Football Violence and Social Identity*. London and NY: Routledge.

Van Limbergen, K., C. Colaers and L. Walgrave (1987) *Research on the Societal and Psycho-Sociological Background of Football Hooliganism*. Leuven: Catholic University.

Van Zunderd, P. (1994) 'Law enforcement responds to sports violence'. Paper presented at conference on 'Sports Violence: Issues for Law Enforcement', University of Illinois, Chicago, 28–30 March.

Vancouver Police Department (1995) *Review of the Stanley Cup Riot, June 14, 1994*. Vancouver.

Viegas Ferreira, E. (1998) *Crime e Insegurança em Portugal. Padrões e Tendências, 1985–1996*. Oreiras: Celta.

Vincze, G. (1999) Az 1956-os magyarországi „események" kihatása Erdélyben (Kronológia, 1956–59) [Effect of the Hungarian events in 1956 on Transilvania], Szabadság Kolozsvári Közéleti Napilap XI /269: 3).

Walgrave, L. and K. Van Limbergen. Unpublished (1989) *Research on Football Hooliganism in Belgium: A Major Guideline for Coping with it*. Leuven: Katholieke Universiteit, Faculteit Rechtsgelleerdheid (A.S.S. en Criminologie).

Warren, I. (1995) 'Soccer subcultures in Australia', in C. Guerra and R. White (eds), *Ethnic Minority Youth in Australia: Challenges and Myths*. Hobart: National Clearinghouse for Youth Studies.

Weinstein, M., M. Smith and D. Wiesenthal (1995) 'Masculinity and hockey violence', *Sex Roles*, 33 (11/12): 831–47.

Wells, J. (1997a) 'Soccer: prime up that chainsaw', *The Daily Telegraph* (Sydney), 22 May: 93.

Wells, J. (1997b) 'Signs of hope on soccer's fateful day', *The Daily Telegraph* (Sydney), 26 May: 52.

Wenner, L. (1997) 'Blowing whistles: mediated sports violence and gender relations'. Paper presented at conference on 'Sport, Youth, Violence and the Media'. University of Southern California, 3–4 April.

West, G. (1996) 'Youth sports and violence: a masculine subculture?', pp. 309–48 in G. O'Bireck (ed.), *Not a Kid Any More: Canadian Youth, Crime and Subcultures*. Toronto: Nelson.

Williams, J. (1985) 'In search of the hooligan solution', *Social Studies Review*, 1: 3–5.

Williams, J. and A. Goldberg (1989) *Spectator behaviour, media coverage and crowd control at the 1988 European Football Championships: A review of data from Belgium, Denmark, the Federal Republic of Germany, Netherlands and the United Kingdom*. Strasbourg: Council of Europe.

Williams, J., E. Dunning and P. Murphy (1984, 1989) *Hooligans Abroad: The Behaviour and Control of English Fans in Continental Europe*. London: Routledge & Kegan Paul.

Wilson, F. and M. Ramphele (1989), *Uprooting Poverty: The South African Challenge*. Cape Town: David Philip.

Winfree, L. T., T. V. Backström, and G. L. Mays (1994) 'Social learning theory, self-reported delinquency and youth gangs: A new twist on a general theory of crime and delinquency', *Youth and Society*, 26 (2): 147–77.

Yeager, R. C. (1977) 'Savagery on the playing field', *Readers Digest*, September: 161–6.

Young, K. M. (1986) 'The killing field: themes in mass media responses to the Heysel stadium riot', *International Review for the Sociology of Sport*, 21: 253–64.

Young, K. M. (1986) '"The killing field": cuestiones que suscita el tratamiento dado por los medios de comunicación de masas a los disturbios del estadio de Heysel', pp. 167–86 in AA.VV. (1994), *Materiales de sociología del deporte*. Madrid: Genealogía del Poder/23, Ediciones de la Piqueta.

Young, K. M. (1988) 'Sports Crowd Disorder, Mass Media and Ideology', unpublished PhD thesis, McMaster University, Ontario.

Young, K. M. (1993) 'Violence, risk, and liability in male sports culture', *Sociology of Sport Journal*, 10: 373–96.

Young, K. M. (1997) 'Women, sport, and physicality: preliminary findings from a Canadian study', *International Review for the Sociology of Sport*, 32: 297–305.

Young, K. M. (2000) 'Sport and violence', pp. 382–408 in J. Coakley and E. Dunning (eds), *Handbook of Sports Studies*. London: Sage.

Young, K. M. (2001) 'From "sports violence" to "sports crime": Aspects of violence, law, and gender in the sports process', in S. Ball-Rokeach, M. Gatz and M. Messner (eds), *A Sporting Chance: The Role of Youth and Sport in Urban Settings*. SUNY Press (forthcoming).

Young, K. M. (2002) 'Standard deviations: an update on North American sports crowd disorder', *Sociology of Sport Journal* (forthcoming).

Young, K. M. and M. D. Smith (1988/1989) 'Mass media treatment of violence in sports and its effects', *Current Psychology: Research and Reviews*, 7: 298–312.

Young, K. and K. Wamsley (1996) 'State complicity in sports assault and the gender order in twentieth century Canada: preliminary observations', *Avante*, 2: 51–69.

Young, K. and P. White (1999) 'Is sport injury gendered?', pp. 69–85 in P. White and K. Young (eds), *Sport and Gender in Canada*. Toronto: Oxford University Press.

Young, K. M., P. White and W. McTeer (1994) 'Body talk: male athletes reflect on sport, injury, and pain', *Sociology of Sport Journal*, 11: 175–95.

Zwane, W. (1991) 'League sets up probe into soccer disaster', *Business Day*, 15 January: 1.

Index